KU-191-643

Island Quest

THE INNER HEBRIDES

by the same author
Movement is Life

Prunella Stack

Island Quest

THE INNER HEBRIDES

Photographs by
MIRELLA RICCIARDI

COLLINS and HARVILL PRESS
London, 1979

The author wishes to express her gratitude to:

Faber and Faber Ltd for permission to quote from
The Journey of the Magi from COLLECTED POEMS 1909–1962
by T. S. Eliot;

Hart-Davis MacGibbon Ltd for permission to quote from
On a Raised Beach by Hugh MacDiarmid;

The West Highland Free Press for permission to quote several extracts;

The Nature Conservancy for information about Rhum,
and Mr M. E. Ball for reading the Rhum text.

ISBN 0 00 262323 4

Set in 11pt Linotype Pilgrim
Made and printed in Great Britain by
William Collins Sons & Co Ltd, Glasgow
for Collins, St James's Place and
Harvill Press, 30A Pavilion Road, London SW1

TO BRIAN
who loves far horizons

Contents

Author's Note

This book sets forth a personal view limited by personal experience. It owes much to the help of my friends. To those who read, criticised and made suggestions for some or all of the manuscript I am most grateful: Sarah Hohler; Professor Hugh Seton-Watson and Iona MacDonald (for Skye); Alastair Nicholson (for Raasay).

I would also like to thank my sons Diarmaid and Iain, in whose homes I wrote much of the text. My husband Brian who shared island living. My Raasay friends for valuable material. Peter Zinovieff for Raasay geology notes. My publishers, Marjorie Villiers and Adrian House for their continual patience, encouragement and advice. Vicki Barter for enthusiastic support and for typing the manuscript. Mirella Ricciardi for her beautiful photographs.

PART I

Skye

Harris
Outer Hebrides
Lochmaddy
North Uist
Benbecula
South Uist
The Little Minch
Kilmaluag
Idrigil
Uig
Trotternish
Rona
Dunvegan
Portree
Raasay
Braes
Kyle of Lochalsh
Kyleakin
Island of Skye
Cuillin Hills
Red Hills
Soay
Elgol
Sleat
Armadale
Canna
Sanday
Rhum
Mallaig
Sea of the Hebrides
Eigg
Galmisdale
Muck
SCOTLAND
Coll
Arinagour
Tobermory
Dervaig
Tiree
Scarinish
Balemartine
Lochaline
Craignure
Ulva
Loch na Keal
+Ben More
Oban
Iona
Abbey
Fionnphort
Ross of Mull
Island of Mull
Inner Hebrides
Colonsay
Kilchattan
Scalasaig
Ardlussa
Oronsay
Jura
Loch Tarbert
Loch Gruinart
Paps of Jura
Port Askaig
West Tarbert
Craighouse
Rinns of Islay
Port Charlotte
Bowmore
Kildalton Chapel and Cross
Loch Indaal
The Oa
Port Ellen
Island of Islay
Airport
0
25
statute miles

I

The Journey North

The journey north from London had been long and tedious. The pitch and clank of the train, heard from my overnight sleeper, mingled with disturbed dreams. Pressures of life left behind in the South still nagged. Hurry, urgency, frustration beat below the tired mind and erupted into nightmare images. Sleep was elusive, coming and going intermittently while the train swayed, gathering speed, or ground to a halt. Lights flashed through the crevices of the blind. Sepulchral voices of loudspeakers on station platforms intoned unfamiliar names and destinations. As we lurched further north their accents sharpened, first into a Yorkshire twang, then into a resonant Scottish burr, and finally into a soft Highland drawl. Heard half-consciously below sleep, these impersonal voices soothed my troubled dreams. With their news of exotic journeys, 'The 8.50 pm from Euston will call at Crewe, Preston, Perth and Aviemore. Change at Carlisle for Dumfries,' they exorcised my anxiety. It no longer mattered if my suitcase was not packed in time, my train not caught, or my ticket not remembered.

At last, early morning light seeped through the compartment The train began to run more smoothly. The air became sharp and cool. Already I could feel the presence of the hills. I rose from my rumpled bed, pulled up the blind, opened the window and leaned out.

From a foreground of heather and rock the great shapes of the Cairngorms towered into the sky. Flank upon massive flank they marched beside the train like ghostly companions, a sprinkling of snow whitening their summits. A small wind stirred the moor and moved among the branches of silver birches and rowans. Patches of water, seen through the gathering light, rippled and gleamed. Silence, space, peace. The austerity and coldness of the North.

'Better close that window.'

The sleeper attendant had entered, bearing a pot of tea and the traditional three biscuits neatly wrapped in cellophane paper.

'It's sharp up here. We're running on time, so don't be too long. Soon in now.'

And indeed the train was tuning up for its approach to Inverness, capital of the Highlands. A draught of mountain air blew away the final vestiges of London tension. The waters of Loch Ness and the stone houses of the town approached, and I began to look forward to porridge and fresh baps for breakfast in the Station Hotel.

This journey, so often undertaken, so well known, is yet always new. My destination, a Hebridean island, can be reached in a few hours by aeroplane. But I prefer the slow unfolding of a journey by train. The three hours on the Highland line from Inverness to the west coast takes on a timeless quality as the train runs slower and slower, stopping at every station, waiting for long conversations between the guard and oncoming or departing passengers. The leisurely tempo encases one like a suit of comfortable old clothes, and gradually the Highland glens disclose their beauties.

Soon the impact of the sea begins to invade the landscape. Long tongues of water, running inland from the ocean, throw up borders of orange seaweed, flashed with brilliant green. Gulls peck among the rocks and wheel against spacious skies. Islands, mysterious with silver birches and pines, rise from clear waters.

Once more I lean out of the window. At all costs I must not miss the first sight of the Skye hills. On a clear day the range of the Cuillins slides into view round a long bend of loch. Far away, over the intervening sea, their purple frieze seems without substance, melting like a dream into the hazy sky. It is the signal to collect luggage, parcels, books, all the paraphernalia which litters the carriage.

The train rounds a couple of sea-girt bends, passes through a tunnel of rock and emerges between cliffs hung with heather and gorse, finally shuffling noisily into Kyle of Lochalsh – the large, ugly, sea-port station. This is the end of the line: a line recently condemned to closure, but given a reprieve by oil-platform construction at Kishorn nearby, and by current naval activity on the coast. A torpedo-testing base has been set up here and workmanlike Naval craft patrol the waters.

The train runs alongside the quays. I dismount, amid smells of oil, tar, fish and seaweed. Tourist cars are stacking up in the ferry bay, waiting to cross to Skye. Hikers, bowed under heavy rucksacks and hung with camping equipment, stride through the streets. Visitors ransack the shops for souvenirs and supplies. In a sudden flash of memory I recall childish forays to this town from neighbouring Skye over forty years ago. Then, the one village store contained everything from household utensils to thick underwear, and the car ferry consisted of two planks strapped across a heaving launch.

I return to the quayside to wait for the MacBrayne steamer from Mallaig. I want to see its departure for Portree, Skye's capital, and the island of Raasay. Opposite, on the Skye shore, stands the ruin of the ancient Castle Maoil, said to have belonged to a Norwegian princess who resourcefully threw a chain across the Kyle and levied a toll on all shipping passing through. Here, too, came the Norwegian King Hako's fleet, anchoring in these waters in 1263, and giving Kyleakin its name. Beinn na Caillich, the hill of the old woman, rearing above the scattering of white houses on the opposite shore, has seen craft of many kinds passing through these straits. Today's squat car ferries and sleek Naval vessels are the descendants of a long line of shipping.

At last a white speck comes into view far down the Kyle. The steamer. For several minutes she appears stationary, poised on the water between steep hillsides, signing her presence only by a flash of sunlight on her white superstructure. Then slowly she draws nearer, gathering speed moment by moment, until the churning of waves at her bow and the cloud of attendant seagulls are clearly visible. This steamer, which today has made the journey from the Small Isles farther down the coast, is the lifeline between the islands, bringing mail, supplies and news, and carrying the inhabitants from their isolated communities to the mainland or to Skye.

With a flourish she pulls up beside the quayside pier, engine revving, bells ringing. A coiled rope flung ashore is secured round a bollard. A gangway is dropped from the top deck at an alarming angle and levered into place on the shore. The quayside bursts into activity. Speed and purpose seize the crew as they heave supplies into the vessel: boxes of groceries, bags of mail, sacks, planks, building materials. Passengers gather up their belongings and manhandle them aboard, time only for a hurried greeting or goodbye.

'Well, then. Have a good trip.'

'Don't forget my love to Katie and Mary.'

'So, Captain, how are ye now?'

'Ah, well, you'll be off. Cheeribye.'

Everyone is impelled by a sense of urgency. Windblown and breathless, they wait for departure.

But now follows a long inexplicable delay. Leisurely conversations start up again between those aboard and those ashore. Nothing moves.

'What are we waiting for?'

'God knows!'

So presumably does the Captain. But he is not telling. Fresh from the orderly South I had forgotten this Highland rhythm of spurts and pauses. All life has now ceased on the quayside. Waves lap the sides of the steamer while a gull, poised on a bollard, eyes it with disdain.

'Is the train from the South in?'

'Ages ago.'

'Why don't we move, then?'

Suddenly, a burly figure is seen hurrying down the quayside, a bottle of whisky protruding from his overcoat pocket. He sights the vessel and breaks into an ungainly trot. The crew, about to draw up the gangway, hesitate.

'Donald. Is it you we've been waiting for?'

Donald's crimson face deepens in colour. With a last spurt he reaches the gangway, grips the handrail, hauls himself up and lurches aboard.

'Well, well, now,' he pants, subsiding on to a seat and gazing gratefully around him. 'Isn't it fortunate she hasn't left yet?'

The siren blows once, twice, three times. The gangway is levered aboard, the watch-bell rings, the engine revs up. With a sharp thrust the steamer tacks away from the pier. Ropes hurtle free and she manoeuvres herself into sailing position. The siren sounds a final toot, and then with a churn of the propeller, a flutter of the mast-head flag and all the dignity of an ocean-going liner, the *Loch Arkaig* proceeds deliberately on her way.

I turn away with a sigh. I wish I was going with her. I chart her route with my eyes, as she grows gradually smaller: past the lighthouse at the narrow Kyle, past the islands of Longay, Pabay and Scalpay, past the serrated Cuillins, until finally far out at sea she reaches the island of Raasay. Its long low contour broken by a hill shaped like an extinct volcano, beckons me with a strange fascination. Remote and mysterious, it shimmers on the horizon. One day, I promise myself, I will explore it.

2

Skye and the Cuillins

But now I must be on my way to Skye. The view of it from Kyle is appealing. The island lies across a narrow stretch of water, and the white houses and hotels of Kyleakin village gleam invitingly as car ferries ply busily back and forth, carrying loads of tourists to the Misty Isle. Skye's fame in story and song has drawn travellers for several hundreds of years. But in recent times the tourist boom has increased beyond all expectations, and now, during the season, the island experiences an influx of visitors which has turned most houses into bed-and-breakfast stands and many beauty spots into caravan sites. Only Skye's weather, traditionally cloudy and rainy (her name is derived from the Norse *Sky* (cloud) and *Ey* (island) saves her from total exploitation.

The island is wonderfully varied, with pastoral crofting land in the north, great bays and sea-cliffs in the west, the wooded peninsula of Sleat in the south and the strange tortured shapes of the Storr and Quirang rocks at each end of the northern rocky spine. Wings of land fly away from the central core in huge peninsulas (the Gaelic name for Skye is Sgiath meaning winged) and the sea is visible everywhere, never farther away than five miles, and usually much closer.

To travel 'over the sea to Skye', albeit on a crowded car ferry, and after a long and tiring journey north, is a passport to another world.

As always, my first glance is for the Cuillins, ranged on the western horizon. Today they are clear, dusted with snow, the sculptured shapes of the Red Cuillin falling in great sweeps to the shore, while the peaks of the higher Black Cuillin fret the sky. The loch below laps a coastline of gentle bays, then narrows to the channel where Kyle lighthouse guards a slim passage between Skye and the mainland. On a wooded peninsula opposite stands a white house, glimpsed among trees. My eyes are riveted to it, for this is Kyle House, once the home of my family and known and loved by me during the impressionable years of childhood.

I watch it disappear among its trees, and the ferry lands. Cars stream off on to Skye, and I look round anxiously to see if I have been met. Yes, my younger son Iain has come, tearing himself away from the house party of his Oxford undergraduate friends for whom I have arrived to cook and cater. We thread our way through the Kyleakin traffic and drive past Kyle House. And as we leave it behind my mind plays with the memories it has evoked.

For more than thirty years, between the two Wars and after, this house was rented by my uncle and aunt who used it as a holiday home, coming to it annually for two or three months in the summer and a month at Easter. I spent many holidays there, and as a result was imprinted for life with a passion for Skye.

My aunt ran Kyle House with apparently effortless hospitality. My uncle, Professor R. W. Seton-Watson, was a historian, founder of the School of Slavonic Studies at London University; and while he wrote his scholarly books in seclusion, a steady stream of visitors came and went, some impinging on his consciousness, some not. My aunt had a talent for imposing harmony on many diverse elements.

She entertained her guests in a variety of ways. She would wander with them round her walled garden on summer evenings, humming a tune to herself in an absent-minded fashion, and encouraging her flowers to grow in the wild Skye climate with loving phrases such as, 'Brave little fellows, aren't you?' or 'Go on trying'. Or, on rare fine evenings, she would take them to the 'Look-out' at the top of the hill behind the house (an old gun emplacement from the First World War) and show them the spectacle of the sun setting in Valkyrian flames amid a vast panorama of sky, sea and islands.

My uncle had a puckish sense of humour and a weakness for puns. When he emerged from his study, the family braced itself for a mixture of learned discourse and spoonerisms delivered with misleading innocence.

In the evenings, all of us – voracious readers – devoured books by lamplight; or sometimes sang Scottish 'Songs of the North', accompanied by my aunt on the piano giving her spirited renderings of,

> Will ye gang into the Hielands, Lizzie Lindsay?
> Will ye gang into the Hielands wi' me?

that to some extent redeemed the self-consciousness of the other performers. At bedtime each person took a candle from a selection on the hall table and mounted the stairs, surrounded by long shadows and the gentle sound of falling rain.

Below the house was a small bay with a shingle beach; there my two cousins, Hugh and Christopher, and I skimmed flat stones along the sea's surface or climbed the cliffs and boulders of the rocky coast. We christened each place with a special name – Long-stretch, Long-long-stretch, Eagle's nest – and ventured farther each day, frightening ourselves on slippery slopes hung with seaweed, or clinging to small holds above the curling water. The feel of rough rock under the fingers and toes, the chuckle of gulls, the smell of sea-wrack and wet heather; all these became an inextricable part of experience, something consistent and unchanging, unaffected by the process of growing-up or the sorrows and joys which life later washed around them.

In the late 1920s Kyleakin was a small village, and my aunt made her purchases at the one shop. If it ran out of whatever she needed, she crossed to Kyle on the ferry – a launch manned by two brothers who wore black oilskins all the year round – and visited a similar store on the mainland. Sometimes I went with her. This shop was a convivial place, stocking every kind of commodity under one roof. Shapeless Fair Isle jerseys hung in a row above the counter, flanked by outsize Harris tweed trousers. There were bales of knitting wool, fresh eggs, kippers, jars of home-made jams, chests of tea and rice, and indigestible 'shop' pastries. A hum of conversation – mostly in Gaelic – permeated the place, and a small purchase could take the inside of an hour by the time news and gossip had been exchanged. Coming from Skye, we were treated as country cousins visiting the mainland metropolis, and given first choice of things which might be running out in the island community.

Kyleakin harbour was picturesque. A fleet of high-masted fishing boats crowded into its narrow waters, and behind rose the ruins of Castle Maoil, standing on its green knoll. Beyond lay Loch na Beiste, a secret inlet of deep-green water which pierced the flanks of Beinn na Caillich, and was only approachable by foot over the hillside, or by boat round the shore. A family expedition there entailed some preliminary organization, for everyone had to be assembled, picnic baskets loaded and transported, and disputes as to who should travel by sea and who by land resolved. Having arrived at last, a ceremonial unpacking took place, and then the picnic would begin, with its usual accompaniment of midges and light rainfall.

My aunt was experienced at settling family differences, but it required all her skill to see that each demanding person was supplied quickly enough with hard-boiled eggs, cold mutton or ham, brown home-made bread and 'dripping cake'. Sitting on the damp slopes, we would gaze at the misty outlines of Beinn na Caillich, or in rare sunshine revel in the honey smell of heather in bloom. After lunch my cousins, keen bird-watchers, tramped the hill with field-glasses; while my uncle rowed his boat quietly about the loch, his high-pitched scholar's voice floating occasionally back to us over the water as he expounded the problems of Eastern Europe to his crony, a Catholic priest from Downside, who spent each holiday at Kyle House. My hospitable aunt, when she had dealt with the food, turned her attention to the youngest or the oldest member of the party, and I, coming in between, was forgotten.

Those endless afternoons of childhood when the grown-ups are busy and invention fails: how well I remember them! I would sit moodily in the heather, the emotions of adolescence boiling up inside me – anger, frustration and boredom, because no one was bothering particularly about me. I longed to do exciting things – to explore the island, climb in the Cuillins, sail across strange seas. In my dreams these adventures were legion, all accompanied by a shadowy Prince Charming who would come to claim me for his own, and by whose side my daring and resource would never fail. The reality was quite different: a podgy schoolgirl wrapped up in her own fantasies, constantly irritating others by her lack of commonsense. Even in Skye fantasy and reality are hard to bridge. Yet in the end some of my dreams came true.

Skye at Easter wears her most beautiful dress. Snow lies on the high hills, daffodils bloom in the cottage gardens, twigs are red with growing buds or green with delicate first leaves, and the sea shines dark-blue, flecked with surf blown up by the strong March winds.

I drove across the island with my son Iain, conscious of this beauty although still possessed by memories, until we reached our destination – the house we had rented for the Easter vacation. It stood on a slight rise two miles south of Portree, a comfortable family house, painted white outside, with a long drawing-room whose end windows faced the Cuillins, an attractive grassed courtyard, and a walled vegetable garden.

My two sons, Diarmaid, then aged twenty-one, and Iain, aged nineteen, had packed this house with their friends and were introducing them to the joys of climbing in the Cuillins under alpine conditions. All day they traversed ridges on hard-packed snow, cut steps up icy faces, and glissaded down snow-slopes. When darkness fell they returned home with gargantuan appetites and, after these had been satisfied, told stories of their climbs which demanded an appreciative audience. I had climbed in the Cuillins only in summer, never in winter, but I knew the areas they were describing and listened with interest, telling them in return some of the history of this extraordinary range of mountains.

The Cuillins are a young range, as the world's mountains go. About forty million years ago the island of Skye appeared, the wreck of a chain of vast volcanoes which had stretched from Britain to Greenland and which also included the islands of Mull, Arran and Rhum. The huge flows of lava which had poured from these early volcanoes survive to this day in basalt sheets and terraces which infiltrate the Hebrides; enormously strong rock, in some places still two thousand feet thick.

Most of the terrain of the Cuillins is rough gabbro, marvellous for the mountaineer, strong and unfriable with good holds. But every now and then a shiny grey intrusion of basalt manifests itself, and this ancient rock has a treacherously smooth surface, as my sons and their friends were beginning to discover.

The Cuillins themselves were produced in a second stage of volcanic activity after the plateaux of basalt had been laid down. They erupted in two separate explosions: first the basic rock which formed the jagged Black Cuillin and later the acid granite masses of the Red Cuillin. The violence of their origin still impregnates their shape.

'Struggling up some of those wild gullies,' Iain said, 'is like opening a gate to the Inferno. Today we went to Coire na Creiche. Isn't that where the last battle of the Skye clans was fought?'

It was, and I told them the story. The MacDonalds and the MacLeods, the two great clans of Skye, were perpetual enemies. They came to the island at roughly the same time during the thirteenth century and for the next four hundred years each harried the other's territory and disputed the other's rights. The climax came with the 'War of the One-Eyed Woman', which occurred because the MacDonald of the day – Donald Gorm Mor – had ill-treated Margaret MacLeod, sister of Rory Mor MacLeod of Dunvegan.

It was the custom then for a couple to spend a year of trial together before marriage. At the end of this year Donald Gorm, instead of marrying Margaret, returned her to her brother. Not only was one of her eyes badly injured, but Donald had mounted her on a one-eyed horse, escorted by a one-eyed groom and followed by a one-eyed dog.

'What happened then?' asked Iain.

'You can well imagine. A furious revenge of the insult by the MacLeods. They murdered and raped and pillaged the MacDonalds who in turn retaliated, and this warfare went on for two years.'

Finally the clans came face to face in Coire na Creiche. In that awesome and deserted place the MacDonalds routed the MacLeods. So the outcome of the feud was unfair to the victim. But the year was 1601. History was changing and the violence of clan warfare was becoming archaic. That clash of the clans among the craggy rocks was the last to take place in Skye.

'But in those days no one ever thought of climbing the Cuillins, did they?' said Diarmaid. 'At a push you might have a battle in one of the glens, but then you got out of the area as quickly as possible to avoid the ghosts and devils who lived there.'

'Yes, indeed. The Cuillins weren't climbed until over two hundred years later. The first to be conquered was Sgurr nan Gillean, the Mountain of the Young Men, which you can see from the drawing-room windows. It was climbed in 1836 by a geologist called Forbes. He also drew the first map of the Cuillins.'

'It must have been fantastic exploring that range for the first time, untrodden and unmapped.'

'It was. The Victorian climbers did it at the same time as the Alps were discovered. One by one the great Cuillin peaks were conquered, and some of them were then named after the first climbers – Sgurr Alastair, after Sheriff Alastair Nicholson, and Collie's climb on Sgurr Dearg after Professor Norman Collie.'

'When was the main ridge first traversed?'

'Not until much later. In 1911.'

'I traversed it when I was a schoolboy at Gordonstoun,' said Iain. 'It's a vast horseshoe six miles long, most of it three thousand feet high. I did it with two other boys and one of the masters. We didn't quite complete it, but we were climbing for seventeen hours. I think the record time for it is about seven hours.'

'It's climbed regularly every year now. So are all the other main peaks. In fact, on a fine summer's day you can see people on almost every major pinnacle.'

'Do you think this influx of climbers has spoiled the Cuillins?' Diarmaid was asked.

'It's hard to say,' he replied. 'As you know, waiting one's turn at the foot of a popular climb is a bit claustrophobic. But once you're on a face or a ridge, the size of the slopes and the exposure of the rock dwarf all human activity. People are redundant in that setting, it's like a Valhalla of the gods. But you can't know that until you've climbed there.'

I agreed. My mind returned to childhood and my first sight of the Cuillins. Then, across the water, they had looked ethereal, their outline continually changing in the shadow cast on them by clouds and by the play of light and shade. Often swathed in mist, their emergence could be as unexpected as a rainbow, with banners of vapour twirling round their peaks, and dark clefts and pinnacles being revealed and hidden again in tantalizing mystery. Sometimes my cousins would set off for a day's mountaineering with one of the experienced climbers whom they knew. I longed to explore this unknown territory with them but I never had the opportunity until, in 1936, they took me up Clach Glas and Blaven and at last a view of the whole Cuillin ridge unfolded before my entranced eyes. A year later, in 1937, I met the Prince Charming of my dreams. He was a Scotsman, David Douglas-Hamilton, tall and determined, who had already climbed in the Alps, and was a keen mountaineer. We shared a love of mountains and wild places, I talked to him of the Cuillins and shortly before our marriage in 1938, he took me to climb them.

We stayed at Sligachan Hotel, the original mountaineers' inn, from which the Victorian climbers had sallied forth to conquer their peaks. Over the years Sligachan had developed into a large comfortable country hotel, and now it catered for tourists as well as mountaineers. It was placed in dramatic scenery among the conical Red Cuillin, and behind it towered Sgurr nan Gillean, the Mountain of the Young Men.

In the hall of the hotel hung two large photographs, each

depicting a precipitous tower of rock. David's brother Malcolm, and his wife Pam, had joined us for a week of mountaineering, and we looked at the pictures together.

'Oh, yes,' said Malcolm. 'Those towers are the Gendarme on Sgurr nan Gillean and the Inaccessible Pinnacle on Sgurr Dearg.'

'We've climbed them both,' Pam added.

I looked again at the daunting photographs, well-named inaccessible in my opinion. 'I don't suppose you'll want to go up there again, will you?' I asked, my courage evaporating. I was the novice of the four, and I wished to be broken in gently.

But the next day I found myself on the Pinnacle Ridge of Sgurr nan Gillean, face to face with the Gendarme. He reared up, blocking any other route, and on each side of him the mountain fell away in a steep drop of many hundreds of feet. It was a clear day, so the doubtful blessing of mist which might have disguised some of the exposure, was denied. The tower of rock was vertical. Perhaps, I thought, it could be scaled direct if it were not for the prospect of balancing on the top, an additional twelve feet or so above the already airy and narrow ridge on which we stood. I wondered if a direct climb was the route, and fervently hoped not.

To my relief, David seized the Gendarme with both arms, pressed his body to the rock, and then wormed his way round one side of it until nothing remained in view but one foot. Finally even that disappeared and I was left alone, gazing at the pinnacle before me, now incongruously decorated with the rope which attached David to me. It tightened round my waist, and then: 'Come on,' I heard David say, in impatient tones.

I embraced the Gendarme with passion. By dint of looking upwards rather than downwards, and by an exercise of blind faith that my toe, stretching sideways round the bulk of rock, would find a foothold, I got round. Malcolm then skipped over the top and Pam followed round the side with enviable aplomb.

From the summit of Sgurr nan Gillean a panorama of the Cuillin range opened out before us. Towering cliffs reared up from bare grey screes. Huge boulders lay scattered about the corries. No grass, heather or flowers masked the stern skeleton of the mountains. I realized that here their shapes were stripped bare. The world of rock, scree and stone was all-powerful and nothing softened its impact. I could understand why the Cuillins have been called savage, malignant, infernal.

'Well, that's your first climb,' said David. 'Just a beginning. There's lots more to come.'

Next day we tackled the Inaccessible Pinnacle. This bastion of rock projects from the south-east side of the summit of Sgurr Dearg, and is about twenty feet higher. For many years it was considered unclimbable, but was finally conquered in 1880 by two brothers called Pilkington. It has a vertical western face of about forty feet, and an eastern spine 125 feet in length which has been described as a 'knife-edged ridge, with an overhanging and infinite drop on one side, and a drop on the other side even steeper and longer'.

The first step on to the Pinnacle is the most difficult. You have to balance on a boulder above a sheer wall of rock and reach up to a sloping ledge. An inlay of basalt makes its surface slippery and devoid of good holds. The ledge, about waist-high, pushed into my stomach and I was very conscious of the drop below as I tried to pull myself up. 'Press down on your left hand and reach up high with your right leg,' called David, from above.

So easy to give instructions once you've done it, I thought. But I followed them, they worked, and soon I was at the top of the Pinnacle.

The descent down the eastern spine above the 'overhanging and infinite drop' was much easier. Stepping from stone to stone on that narrow knife-edge I felt closer to sky than earth, companion to some eagle of the crags and one with the elements of sun, wind and air. At last my dreams of climbing in the Cuillins were finding fulfilment.

I had hoped that the traverse of the Inaccessible Pinnacle would be the main challenge of the day. But I had reckoned without Malcolm. It was still early, only just past midday, and the sun blazed on dry rock.

'Think I'll have a look at the south crack,' he said.

This narrow fissure, which cuts the face of the Pinnacle's south-west wall, provides very small holds on an otherwise blank and perpendicular cliff. Malcolm changed into rubber-soled shoes and started to swarm up it. About thirty feet up a slab of rock jams the crack, jutting out into a slight bulge. The climber has to lean out from the face and pull up over this obstacle, the crux of the climb. Malcolm hesitated below it, poised on toenail footholds. For what seemed a long time he hung there, searching for some way round the difficulty. Then he began to descend.

'Got to change my shoes,' he muttered, the light of battle still in his eye. Shod now in paper-thin bathing shoes, he tackled the crack once more. Moving in easy rhythm to the bulge, he hardly changed his pace as he pulled up over it, stood on the holds above it and continued to the crest. We watched him with stiff necks, then saw his smiling face outlined against the sky.

He made himself fast on the ridge, then shouted for David to follow. David, held on a rope from the top, skimmed up with ease. And then it was my turn.

The only compensation of a really severe climb is that the situation is so extreme that you have no time to feel afraid. The instinct for self-preservation and the adrenalin flooding through your system make you grasp the rock with manic force.

The first half of the climb was comparatively easy, for the holds, though very small, were well-placed and firm. But the exposure was horrifying. The cliff was perpendicular and the ground below receded in a swiftly accelerating fall. I reached the bulge and as I leant out to circumvent it I felt the full force of gravity about to pluck me off the mountain. For an instant I swayed, then my fingers tightened on the holds above and pushing with my toes, I pulled myself up and over. Now I had only to refrain from looking down and to command my tense hands and toes to keep moving in rhythm from hold to hold. Gradually the face fell away behind me and the length of cliff above decreased. At last David leaned over and grasped my hand to lever me up over the last few feet. I sank gratefully on to the narrow ledge, the hot hard rocks a welcome contact with earth after my airy ascent. I did not dare to look down, where Pam was following up with quiet competence, because rock, sky and distant sea were revolving slowly before my eyes in a giant cyclorama.

The reward of such climbs is the stretching of one's powers to their fullest limit. The catharsis which the effort, mental and physical, entails also brings an awareness of beauty which seems unique. When the world had stopped revolving I realized that I was now part of this mountain scene in a new way. I had earned my place there, I could identify with the texture of the rock and the sweep of the face; the mountains would disclose for me their private beauties of crag, crest and ledge, unknown to those who never climbed into their midst.

Far away gleamed the western sea, dark shapes of islands grazing upon it like sheep on a cobalt plain. Below shone Loch Coruisk, the most famous loch on the island, ringed by the horseshoe range. And all around rose the magnificent Cuillin ridge, mile upon mile of shattered rock, gathering itself into knife-edges, lifting to towers of fantastic shape, and dropping to precipitous cols, a 3,000-foot-high roadway of the gods. I felt I had earned the right to tread it and a new dimension was added to my love for Skye.

I often remembered that climb during the dark days of war which followed so soon afterwards. David, by then my husband, and Malcolm were called up into the RAF. David became a fighter pilot and in the following years my two sons were born, one in 1940, the second in 1942.

Skye was a prohibited area during the war and any hope of visiting it or climbing in the Cuillins was out of the question. Naval craft patrolled its coasts and only inhabitants or their close relatives were allowed to come and go.

So it was six years before I stood again on a Cuillin peak. I returned to the mountains bereaved, as had been so many others, by the war. My brother-in-law Malcolm came with me. He had lost a brother, I a husband. We both hoped that somehow the healing power of these mountains might bring back to us the one we had lost, in the terrain he had loved.

At my suggestion, we climbed Blaven, and once again from its summit I had a magnificent view of the whole Cuillin range and of Loch Coruisk shimmering far below. This loch was one of my favourite places in Skye. As a child, I had sailed across to it from Elgol in an old fishing smack, a never-to-be-forgotten journey with water lapping at the tarry sides of the boat, beams creaking, wind tugging the canvas and dark-blue waves undulating away in gleaming folds. Near Coruisk's shores the sea shallowed to a brilliant emerald, and stones in its sandy bed had shone like buried gold.

With David I had walked round the shores of Loch Slapin, feared for its sudden storms, and reached Coruisk by the Bad Step, a scramble over an exposed slab of rock near the loch itself.

Famous ever since Sir Walter Scott first romanticized it in *The Lord of the Isles*, Coruisk is now a tourists' Mecca, yet human beings are still dwarfed by the 'grim and awful giants keeping their eternal watches' which surround the loch. 'Monsters of the Primal turned into stone, yet with a strong life and consciousness in their fixed look and stern sphinx-like response,' was how Sheriff Nicholson, pioneer of so many Cuillin climbs, described them.

But perhaps the most perfect way of all to come upon this loch is to descend to it after a climb up and over the ridge from Glen Brittle on the other side. This, almost at the end of our visit, was the approach which Malcolm and I chose.

We started with a trudge up Coire na Banachdich until we reached a wall of rock on the left side of the Banachdich Gully. On this wall was a climb which offered a long stretch of good rock. We set off up it, leading alternately. Conditions were ideal. The rock was firm and dry, and the sun hot; and feeling again the rough stone under our fingers, the strains and horrors of war began to diminish. When we reached the crest and looked down at Loch Coruisk it seemed to reflect our mood, as it lay gleaming far below in the heart of the Cuillin horseshoe, all menace dissolved by the radiant summer sun.

We lunched on the summit, then descended to Coruisk by

the Coireachan Ruadha – the red corrie – a wild place ringed round with peaks jutting up from steep scree slopes. As we neared the loch the ground grew wetter and wetter, and hotter and hotter shone the sun. We longed to bathe. We still had a strenuous climb ahead of us, back over the ridge and down to Glen Brittle on the other side, and it was already 4 pm. But the loch sparkled invitingly and when we reached the slabs at the foot of the Dubhs we could no longer resist. We plunged in, breaking the mirrored reflections of the Cuillins.

Sgurr Dubh Beag and Sgurr Dubh Mor – the small black peak and the big black peak – soared up from the shore. After only a short rest, rejuvenated by the icy water, we started up Dubh Beag; as we climbed its rough slabs, Coruisk fell away behind us, sinking farther and farther down, becoming remote and inaccessible once more. The sun was dropping towards the horizon, casting long shadows, and mist began to cloud the peaks. The view of the islands out to sea grew hazy. We roped for the pitch off Dubh Beag, then walked along the fine ridge to Sgurr Dubh Mor. The third peak, Dubh na da Beinn, loomed high ahead. To reach it we had to climb a tower and negotiate a very exposed corner with an alarming drop. The mist was thickening, and I began to wonder if we would get off the mountain while it was still light. We were short of time, and the final hazard, the Thearlaich-Dhu Gap, still lay ahead. This place has an awesome reputation and had been haunting me all day.

By the time we reached it the rock was very wet. We roped thirty feet down the Dubh side and the Gap disclosed itself as a narrow ledge with a precipitous fall on each flank. Ahead towered the wall of Sgurr Thearlaich, slashed by an eighty-foot vertical chimney, the only means of exit. The light waned, the mist deepened and the wind rose. I was reminded of the advice given in the *Scottish Mountaineering Club Guide*: 'The passage not being absolutely simple, it is recommended that a party of tourists should not all descend into the Gap at one time, in case they might have to remain there permanently.'

I watched Malcolm swarm up the chimney and reflected,

not for the first time, on the mixed joys of mountaineering. Then my turn came. I laboured up, the heavy rucksack which I was carrying continually sticking in the narrow cleft. Half-way up, an unsteady chock-stone wedged in the chimney entailed a traverse out on to the face. I accomplished this to the right instead of to the orthodox left side, thus adding to my difficulties, and reached the top panting for breath and with shaking hands.

There was no time to rest. Darkness was gathering and we had to press on to the summit of Sgurr Thearlaich, our final peak. But when we reached it at last, it was cold and wet, and thick mist obscured any view. We made haste to descend, but in bad visibility the route over the rocks was hard to find. By the time we roped down the final pitch it was 9 pm.

The long Highland summer evenings have a magic of their own even when, as then, they are overcast. Twilight comes slowly with a glimmer of water and the sound of the last bird's cry. We looked down at Loch Coire Lagan, grey under the grey sky, and saw beyond it the path home winding through the glen. Our climb was over. In the hills we had found some solace for our grief and some measure of peace. But now we must return.

Swiftly we ran down the scree slope and when we reached the path we turned with one accord for a last glimpse of the peaks. They were invisible. Swathed in mist, guarding their jewel of Coruisk, symbol of beauty, the Cuillins had withdrawn once more into their own mysterious isolation.

3

Some Island History

Skye was my first love among the Hebridean Islands and I tended to think that no other could surpass it. In fact all possess a special beauty derived from their sea-girt position and the luminous quality of their light.

The Norse named them *Havbredy* which means 'Isles on the Edge of the Sea' and although all share a common origin and history, each is unique. As I grew to know them better and love them more I found myself searching out the facts of their existence. For an island, a microcosm of a macrocosm, presents a view of history which is at once clear and dramatic, like the view through the wrong end of a telescope. Its size limits complexity.

During the course of the centuries many of the same things happened to each of the Islands. But geography has divided them naturally into two groups – the Outer, which lie far from the mainland coast and stretch in a long line for 130 miles along the Atlantic seaboard; and the Inner, closer inshore. Skye belongs to the Inner group, and is the farthest north. South and south-west of her lie the remaining islands of the Inner Hebrides, and these are scattered over a wide area, some near the mainland, others out in the western sea within sight of Ireland.

The bones of all these islands lie bare. There is little superstructure of roads, houses, or human habitation to cover them. Much of their land consists of heathery moor sweeping up to rough hills. And stone, an integral part of it, keeps breaking through in the form of boulders, rock-faces, pebble beaches, and sea-cliffs pounded by the constant surge of waves.

Here man has made little mark. His presence, as recent as the last few thousand years, is infinitesimal in comparison to the time-scale of the geological changes, some violent, some gradual, from which this land has emerged. A portion of the world's most ancient rock is found here: schist, gneiss and Torridonian sandstone which have undergone vast tectonic stresses. Here

> . . . a man must shed the encumbrances that muffle
> Contact with elemental things, the subtleties
> That seem inseparable from a human life, and go apart
> Into a simpler and sterner, more beautiful and more
>   impressive world,
> Austerely intoxicating . . .*

And because the landscape still shows signs of its origin (on Skye's coastline you can see clearly the raised beaches, the tiered escarpments cut in ancient lavae, and the deep sea-lochs – in reality drowned glens) it is easy to imagine how it looked before the advent of man. Scotland, in fact, was under ice for so long a period that the history of the human habitation of the Highlands extends back only a few thousand years. In the Hebrides, the landscape still seems to dwarf the people who live in it; while the inescapable sea, at once the source of their sustenance and their isolation, beats without remittance on their shores.

It was from the sea that the first settlers came, probably from Ireland and probably by coracle (a boat made of hides stretched over a wooden frame and used up to the time of St Columba and his emigrant monks in the sixth century AD). All is conjecture, but the primitive stone artifacts which these first men made, and which have been found on Skye and several of the other Inner Hebrides, are similar to those discovered at Larne, on the Antrim coast of Ireland.

The Mesolithic hunter-gatherers who arrived about 4600 BC

* Hugh MacDiarmid: from 'On a Raised Beach'

lived precarious lives, existing on raised beaches twenty-five feet or so above the sea. They hunted seals and deer, and made spears and harpoons of bone with which they caught fish. Their shallow caves and flimsy shelters afforded not much more protection than the nest of a seabird or an animal's lair and, like an animal, the fear of death must have been their daily companion, a familiar which never left them and often struck.

History unfolded slowly in those days and it was many hundreds of years before the next colonizers arrived: Neolithic men who came around 3300 BC bringing with them their stone axes, flint tools, domestic animals and grain seeds. During the next two thousand years these colonizers spread to all the larger Hebridean Islands, and they left many traces, including chambered cairns which they used for burial and huge standing stones and stone circles similar to Stonehenge.

We can only guess how these great blocks, some up to seventeen feet high, were erected. To stand in the midst of them, as at Callernish in Lewis, or Brogar in Hoy, one of the Shetland Isles, is a mysterious experience. The stones now are no more than a majestic pattern on the lonely moor. But once they were structures for sacrifices which would make corn grow and animals breed, their circle representing the sun's journey and the year's calendar, calculated through their alignment. Life then did not end with death. Favourite possessions were placed in the tombs and accompanied those travelling to the next world. And when, later, Bronze Age immigrants – Beaker Folk – came from the Rhine, bringing with them pottery, metal bracelets, and earrings and necklaces of amber or lignite beads, these too found their way into the graves and remained there for thousands of years, quietly waiting to become the means whereby their owners' lives could be reconstructed.

During the Bronze Age the links between Ireland and the Hebrides became even closer. The Irish Sea was by then a waterway for colonizers not only to Ireland but also to the north of Scotland, the Orkneys, Shetlands and Scandinavia. Trade flourished as far south as Cornwall, as far west as the Baltic and Spain, and the Hebrides received their share. From

Ireland came designs for the hammered bronze shields of the Hebridean warriors, artifacts which influenced the people's daily lives, and legends of gods and heroes which fed their imaginations. In Irish mythology there was no clear division between natural and supernatural experience. Irish seers were able to visit the lands of the dead as *echtrai* (the adventurers) or *baili* (those who possessed ecstatic vision). They were freed from the limitations of time and space and after their sojourn they could bring back the wisdom of the supernatural world. Today some old Highlanders still possess the gift of second sight, and can foretell future events, usually, it must be admitted, unpleasant ones. But this capacity is becoming rare. Radio and television have exorcized it, and the voices heard now in the Hebrides are no longer those of spirits, witches or fairies.

Anyone who visits Skye will be impressed with the number of *brochs* or *duns* (crumbling stone forts) which abound there, particularly in the north of the island. How did they come to be built and why do they always occupy a prominent position on a headland, usually within sight of one another? They were obviously erected as a means of defence, but against whom?

Their origin is unknown, but it is likely that the forts which first stood on these sites were built in the late Bronze Age and were used against the bringers of iron, the Celts, who appeared in the Hebrides from 500 BC onwards.

The Celts came from Europe via Britain, Ireland and Northern Gaul. They conquered the territories bordering the Irish Sea which are still associated with their name, settled there, and mixed with the local inhabitants, bequeathing to them the red hair and blue eyes which are a Highland characteristic to this day. Once established, the Celts in their turn re-built the hill forts they had destroyed, and prepared to defend them against invaders.

The Southern Islands meantime were busy resisting a different enemy: the powerful forces of Rome. It is difficult to visualize Roman legions in Scotland, although one can clearly imagine how uncomfortable they must have been. But in spite of the climate and a less than friendly welcome, they came in AD 79 and stayed for three hundred years. They were continually harassed by a confederation of tribes whom they named Picti or Pictones, and who around AD 300 united to form a Pictish kingdom. The Irish joined in the battle (the Romans named them Scotti to add to the confusion) and while the Romans manned the Antonine and Hadrian walls, these Picts and Irish-Scots warriors flung themselves against the Roman fortifications, fighting naked, their bodies painted with vivid identification colours – a habit which sent a chill through Roman hearts. At last, about AD 385, the Romans withdrew and the field was left clear for the Picts and the Irish-Scots, who by this time had colonized Kintyre on the West Scottish coast and the island of Islay, and had joined the two into a kingdom, Dalriada, which was linked to the Irish King of Antrim.

Ireland's heroic age, the age of mythical kings and warriors, had already spilled over into the Hebrides. Ireland had sent the islands their first colonists, first boats, first tools, and first beliefs. Now the first of Christianity was to appear, and again it came from Ireland.

Nothing is more poignant than to stand beside the remains of one of the early Hebridean foundations, sited for beauty as well as remoteness, and to re-create in one's mind the mission of those saints who 'left all to journey over the sea for Christ's sake'.

St Columba is the most famous, but he was preceded by St Ninian, St Brendan and many others. Some sailed their boats from the Irish shore, committed themselves to God, and let the wind and tide take them where they would, careless of their destination. Some may have reached Iceland, Greenland and even America. Some were drowned. But all were inspired by the extraordinary missionary zeal which exploded in Ireland during the fifth and sixth centuries.

St Columba came to Iona in 563. By then war was raging between the Picts and the Irish-Scots colonists. Pockets of Christianity had been established in the Irish-Scots kingdom of Dalriada, and in a few places farther north, but the Picts were heathen, followers of the ancient religion of the Druids, first established in Neolithic times. It was probably Druids who raised the huge standing stones and stone circles of Callernish and Brogar, and used them for human sacrifice. Yet much of the Druid morality was chivalrous, generous and compassionate to the weak.

'Though near to stone is the earth, nearer than that is the help of the Druid,' says one of their proverbs. And the beautiful prayer used in their May Day rites of the lighting of the Bealltuinn fires, could have been composed by a Christian saint:

O God, kindle in my heart
A glimmer of the sun's warmth towards my neighbour,
Towards my enemy, towards my friend,
Towards the free, towards the slave, towards the bondsman –
O Sons of the Earth soft and fair,
From the lowest created thing
Up to the Circle most High.

Many of St Columba's foundations were established on Druid sites, including the mother house of Iona itself, from which flowed forth such a stream of missionary activity; and the Druid sun-circle was incorporated in the Celtic Christian cross.

By the time of St Columba's death in 597, his mission had been achieved. The Highlands and the Hebrides were Christian. A hundred monasteries and several hundred churches had been established and Christ's gentle doctrine had entered men's hearts. It was never thereafter entirely forgotten. Succeeding generations of Christian saints consolidated Columba's work and built chapels and oratories in the most remote places, in spite of unremitting Picto-Scottish strife. Ireland's influence in the Hebrides had reached its height. But now, from an entirely different quarter a force of unparalleled violence was about to erupt.

I have often stood on a headland in Skye and looked northwards. The sea stretches to the horizon, vast and limitless, and one's eye is drawn to its farthest extremity. There sky and water meet in an uncompromising iron-grey line. And it was from there, in 795, that Viking invaders struck. Their invincible dragon-prowed longships swarmed into Hebridean waters and the islands were submerged by a tide which did not recede for four hundred years.

Iona was sacked three times, and the mainland Picts so weakened that in 843 the Scots King, Kenneth MacAlpine, was able to join the Pictish and Scots kingdoms into one people: Scotland.

The Islands took the main brunt of Norse invasion. Coming first as piratical raiders, a later wave of Norsemen arrived around 875, and stayed as colonizers, treating the conquered territory as their own and often refusing to obey the feudal demands of their Norwegian king. Celtic and Norse races intermingled and produced a mixture of the two called the Gaidhal – 'a restless and ungovernable people'.

The islemen's fury against Norse domination erupted from time to time, but power was on the side of the invaders and even the Scottish king was forced to acknowledge Norse suzerainty over the Hebrides. Norse influence was profound, especially in the Northern and Outer Isles, and traces of it can be seen even today in the number of place names (two-thirds of the total in Skye alone) and the Scandinavian appearance of many islanders.

The Norsemen stayed in the Hebrides until the mid-thirteenth century. The Southern Islands were freed first, in 1156, by Somerled, King of Argyll, who defeated the Norse King of the Isles and then annexed all islands south of the Ardnamurchan peninsula. A hundred years later Skye was devastated by an attack from the mainland, probably instigated by the Scottish king. In reprisal, King Hako of Norway sailed from Bergen with a fleet of 120 ships. He anchored at Kyleakin, and then his whole armada sailed on down the coast to Largs. There, in August 1263, they were decisively defeated by the Scottish King Alexander III. A gale overtook King Hako as he escaped, and most of his galleys were wrecked on the coasts of Larne, Mull and Skye. He himself took refuge in Loch

Bracadale, in Skye, then sailed for home, but died in the Orkneys before he could reach his journey's end. The Hebrides were ceded to Scotland, and Skye was added to the territory of the Lord of the Isles.

The title, 'Lord of the Isles' is a romantic one, suggesting an era where everything is larger than life: chiefs more noble, clansmen more fierce, loyalties more powerful and battles more heroic.

Victorian writers like Sir Walter Scott, Ossian, and others who popularized this period, tended to extol its primitive virtues, so different from those of their own age, and gloss over its defects. In fact it was savage, barbaric and cruel, torn with clan feuds and clan warfare. Life was precarious and liable to end swiftly. Yet it was during this era that the Isles were united for the first time under firm rule and thus enabled to develop into a powerful entity of their own.

Somerled was the first Celtic King of the Isles (his predecessors had all been Norse) and the Gaelic kingdom which he founded was of great importance to the Hebrides. Somerled was also the founder of Clan Donald, the clan which later gained suzerainty over a huge area which included all the Hebridean Islands as well as the mainland from the Assynt coast to the Mull of Kintyre. From this position of strength, acquired through judicious marriages and royal gifts from the King of Scotland, the MacDonalds granted lands to vassal clans. Each clan had its own chief, but all were subject to the Council of Fourteen who met annually on Islay to dispense justice and discuss Hebridean affairs.

Islay, Mull, Skye and Lewis, were centres for regional administration, and every large island had its own court of justice. In addition, each clansman possessed the right of appeal to the Council at Islay. Over all ruled the chief of Clan Donald – *Buchaille nan Eileann* – the Herdsman of the Isles. Like all good shepherds, he was expected, if necessary, to give his life for his sheep. At his ceremony of inauguration he placed his bare left foot in a stone footprint as a symbol of his intention to walk in the steps of his forefathers, and the tradition he followed was one of service as well as power.

The Gaelic kingdom of the Lords prospered. Although clan feuds were never eradicated, they were considerably modified. During three hundred years of relative peace, the Lords ruled their territories, pursued their own policies and negotiated their own treaties with England, Ireland and France.

But it was inevitable that their power should begin to challenge the power of the Kings of Scotland. A particular bone of contention was the doctrine of feudalism. Feudal institutions, derived from the Anglo-Normans, had been established on the Scottish mainland during the eleventh century. They entailed obligatory serfdom. But the tradition of the Isles, both Celtic and Norse, was one of freedom – the clansman bound to his chief by ties of blood and loyalty, never of servitude.

In 1543 the crisis came. James IV of Scotland forced John II of Islay to relinquish his title of Lord of the Isles. The Donald line continued on Islay; but with no focal point and no common interest, each island chief plotted against his neighbour and appalling internecine strife took place.

Finally James VI of Scotland and I of England decided to put an end to this anarchy. In 1609 he summoned the Hebridean chiefs to a Council in Iona, where he imposed on them nine statutes, one of which was that bards who glorified war should be suppressed. Soon after, at the instigation of the Earl of Argyll, the King transferred the ownership of Islay to the Earl's kinsman, Sir John Campbell of Calder, and in 1615 the last of Somerled's line, Sir James MacDonald, fled from Islay and was imprisoned in Edinburgh.

So ended the era of the Lords of the Isles. Skye was one of the regional centres and played an important part, the island being divided between the MacDonalds (Clan Donald of Sleat) and the MacLeods (Clan Leod of West Skye). The MacLeods claimed as ancestors the Norseman Olave, King of Man, whose grandson, Norman, became the first of the Skye MacLeods. The MacDonalds descended from Somerled. So the pedigrees of both clans extended back into the mists of time and the honour of each was jealously guarded.

Skye abounds in places where bloody battles were fought between the MacDonalds and the MacLeods, and their feuds spread to the surrounding islands, over which they had suzerainty. Galleys sailed across the sea on punitive raids. Populations who took refuge in caves or churches were smothered or burned. And violence bred counter-violence down to the third or fourth generation.

Such a way of life was only possible while the clans flourished, for it depended on a close-knit loyalty which bound the chief and his clansmen in an indissoluble pattern. The clansmen provided the fighting force. The chief gave them leadership, sustenance and protection; and all shared the same name, the same blood and the same tradition. They lived or died together.

But with the break-up of the Lords of the Isles the first seeds of destruction of the clan system were sown. The two hundred and fifty years of violent clan feuding which followed, weakened the clans still further and the ill-fated Jacobite rising of 1745 delivered its *coup de grâce*. Ironically, it is this event by which they are best known and most widely remembered.

4

The Prince in the Heather

Prince Charles Edward came to Skye in 1746 with a price of £30,000 on his head. The time was late June and it was not a year since he had first set foot on Scottish soil. His desperate venture – to regain the crown of England for the Stuarts – had met with initial success. Some of the most powerful Highland chiefs had joined his cause, his troops had occupied Edinburgh, and his army had marched as far south as Derby, causing the English King George II to make hasty preparations for flight to Holland. But then the tide had turned, and the long slow dispiriting retreat back to Scotland had ended in the disaster of Culloden, a defeat from which the clans never recovered. The broken remnants of the Jacobite army fled into hiding in the heather and the Prince escaped to the Outer Isles.

He stayed there for almost two months. He had hoped to hire a ship which would take him to Orkney and then Norway, or to be rescued from France. Instead, the net of his pursuers grew ever tighter, Government troops and ships closed in, and only the expedients of a few devoted Jacobites saved him from discovery. It became imperative that he should leave the islands. But how? It was then that a young woman of twenty-five, Flora MacDonald, appeared. Boswell, in his *Journal of the Hebrides*, tells us that she offered 'with the magnanimity of a Heroine, to accompany him in an open boat to Skye, though the coast they were to quit was guarded by ships'.

In fact, Flora was at first unwilling to undertake such a

dangerous enterprise, but once committed she showed great resourcefulness. She persuaded her stepfather, Captain of a company of militia from Skye, to give her a pass for herself, her manservant and her maid, an Irish girl called Bettie Burk. Bettie Burk was in reality the Prince. Flora procured women's clothes for him (refusing to allow him to hide a pistol under his petticoats), arranged several rendezvous in the teeth of Government troops and finally, after a week's anxious comings and goings (at the end of which the Prince was reduced to hiding under a rock in Benbecula), embarked with him for Skye.

They left at 8 pm on the evening of 28 June, and the crossing was stormy. In Flora's words, 'They had not rowed from the shore above a League till the sea became rough, and at last tempestuous, and to entertain the Company the Prince sang several songs and seemed to be in good spirits.'

Danger often evoked from him a courageous and optimistic response. But if he expected help from the Skye lairds his hope was ill-founded. Neither Sir Alexander MacDonald nor the MacLeod of the day had come out for the Jacobite cause, and the island was swarming with militia. Nevertheless, remembering Clanranald, head of the MacDonalds, and MacDonald of Keppoch – both of whom had supported him – the Prince felt that he was 'sure to meet with greater favour among the worst of the MacDonald men than among the cold MacLeods'. So, when they landed in north-west Skye, it was to Sir Alexander MacDonald's house that Flora fled.

Sir Alexander's wife, Lady Margaret MacDonald, was an ardent Jacobite. Her family, like many others, had been divided by the '45, and at that moment her husband was at Fort Augustus on the mainland, serving with the notorious Duke of Cumberland, King George's son and General. One of the Government militia officers, a Lieutenant MacLeod, was actually in her house, about to dine at her table, having arrived shortly before with a party of men in search of the Prince.

The bravest heart might have quailed at these circumstances, but Lady Margaret 'showed a perfect presence of mind, and readiness of invention, and at once settled that Prince Charles should be conducted to . . . some select friends'. She and Flora entertained the Lieutenant at dinner while her factor, MacDonald of Kingsburgh, was despatched to the shore where he found the Prince and informed him of his danger. On the way to Kingsburgh's house the Prince, forgetting his woman's attire, held his skirts up so high as he leapt across a Highland burn, and took such large strides that 'some women they met reported that they had seen a very big woman, who looked like a man in woman's clothes, and that perhaps it was . . . the Prince'.

This Ruritanian atmosphere was further prolonged at Kingsburgh's house. Kingsburgh's wife, reporting on the events afterwards to Bishop Forbes,* said, 'I saw such an odd muckle trallup of a carlin, making lang, wide steps through the hall that I could not like her appearance at all.'

The evening developed into a convivial one and the good wife's first fears were confirmed. She was told that her guest was the Prince.

'O Lord,' she cried, 'we are ruined and undone for ever! We will a' be hang'd now.'

'Hout, goodwife,' Kingsburgh replied, 'we will die but ance, and if we are hanged for this I'm sure it will be in a good cause.'

These sentiments were echoed wherever the Prince fled. In spite of the danger to life and fortune of his protectors, and the reward of £30,000 for his head, he was never betrayed.

Lady Margaret had planned that the Prince should be conducted to the old chief of Raasay, a MacLeod, but one who had brought out a hundred fighting men for the Jacobite cause. But the island of Raasay, between Skye and the mainland, had recently been visited by Government troops and it was now destitute, and its chief a fugitive, hiding in the heather in Knoidart farther down the coast. Raasay's son John, the young chief, volunteered to bring the Prince to his island nevertheless. But how to get him there?

* Robert Forbes, author of *The Lyon in Mourning*, a collection of first-hand accounts of the aftermath of Culloden.

'They could not trust a Portree crew, and all the island boats had been destroyed, or carried off by the military, except two.'

These two, however, belonged to Captain Malcolm MacLeod, nephew of MacLeod of Raasay and a devoted Jacobite. Malcolm was also a man of courage and resource. He had concealed his boats from the raiding militia, and when he heard of the Prince's need 'with the utmost alacrity he got ready one,' and sailed it to Skye, accompanied by the young chief, his brother Murdoch and two strong boatmen. They landed within half a mile of the inn at Portree.

By this time Prince Charles and Flora had also reached Portree. The Prince had changed his clothes to a kilt, a plaid, and a tartan coat and waistcoat, and was sitting in his shirt-sleeves at the inn, consuming a meal of fish, bread, butter and cheese. The Raasay men waited in impatient anxiety by their boat, every moment bringing fresh danger. But the Prince was enjoying his sojourn at the inn and it was not until the small hours of the morning that he joined them. He had said good-bye to Flora (whom he never saw again) and came bearing with him a bottle of whisky, a bottle of brandy, a cold roast chicken and four clean shirts. Thus equipped he set off over the water to yet another island, guarded this time by the three loyal MacLeods.

Seven weeks before, Captain Fergussone of the Royal Navy ship *Furnace* had been cruising off Raasay. He decided to punish the island for the hundred fighting men its chief had led to the Jacobite cause. His ship's log recorded briefly, 'Set Raasa Isle afire', but the account he sent to his Commodore was more explicit, '. . . my boats manned and armed [went] ashore, burning and destroying the laird's houses with some others that belong to their officers'. He left the island a ruin.

When the Prince landed, shortly before daybreak, the only lodging the MacLeods could find was a 'little hut, which some shepherds had lately built; and having prepared it as well as they could, and made a bed of heath for the stranger, they kindled a fire and partook of some of the provisions which had been sent with him from Kingsburgh'. The Prince, by now exhausted, 'His health . . . a good deal impaired by hunger, fatigue and watching, slept a long time but was frequently disturbed.' In his dreams he cried, 'Oh, God, poor Scotland.'

The two boatmen had been posted as sentries, and the next day an incident happened which involved them:

Cold mist, wind still,
Dank weather.
Over the brow of the hill
A man in the heather.
Sentinels hiss:
'A stranger!'
Hearts lurching to danger.
'Coming this way
Selling tobacco, he'll say.'
Dragging one foot, head bare
The man draws near.
Twelve eyes glare
Hands clench in fear.
'He must die,
We cannot risk a spy.'
Walking slowly, eyes on the ground
What is it that he has lost or found?
The Prince speaks: 'God forbid
we should take away a man's life.
He may be innocent.'
'Sire, he cannot live.'
'I'd sooner shoot my own brother
If in doubt. Why spare another?'
Voices rise in strife.
'We are many. You are one.
Prince – yes. But we your Parliament.'
The deed hangs in the balance – almost done.
Slowly the stranger passes
Still alone
A messenger, a victim? He has gone.
Fear turns to mirth.
'My loyal Parliament. I know your worth!'

The fugitive soldier of the Highland army
Limps towards home.

Later, amid the sycophants of Rome,
Remember, jaded Prince, the hour of danger
Found you merciful to this stranger.*

The Prince expected a French ship to come and take him to Loch Broom, in the territory of the Mackenzies. The MacLeods discussed sailing there in one of Malcolm's boats, although the distance was far – 'fifteen leagues coastwise'. However, after receiving information that there was no appearance of any French ship in the vicinity, they decided to return to Skye. They landed in Strath, after a very rough crossing, during which the Prince again 'sung an Erse song with much vivacity'. He then embarked on a strategy which showed how little he trusted even his most loyal supporters.

'With such earnestness, [he] charged MacLeod to have a boat ready at a certain place about seven miles off, as he said he intended it should carry him upon a matter of great consequence; . . . but all these orders were only blinds; for he had another plan in his head, but wisely thought it safest to trust his secrets to no more persons than was absolutely necessary. Having then desired Malcolm to walk with him a little way from the house, he soon opened his mind, saying, "I deliver myself to you. Conduct me to the Laird of Mackinnon's country." ' Malcolm objected that it was very dangerous, so many parties of soldiers were in motion. The Prince answered, 'There is nothing now to be done without danger.'

So the two set off across country over the hills, the Prince disguised as Malcolm's servant. They proceeded through the mountains, taking many a circuit to avoid any houses, discussing what they should do if they fell in with a party of soldiers. 'Fight, to be sure!' said the Prince. Fortunately, they met no one except a man called Ross, a former soldier in the

* Poem by the author.

Highland Army, who recognized the Prince immediately.

'Malcolm asked, "What's to be done?" "Swear him to secrecy," answered Prince Charles. Upon which Malcolm drew his dirk, and on the naked blade made him take a solemn oath, that he would say nothing of his having seen the Wanderer, till his escape should be made public.'

They reached the house of Malcolm's sister, near Elgol in the south-west of the island, in the early hours of the morning. Her husband, John Mackinnon, was out, but she set a 'plentiful breakfast' before her brother Malcolm and his supposed servant. They then slept for some time, until the vigilant Malcolm, first to awake, heard that his brother-in-law was now in sight. 'He sprang out to talk to him before he should see Prince Charles. After saluting him, Malcolm, pointing to the sea, said, "What, John, if the Prince should be a prisoner on board one of those tenders?" "God forbid!" replied John. – "What if we had him here?" said Malcolm. "I wish we had," answered John: "we should take care of him." – "Well, John," said Malcolm, "he is in your house." '

At this dramatic disclosure John, 'in a transport of joy, wanted to run directly in, and pay his obeisance: but Malcolm stopped him, saying, "Now is your time to behave well, and do nothing that can discover him." '

A few hours later Prince Charles was taken to a cave on the coast nearby, where he was greeted by the Laird of Mackinnon and his wife, and 'entertained with cold meat and wine'.

Malcolm, 'being now superseded by the Laird of Mackinnon, desired leave to return, which was granted him, and Prince Charles wrote a short note . . . informing his friends that he had got away from Skye, and thanking them for their kindness; and he desired this might be speedily conveyed to the young laird, that [he] might not wait longer in expectation of seeing him again. He bade a cordial adieu to Malcolm, and insisted on his accepting a silver stock-buckle and ten guineas for his purse.'

So the Prince finally left Skye, conducted to Knoidart on the mainland opposite by the Laird of Mackinnon. He had been in constant danger on the island, troops having traced him from the Outer Isles and across Skye to Portree, there having lost him. If he had not met with such devoted loyalty he would undoubtedly have been taken prisoner. He still had six weeks of fugitive life ahead of him on the mainland before a French ship finally took him off from Loch nan Uamh, near Arisaig, on 19 September 1746.

Boswell relates that 'the gallant Malcolm was apprehended about ten days after they separated, put aboard a ship and carried prisoner to London'. He said, 'The prisoners in general were very ill treated in their passage; but there were soldiers on board who lived well, and sometimes invited him to share with them.'

Malcolm was tried in London, but 'to his astonishment, only one witness could be found against him, though he had been so openly engaged; and therefore, for want of sufficient evidence, he was set at liberty'. He had thought himself in great danger, yet said 'he should never be so ready for death as he then was'. However, instead of dying he had a triumphal return to Scotland. Flora MacDonald, who was also then in London, chose him as the friend she most wanted to accompany her North. 'So,' said Malcolm, 'I went to London to be hanged, and returned in a post-chaise with Miss Flora MacDonald.'

Flora married Allan MacDonald in 1750 and later emigrated to North Carolina, where she was caught up in the American War of Independence, supporting the Royalist cause for which her husband fought. In due course she returned to Skye and lived long enough to entertain Dr Johnson at her house at Flodigarry. She gave him the same bed to sleep in as that used by the fugitive Prince Charles twenty-seven years before. In return, he paid her a tribute which is carved on her granite memorial in Kilmuir churchyard,

FLORA MACDONALD
A name that will be mentioned in history,
and, if courage and fidelity be virtues,
mentioned with honour

The story of Bonnie Prince Charlie, in which Flora played so crucial a part, has a perennial glamour. It has survived the ravages of time and been widely told. Those clansmen who, after the defeat of Culloden, were forced into exile, took the story with them and passed it on to their descendants. And in America, Canada or the Antipodes, far from the homeland, its romantic ingredients – danger, courage and sacrifice – shone even brighter, kindled by the well-remembered Jacobite songs.

In our times, Highland expatriates who return seeking Jacobite relics are not disappointed. The Prince has now become a commercial proposition and his traces have been exploited in many parts of the Highlands. Yet, despite all, his fascination remains.

In Skye some of his most exciting moments were spent. His sojourn there during his wanderings in the heather after Culloden was vital to his escape, and in the island he has left an undying memory.

5

Life on Skye

The Braes peninsula, where our house in Skye was situated, is a long tongue of land south of Portree. The island of Raasay rises across the waters of its eastern shore, and the Cuillins bar its southern horizon with a high purple mass. The Braes road runs parallel to the sea – a narrow road with twists and turns which explores the terrain imaginatively, unlike the surgical highways now bisecting much of Skye. After a few miles it comes to a full stop, ending abruptly above the shore of Loch Sligachan. Small white houses are scattered along its route – some crofts, some holiday homes, frequently unoccupied. But enough people live here all the year round to make a community, and a Christmas party for the children of Braes is a lively and crowded affair, attended by newcomers as well as permanent inhabitants.

I often drove along this road, as I fetched or took back our daily help who lived in one of the cottages. Sheep and cattle wandered across it, and one day I came upon a new-born lamb lying slap in the middle of the road, its placenta strewn on the tarmac beside it. In the summer, hay was stooked in the small fields, and oats and barley shone yellow against the blue of Raasay Sound. Heather clothed the reaches of moorland and bracken glowed tan on the hill slopes. Wild flowers clustered thick on the verges of the road, springing miraculously from cold soil in the spring, blooming all summer and sinking to sleep again under winter snow. And in the silence, the presence of the sea could always be felt and often seen as it came into view round each bend, vivid blue, misty-grey, or opaque with angry white flecks, a reminder of island solitude.

Here, as in so many other parts of Skye, were groups of ruined cottages, relics of the emigration that had taken place throughout the Islands during the last two hundred years. It began when Jacobites were press-ganged to the Colonies after Culloden or fled to exile in France. At that time, clansmen were disarmed and Highland dress and music prohibited, while the chiefs who remained set their faces to the south, as economic profit replaced the old patriarchal relationship of clansman and *Buchaille* (shepherd). Yet, in spite of the exodus of 20,000 Highlanders and Islanders between 1763 and 1775 (many of them transported under appalling conditions, reaching the Colonies destitute and then being sold into indenture), the Hebridean population continued to rise. There was a brief period of prosperity around the turn of the eighteenth century, when herring fishing and the sale of black cattle flourished, and the discovery of kelp (an alkaline ash produced by the burning of seaweed and used in the manufacture of glass, soap and linen) brought employment.

Then in the 1820s and '30s the kelp market was killed by cheaper imports from Spain and Germany. The herring shoals disappeared from the sea-lochs of the Inner Isles. And sheep farming, an activity which brought quick profit to the landlords and required infinitely fewer men for animal care, displaced cattle rearing.

To this day the 'Coming of the Sheep' is looked on in the Highlands as a momentous event. It changed the face of the country. The old husbandry, where each crofter had his own fields of barley, oats and potatoes, and his own modest herd of a few sheep and cattle supported on his own land, gave way to a heavy stocking of sheep on the hill, tended by a few shepherds, and needing winter pasture on crofting grounds in the glens. In this impasse, something had to yield. The sheep or the people must go. The sheep brought profitable returns to the landlords – many of them absentees. It was the people who were cleared from their homes.

The crofters had no security of tenure. The old system, where the land was held in trust for the clan, had long since passed. The laird or the tacksman (a gentleman farmer appointed by the laird) could evict a crofter at his will, and many of them did. Homes were burned. Old people died of exposure. Throughout the Highlands and Islands glens, once alive with people and cattle, became deserted. Many thousands emigrated; others were pushed to coastal strips where in some places the poverty of soil and exposure of climate were so extreme that it proved impossible to grow crops. And yet, in spite of extreme destitution, the population continued to rise until the failure of the potato crop in 1835, and again in 1846 for four consecutive years, brought famine and disaster.

In Skye the MacLeod and MacDonald chiefs did what they could. They ruined themselves in their efforts to feed their people and buy them a passage abroad. But the problems were too great. An old way of life was ending. A new one had not yet been born.

Why, I wondered, as I looked at the derelict ruins and reflected on their sad history, why had there not been more resistance? The force which had displaced families from homes occupied for generations, had seldom been met with counter-force. The teaching of the Church was part of the reason. It had a profound influence over its flock and it warned them not to resist. There was also a residual clan loyalty, a legacy from the past which could not conceive of disobedience to a chief. Yet the modern world into which the people were moving was a democratic one.

Then I remembered that in fact here, in Braes, a battle had taken place: the last battle to be fought on British soil. I had heard about it from an old man called Calum Nicholson, a bard who lived in Camus Tianavaig, the hamlet at the foot of Ben Tianavaig, northern boundary of the Braes. Standing outside his cottage one day, and gazing across the sea to Raasay, he had told me of the time when the sobbing and wailing of those turned out of their homes in Raasay could be heard by the people in Braes.

'And when it came to be their turn to go, the people in Raasay could hear the crying of the people in Braes.'

Listening to him, with the shadows lengthening and the light deepening, with the gulls flying in from the water towards their night's resting place and silence wrapping us round like a soft sea-mist, the ghosts of those who had mourned when they left this place seemed near.

Then Calum Nicholson had stirred and broken the trance and offered to tell me the story of the Battle of the Braes.

'It was a great battle. A famous one,' he had said. 'It changed the crofting laws, though that wasn't what the people had in mind when they fought. They only wanted justice for themselves and their families. And they were desperate to get it. It was the women of Braes who started the resistance. The grazing on the hillside belonged to their men. They'd taken their sheep and cattle up there for generations, as long as anyone could remember. Their living depended on it. But one day – in 1882 it was, that was the year – a Sheriff's officer came out from Portree and he had with him an eviction notice. The crofters were to be deprived of their hillside grazing.

'When the women of Braes understood what this meant they surrounded the Sheriff's officer and they forced him to burn his papers and sent him scuttling back to Portree without them. But they knew that wasn't the end. The Sheriff would return in a few days or a few weeks. So they made preparations to welcome him.

'Sure enough, back came the Sheriff at sunrise one morning two weeks later, and this time he had another Sheriff with him and not only that, but also sixty policemen from Glasgow. Coming so early, this force surprised the crofters. The Sheriff produced another warrant and the police tried to make an arrest. At this the fury of the men broke loose. They attacked the police with stones and flails, and their women joined in, fighting side by side with their men. Many were injured.

'Before long the police were forced to retire back along the road. And then came the crux of the battle. The crofters had gathered a pile of boulders on top of a cliff overhanging the road. As the police passed below they hurled the stones down on top of them. And that was the end. The police withdrew as best they could, and the crofters won the day.'

Calum had gone on to tell me that nevertheless five men

had been arrested and taken to trial in Inverness. By then the whole of Skye was seething with fury, and though the Government had sent warships and troops to subdue the island, it had refused to be intimidated. The revolt had spread to other islands and led to the appointment of a Royal Commission, charged to report on the state of the Highlands.

Four years later, in 1886 an Act was passed through Parliament which gave the crofters security of tenure, and at the same time the Crofting Commission was set up to look after their interests. Their protected position remains to this day, reinforced by subsidies for stock, and, in 1976, by the Crofting Reform Bill which enabled a crofter to buy and own a house and land.

Today Skye is one of the most heavily crofted islands in the Hebrides and crofting continues to give an important contribution to its life, aided by the opportunities for other work which tourism has brought.

From the dining-room window of our home we had a splendid view of Portree with its cluster of houses grouped round the placid bay. Port Righ, the Port of the King (so named after a visit by James V), is the administrative centre of Skye with a population of around two thousand, a magistrates' court, police, a hospital and a fine secondary school, recently rebuilt, which draws children from all over the Northern Islands.

Portree has a spacious square, three churches – Presbyterian, Episcopal and Free Kirk, streets of shops, several hotels (among them the Royal Hotel where Prince Charles parted from Flora MacDonald) and a picturesque harbour. The eighteenth-century stone houses on the quayside give a charming welcome to anyone approaching the town by sea. Also on the quayside are several old-fashioned shops, including a tailor's, whose owner sits cross-legged on the counter, stitching amid bales of strong-smelling tweed. My son, Iain, ordered a suit from this man, chose the material, and fixed an appointment for a fitting. The evening before, the tailor telephoned, 'I just wanted to confirm the time of your fitting tomorrow,' he said.

'Ten o'clock. I'll be there,' answered Iain.

'Good, I'll look forward to seeing you.' There was a pause, during which Iain nearly rang off. 'Oh, there's just one thing,' the tailor said. 'I forgot to take any measurements.'

With around 360,000 tourists coming to Skye every year, Portree is apt to get crowded during the summer season. The square is jammed with cars, and on rainy days people wander disconsolately up and down the streets, sucking ice-creams as though imploring the sun to shine. This is depressing. On the other hand, few sights are more invigorating than the Portree Pipe Band marching through the town, instruments blaring, tartan ribbons fluttering, kilts swinging and heavy feet slapping the pavement in energetic unison.

When I stayed in Skye as a child it had always been in the south at Kyleakin. Now, based in the north, I could enter more easily into the island's activities. We made friends with several families living near Portree and saw a different aspect of Skye life; that of the retired gentry with their estates, their shoots, their fishing and their kinship groups. MacLeods and MacDonalds still dominated the social life of the island, though clan feuds between them had long ceased to exist.

As newcomers we were welcomed with hospitable friendliness, and it was not long before my sons were taking MacDonald girls climbing in the Cuillins and initiating them into the mysteries of mountaineering. I saw history repeating itself as they hung apprehensively on to ropes, abseiling down the Inaccessible Pinnacle, or clasping the Gendarme with desperate force.

I, too, climbed once more in the Cuillins, sometimes with Iain, sometimes with an old friend, Evelyn Baring (the late Lord Howick of Glendale). A veteran mountaineer, he discovered the Cuillins with joy and came year after year. Iain took him up most of the classic climbs during the day and in the evenings he recounted them, hold by hold, and we compared them with ascents we had both made on Table Mountain in Cape Town. The Bhastair Tooth, which entailed a 400-foot abseil, was his favourite Skye climb, often repeated. My zenith was reached when Iain led me up Cioch Gully, a difficult climb of three pitches ending in a 'trap chimney with few holds'. As

I emerged at the top of it, I received my accolade, 'Well, Mummy, you're not past it yet!'

On Sundays the house party trooped off to the well-filled Presbyterian Church. Squeezed into one long pew we listened to the minister, Mr MacLeod, as he declaimed the extempore prayers and preached to us with great sincerity. The hats of the choir ladies were a feast for our eyes, while our ears were beguiled by the descants they sang to the hymns.

One regular attendant at this church was Colonel Jock MacDonald, who lived in his family home not far from Portree. Brought up in Skye, he could remember the island in its Victorian days when Portree was a small village with only one shopping street, and a cattle market was held each week in its central square. Then the year's chief event had been the Skye Gathering, which consisted of a regatta, the games and two balls. Organized by the local lairds and their families, these three functions attracted people from all over Skye, from the mainland and from neighbouring islands.

During the regatta Portree harbour was crowded with red-sailed fishing smacks. Races and competitions for local boats were keenly contested and visiting yachts came from far and wide, joining in and bringing participants who stayed on for the games and the balls. In the beautiful setting of hills and sea, and invested with Victorian grace and leisure, all three events must have possessed a unique period charm.

They continued well into the twentieth century, motor boats and steam launches reinforcing the yachts and fishing smacks. Then the regatta ceased. But the games and the balls survived, and in spite of two World Wars they have continued to this day.

The games happen first, at the end of August. They take place in a picturesque setting, on a small hill above the harbour, and attract a large and varied audience. The day's programme is crammed to bursting point, and everyone comes: island characters (ancient mariners ready to buttonhole the unwary), kilted lairds and their ladies, crofters, farmers, shopkeepers, seamen, visitors, tourists, and many many children. Though it almost always rains, a series of activities ceaselessly unfolds. Local Highland men toss the caber, put the shot, run, jump and perform prodigious feats of strength in mammoth tugs-of-war. Young girls, immaculate in velvet doublets and bonnets and tartan kilts and plaids, dance in competition, their footwork as swift and neat as ballerinas. Pipers assemble from all over the Highlands and are judged by meticulous standards, as they intone their strathspeys, marches and pibrochs for hours and hours. The day wears on and the refreshment tents are visited more and more frequently. The scene gains in animation what it has lost in pristine freshness. The grass is churned up by many footsteps. Paper cups and sweet-wrappings blow in the wind. Then into the arena stagger several weary figures – competitors in the marathon race, back from scaling a mountain nearby, forgotten by all, but now given a ragged cheer.

At last the time for the presentation of the highly-coveted awards arrives. The victors receive their prizes for sporting events, for dancing and for piping, and are warmly applauded. And so the games end for another year.

No wonder they attract such a crowd. They still provide a unique occasion, and bear witness to a vitality and sense of tradition in Skye life which has continued for over a hundred years.

The summer season is rounded off by the Skye Balls which are held on the first Wednesday and Thursday in September. These are a more exclusive affair, as befits their origin, for they started in 1889 as a party for the landed gentry of Skye and the West Highlands. They take place in the Skye Gathering Hall and an old-fashioned atmosphere still prevails, with programmes for dances, lists of the various hostesses' guests published in the *Oban Times*, sitting-out rooms, a supper-room, and a balcony – originally occupied by chaperones, now a haven for the elderly, who cast appraising eyes on the youth and beauty below. About two hundred and sixty people attend, the majority from the Highlands, the men in full Highland dress, the girls wearing family tartan sashes. Highland reels and country dances are performed with verve and skill from 10 pm until 7 am for two nights in succession. And although strict standards of dancing and behaviour are expected by the doyens of the Skye Gathering (who organize the balls and whose fifty members invite the guests) great gaiety prevails.

We took a party to the Skye Balls for a number of years and many vivid impressions remain. The moment in the foursome reel when the men meet in couples, each contriving to swing the other off his feet, with flying kilts, stylized yells, flashing leaps and an expense of libido which can only be equalled in primitive African hunting rituals. The decorous, fresh-complexioned girls performing prim and unobtrusive steps below their long skirts. Dawn breaking over Portree harbour, gleaming water and the shapes of hills slowly emerging in contrast to the brightly-lit room. Breakfast at 6 am and the last gallop an hour later, followed by the dispersal of the dancers into the silent town, some to catch the steamer south, having first danced a final reel on the jetty.

One year we sailed away from the balls in a friend's yacht, changing from our evening clothes into oilskins and steering east into a newly risen sun. A rainbow arched over the Red Cuillin and a concourse of gannets circled a primrose sky, diving one by one into the dark sea. The mountains drew farther away, changing from black to hazy-blue. And looking back Skye seemed indeed the essence of all romance, remote and inviolable.

With the games and the Skye Balls over, September draws to a close. The last tourist leaves and Portree reverts to a quiet island town. But a vigorous social life, for inhabitants only, continues. Amateur dramatics, dances, whist-drives and meetings of the Scottish Rural Institute flourish. And the number of *ceilidhs*, always fairly frequent, burgeons.

Ceilidh is a Gaelic word meaning 'to visit'. Originally a ceilidh was a gathering held in a home. Its origin was often spontaneous. A friend visited another friend and started to sing. Several more friends dropped in and each contributed something: a story, a song, a pipe tune or a dance. Gaelic was the only language and the whole gathering was impromptu and unplanned. Often fiddles or small harps called *clarsachs* were played. Legends, fairy stories and the history of the clans were passed from one Gaelic mouth to the next, and thus the long winter evenings were whiled away and the Gaelic oral tradition was kept alive.

Today ceilidhs are more sophisticated affairs, often laid on for the tourists with an influx of music and visitors from outside the Highlands. But the spirit of hospitality still prevails and is usually reinforced by the mandatory dram of whisky.

The ceilidhs we most enjoyed were those held by Colonel Jock MacDonald and his wife in their large Victorian family mansion near Portree. This splendid house, with its antlered walls, Daniell prints, stuffed owls and eagles, tartan furnishings and rare Scottish books could only be preserved by its owners taking in bus-loads of tourists during the summer season.

Those who stayed there never forgot their visit, spiced as it was by Colonel Jock's sardonic sense of humour and his wife's lavish catering. Dinner was eaten in a room lit by candle-light, resplendent with the family silver, and ended as often as not with a tune on the pipes played by the host. First thing next morning, he could be seen at the Portree bakery, collecting fresh rolls for his guests' breakfast.

Occasionally, when the strains of hospitality became too intense, we would receive an urgent telephone call, 'We're having a ceilidh tonight for our visitors. Please come and bring your house party.'

We would arrive, complete with whatever musical instruments we could muster, to find the tourists sitting in a bewildered and comatose semi-circle, punch-drunk from the day's bus-tour of Skye.

'The artists are here,' Colonel Jock would announce, while I struggled to eject my recalcitrant clarsach from its canvas cover, and someone else unpacked a guitar.

'Now, Prunella,' our hostess would command, 'let's have that song about the woman who put her baby down somewhere and then couldn't find it again. So careless of her, I always think.'

'I left my baby lying there, lying there, lying there . . .' I began to sing, amid some surprised looks from my audience. Fortunately most of them knew the refrain and soon joined in. The ice once broken, talent flowed fast. Songs ranged from the Hebrides to Australia, including a Russian saga, the words of which we had been taught at lightning speed by my elder son, Diarmaid, shortly before arriving. The energetic danced a reel, and this was followed by a sword dance (intricate steps over crossed swords laid on the floor) performed with great expertise by a young MacDonald member of our party who also gave us an Indian dance, wrapped in a white sheet as a sari and with a pillowcase for a turban, the subtle sexual undertones of which we hoped escaped our audience. By the time tea-trolleys were wheeled in at about 10.30 pm the guests were as exhausted as ourselves.

Such a ceilidh was far from traditional, but it was contemporary in the range of its material, gathered from different parts of the world through the far-flung travels of the young. After the tea interval it became more Highland, when the Skeabost schoolmistress contributed some *port a beul* – Gaelic words sung rapidly to a rhythmic lilt; a type of tune used in former times as 'mouth music' to acompany dancing in the absence of either a fiddle or the pipes. The words are often nonsense rhymes: 'There are three hind legs on the cock that was in Kerrera,' is the translation of a typical refrain.

Then it was time for the pipes. This ancient music, still played throughout the Highlands, is kept at a level of excellence by regular competitions held at all Highland Games and Gatherings. Colonel Jock, himself a first-class piper, was also a competition judge with a profound feeling for the music of the Gael. He had a small set of pipes, specially adapted for performance indoors, and on these he now played us some gay reels and stirring marches. Then his mood changed, and he drew forth from his instrument a traditional pibroch, the classical music of the pipes. These haunting primitive melodies are decorated with intricate grace-notes whose accuracy demands great skill, as do the slow tempo and long-held notes of the score. The music penetrated the silent circle of listeners, and rang farther out into the night with its cloud-filled sky and solemn hills. Ancient and poignant, it spoke of valour and sorrow, of exile and grief, of the great events of the clans, and the beauty of places long known and loved. The whole fierce, sad, wild history of the Highlands and Islands is in the pibrochs; the *Ceol Mhor*, the great music.

Skye is famous for its pipers. From early days each Highland chief had his own piper and the office was handed down from father to son. Great rivalry existed, but the MacCrimmons, hereditary pipers to the Skye MacLeods, were acknowledged by all to be supreme. At Boreraig, near Dunvegan Castle, the MacLeods' home, the MacCrimmons set up a college, and pipers from all over the Highlands and Islands came to learn from them.

Many of the tunes they played were laments, recording the death of the clan chief or his son; others were concerned with the '45, such as 'My King has landed in Moidart', or 'Lament for Prince Charles' (written by Captain Malcolm MacLeod who conducted the Prince to Raasay). Others again were stirring Salutes to MacLeods or MacDonalds; yet others were celebratory paeans like, 'I got a kiss from the king's hand', which was composed by Patrick Mor MacCrimmon in 1651, when Norman MacLeod joined the army of King Charles II:

> I have had a kiss, a kiss, a kiss
> I have had a kiss of the king's hand –
> No one who blew in a sheep's skin,
> Has received such an honour as I have.

After Culloden, pipe music was banned, along with Highland dress. But with the recruitment of the Highland regiments towards the end of the eighteenth century, both were revived and piping was given a great impetus by the creation of Regimental Pipe Bands.

The art also flourished overseas where it was taken by the emigrants of the '45 and the Clearances. And in due course, like the descendants of those who were exiled, pipe music returned again to its homeland. On several occasions in recent years, the accolade of Highland piping has gone to a piper from Canada.

The evening having now taken a Jacobite turn, we ended with a mass singing of the clans' lament for Prince Charles.

Bonnie Charlie's noo awa'
Safely o'er the friendly main
Mony a heart will break in twa'
Should he ne'er come back again.

Will ye no' come back again?
Will ye no' come back again?
Better lo'ed ye canna be
Will ye no' come back again?

This request, transferred now from the Prince to the tourists, was sung with commendable feeling. After which, spiced full to overflowing with Gaelic nostalgia, we staggered to bed.

To stand beside the ruined home of one's forebears must be a poignant experience, bringing with it a strong sense of identity and of the mysterious roots of being. Some visitors come to Skye with such a quest in mind. But for the few who return as pilgrims there are many who want only a superficial stimulation. For them, the Jacobite trinkets, the highly-coloured postcards, the tartan objects and the lightning bus-tours are produced. Tourism is Skye's chief industry. Crofting is no longer viable as a way of life. It must be supplemented by a number of other activities – road work, forestry, building, weaving, fishing and distilling. All these exist on Skye, but even taking them into account, there is still heavy unemployment, and without tourism the population would quickly decline.

Such attractions as Dunvegan Castle, ancestral home of the MacLeods (to which around 73,000 people come each year), Skye Agricultural Week, and the Skye Games bring many visitors and create revenue for the inhabitants; and there are few houses during the season without Bed and Breakfast signs, or (the next step) space for a caravan to park or be let out.

But the season is a short one. It lasts only for about four months. And during that period money must be made for the whole year.

Yet the Hebrides hold great treasures for those who venture there at other times. When the brief summer is over and the long autumn nights close in, when winter snows whiten the summits of the hills and the bracken and tips of the birches flame a dark-red, when early spring winds toss the catkins on the hazels and sudden shafts of sunlight rain on to opaque seas; then the real flavour of the Isles manifests itself. Wild weather, mist, rain. All these must be accepted, sometimes for days on end. It is the contrast of wet and fine, storm and calm, which creates the magical rain-washed Hebridean light, translucent as with the radiance of another world.

People who live here all the year round are aware of these things. The beauty of their surroundings is not taken for granted. There is a Highland type which persists.

> In the Highlands, in the country places
> Where the old men have rosy faces
> And the young maidens quiet eyes.

Robert Louis Stevenson's description fits many of them yet. Slow and soft-spoken, they have not changed, and even amidst the tourist flurry, they still reflect the peace of their remote hills and glens.

It is for this peace, coupled with a sense of adventure and discovery, that people come to Skye. When, after the Second World War, the island took its deliberate turn towards tourism (encouraged by several of the local lairds who could see that crofting as a sole means of livelihood was no longer possible), plans were also made to preserve Skye's unique beauty. The Skye Council of Social Services was set up, and means to contain as well as encourage the tourists were planned. As a result there are still many places in Skye which have remained remote, places where the inhabitants still live as their forebears did, with a traditional simplicity.

Like an accomplished courtesan, Skye has many moods. She

can retire into solitude, repulse with rain and storm, smile under glancing sunshine, or languish in exotic heat. Perhaps her favourite role is that of the mysterious virgin, withdrawn and undefiled. This is how her lovers have always thought of her. And, far as the picture may be from present-day facts, her spell is such that this is how they think of her still.

PART II

Raasay

6

We Find a Home

Skye has a number of off-shore islands, large and small. The chief of these is Raasay, four miles to the east, connected to Skye by a similar history and geology, but nevertheless possessing a distinct personality of its own. Fifteen miles long and four miles wide, the land mass of Raasay protects Portree harbour and stretches down the Skye coast from the Storr mountains to the mouth of Loch Sligachan. The Lairds of Raasay were also MacLeods but of a different origin from Skye's. The Raasay MacLeods stemmed from the MacLeods of Lewis, in the Outer Isles. Under their rule the island acquired a reputation for poetry and music which became deeply embedded in the Gaelic oral tradition and which is remembered to this day.

After the break-up of the Lords of the Isles Raasay had its share of bloody clan warfare, and during the troubles of the sixteenth century it became the refuge of robbers and pirates. It played a gallant part in the '45, suffered for it by a terrible devastation, but nevertheless sheltered Prince Charles after Culloden. Boswell and Johnson's visit to it in 1773 brought it permanent literary fame.

An excellent microcosm of the varied geology of the region is to be found on Raasay. In the north and on its sister island, Rona, there are ancient schists and gneiss which are the transformed remnants of rocks formed when the world was still in childhood. They weather into smooth Scandinavian-like seascapes with beautiful rocky inlets and smooth, reddish quartz-veined rocks. Also in the north and stretching south to the neighbouring islands are the red desert sandstones of the Torridonian.

The fertile southern part of Raasay is made up of Jurassic shales and sandstones, often full of fossils, lying on a rough ancient Triassic desert landscape.

The highest and most distinctive hill, which makes Raasay recognizable from all sides and far away, is Dun Caan. It is a cap of lava; a reminder of the huge volcano that once stood above the present Cuillins.

It was this hill, sliced flat at the top as though by a giant knife, which intrigued me when I first saw Raasay from Kyleakin in the days of my youth. Later, I watched the MacBrayne steamer depart for Raasay from Kyle. Later still, when we lived on the Braes peninsula I climbed Ben Tianavaig, the hill behind our house, and gazed at Raasay's coastline across the water; wooded, peaceful, serene, dreaming away the hours in sunshine while rain clouds threatened Skye. Last of all, I read Boswell's account of his sojourn at Raasay House, and that clinched my determination to visit the island. So, one morning I hired a boat from Portree and I, my son Iain, and two friends set off across the Sound to Raasay.

We landed on Holoman's Island, a small tidal island a third of the way up the west coast. This stretch of Raasay's shore is bleak and the rough pebble beaches looked uninviting. Above stood an unoccupied manse house, with the ruined walls of the church alongside; a typical Scots stone building, grey and rather forbidding. We climbed the slope to the house and, pushing between briars and nettles, explored the garden and peeped through the windows. Our boatman had told us the house was for sale.

'Would it be fun to live on Raasay?' asked Iain.

I viewed the bleak terrain with distaste. Where, I wondered, were the woods and fields I had seen from Ben Tianavaig? 'I'd rather be on Skye,' I replied.

Beyond the road was a moorland slope which we mounted for a better view. Nothing but peat and bog met our eyes. Then suddenly, ahead and above, yet seeming tantalizingly close, rose the rock-crowned summit of Dun Caan. Its straight truncated shape gave an impression of great height and solidity. To climb it and dance a reel on the top, as Boswell had done, was one of our objectives; so forgetting about houses, fields and woods we set our feet to the hill.

Highland summits have one thing in common: they are always farther away than they look. Dun Caan was no exception. We ploughed across country, over three deep valleys and up three steep slopes until at last we stood on what we hoped was the final crest. A small loch, blue with reflected sky, rippled in the wind. Beyond, the ground fell steeply away into a face of shale, marked by a winding sheep track. At its foot lay a large sheet of water, dark and eerie, edged with thin reeds. And from the farther shore rose the last of Dun Caan's slopes; steep short turf pitted with rabbit holes and ending in a mass of loose boulders. Above this towered the summit, still the best part of an hour's walk away!

When at last we reached it, the island lay below us spread out like a map. To the north were wild and uninhabited moors, broken only by four small croft houses whose white paint flashed on the north-westernmost tip of land. The ruins of an ancient castle merged with the grey rock of the eastern shore, while stretching away to the south, the coastline broke into a series of dramatic cliffs and bays. The only sounds came from gulls circling the sea or sheep browsing on the green and brown slopes which undulated towards it. The island seemed enchanted, caught in a spell; akin to its spectacular sister Skye whose mountains shadowed it, yet unique. Brilliant sea surrounded it, and above it the sky curved in a dome of melting blue. On the horizon were the shapes of mainland hills, while far across the western sea the Outer Isles shimmered, remote and mysterious. Days of such weather are rare in the Hebrides. I was happy that Raasay welcomed us with one of them.

We ate our sandwiches and we danced our reel and then we started to descend. Once more, the way was longer than expected. Identifiable at first as a track across flat stones, the path ran through a region of extraordinary rock crevasses and caves which yawned on each side to a depth of thirty or forty feet. Later it petered out over anonymous boggy wastes and we lost it, ending up in a forestry plantation full of young and spiky fir trees.

We reached the road at last, scratched, irritable and weary. A post-van approached, and we begged a lift to Raasay House.

'Did ye not find the path?' asked its driver, his lifted eyebrows expressing faint disapproval. 'There's a path from the top road will get you to the summit of Dun Caan in less than an hour.'

I murmured something about Boswell and Johnson.

'Och aye, that'll be the path Boswell took. It was there in his day.'

'And Raasay House is a hotel now?'

'It is so. I'm thinking it's some tea you'll be wanting there?'

The hotel was quiet and unpretentious; its view of the Skye hills superb. Walking down to the old pier after tea, the ghosts of the friendly company who had emerged from Raasay House to greet Dr Johnson seemed near. In this island the two gentlemen had spent the happiest days of their tour and witnessed a Hebridean gaiety and hospitality which had made Boswell declare: 'Can there be no misery here?'

As our boat drew away from the shore, I looked back at Raasay House. It was standing, in Boswell's words, 'well defended by a rocky coast with a fine verdure about it, and beyond it the hills and mountains in a gradation of wildness'. Yet something about its appearance and its poetic site was infinitely poignant. It had obviously been a grand mansion in its day, a family home beloved by its occupants, a source of pride and affection for the islanders. Now it was a hotel, but even that function seemed in jeopardy, for I had the impression that the hotel was in decline, that there was difficulty in making ends meet.

Is Raasay House falling on hard times? I wondered, as I watched it fade into the distance. What will its future be? What secrets does it hold?

My next visit to Raasay took place two years later. After a series of holidays in Skye my sons and I longed to find a permanent base in the Hebrides which could be a home, not only for holidays but also throughout the year.

We had cast around for somewhere in Skye without success. Then early in 1962 we heard of four croft houses on Raasay, belonging to a former small crofting community. Peter Zinovieff, the friend who told us of the houses, had seen them when studying geology in Raasay some years before. They were now deserted and he thought they might be for sale. We decided to visit them.

The steamer for Raasay left Portree at 8 am. I recognized the *Loch Arkaig*, the same boat I had seen departing for Raasay from Kyle, and we boarded her as the sun flushed the sky. Ben Tianavaig's rugged cliffs changed shape while we swung round them into the open sea, and Portree's church spires and stone houses disappeared. The Cuillins' snow-clad peaks came into view and a sharp wind ruffled the Sound. We sailed across it to Raasay, an hour's journey away.

The *Loch Arkaig*'s route took us along the island's west coast, past Holoman's Island where we had landed, past Raasay House and its wooded enclave, and past the village of Inverarish with its white houses clustered above the bay. Farther on, a long, high, wooden pier jutted into the Sound. This pier was built in 1913 by Baird and Co., who mined iron-ore on Raasay during the First World War. It was the steamer's stopping place and our destination. Here we disembarked. The *Loch Arkaig* unloaded mail and some supplies for the island and then resumed her journey to Kyle. We were left on the draughty pier, viewing the scene.

It was one of some desolation. Decaying mine buildings stood against the skyline. A rough hill of peat and heather fell to an empty road. A stone quarry rose above a black pebble shore. No crofts, fields or cattle were visible. The road wound away over the horizon and we set off along it while indignant seagulls screeched and the wind blew. We had to walk for two miles along the road, and another two over a heathery moor before we sighted the houses. They were spread out across the hillside, a road running above them, a steep drop to the sea below. Stone dykes, boundaries of old fields, still patterned the ground. Sheep grazed where crops had once stood. A burn cut deep into the hillside and a small wood softened the lower slopes with birch and hazel just coming into bud.

The houses faced the sea and gazed across six miles of it to one of the finest views in the Hebrides. Glancing water stretched away in a widening curve, its surface broken by skerries and small islands ringed with foam, until it reached Kyle lighthouse and the houses of Kyleakin, strung like pearls below the soaring shapes of the Kintail mountains. To the west the great mass of the Cuillins' strange outline filled the sky; and to the east rose the mainland hills of Torridon and Applecross, far away and tenuous as a dream.

The houses were typical Highland croft houses, built like a child's drawing, two up, two down. Unlike the grey stone manse above Holoman's Island they welcomed us with a smile, their charm surviving their decay. Three of them were strung along the road, a quarter of a mile or so between each. The fourth lay against the side of the hill two hundred feet or so below the others. Not even a sheep track led to it, although sheep browsed all around and had eaten its surrounding grass short, making a natural lawn. A willow tree in front of this house frothed in full bloom, its fuzzy buds vivid against the blue sky.

We sat below the cracked and broken window-ledges and ate our sandwich lunch. We had been told that it was twenty years since anyone had occupied this house, and fourteen or so since the others along the road had been lived in. Like many crofting communities in the Hebrides, this one had gradually declined. Young people had left. The old had stayed until they were no longer able, and then had gone. Finally, mice, rabbits and sheep had made their homes in the houses, which were still owned by the families of the original crofters. It was unlikely that they would ever live in them again though their sheep continued to graze the surrounding land.

The houses had an attractive exterior although their white-wash had faded and slates were missing on their roofs. But inside, all was dilapidated and depressing. A broken door revealed a pile of sheep dung in the hall. A rickety stair led to two upstairs rooms, one of which had a large hole in the floor. Wind blew through a gap in the roof. Wallpaper peeled off the walls. The grime of ages had settled on the rusty old stove, and rotten floorboards gave way to mud and earth. The windows were broken and coated with dust. A smell of damp and decay permeated everything.

What to do? The site was enchanting, the houses appealing, but could they ever be converted into practical homes? Logic said no. They were too remote, too dilapidated; the problems of labour and transport would be too severe – three miles from the village, two miles from the nearest neighbour. It was not even certain that they would be available for sale.

But on that Easter day logic had little place in our minds. Sun dazzled the sea. Snow shone on the hills. Birds heralded the spring, and we stood in a place of such beauty that it caught the heart. We realized that we had fallen in love. And love demands possession. Come what may, we would strain every nerve to possess these houses, this view.

Raasay is owned by the Department of Agriculture and Fisheries. Next day we paid a visit to its Portree branch. We had decided to make an offer for all four houses; one each for my two sons, the other two for Peter Zinovieff and his wife Victoria. We knew that croft houses were extremely difficult to buy. The policy of the Crofting Commission was to refuse a sale unless it was established beyond doubt that no crofter would ever again wish for occupation. Crofters, not tourists or holiday-home-makers, had the first right to croft houses.

We were told by the Agriculture Department official that the houses would probably come up for sale since they had been unoccupied for so long. In this case, they would be advertised, tenders for them sought, and the most suitable offer accepted. There was no guarantee when or if this would happen. The best we could do would be to seek a solicitor's advice on a suitable price to offer, and meanwhile leave our names with the Agriculture Department so that we could be notified if the houses became available.

We left the office somewhat deflated. However, we did

decide on a price, sent our offer and mustered what patience we could to await developments.

We had to wait a long time. It was not until the following Easter, 1963, that a typewritten sheet, containing particulars of the houses and asking for offers, reached us. The Scottish system of tenders is disconcerting in that one has no means of knowing what prices may be put forward by other interested purchasers. All tenders must reach the Department of Agriculture by a certain date. They are then considered on their respective merits, but most likely the highest bid will be accepted. Thus one might lose one's house for the sake of a few pounds.

The months went by and we heard no more. Finally, in June, my son Diarmaid, who happened to be in Edinburgh, made enquiries at the Department. He was told that a description of the houses had recently appeared in a London Sunday newspaper, and by the following post had come offers at high prices, enclosing cheques from intending buyers.

Were we to lose these houses after so many months of waiting? Diarmaid reiterated our original offer, and pointed out that we were prepared to buy all four houses, to use them continually, and to establish a community after years of neglect and decay. We waited in suspense. A few weeks later a letter arrived to tell us that the houses were ours.

Peter and Victoria, on holiday with their young children in France, returned at once, bought a lorry load of camping equipment, and drove up to Raasay, prepared to start work on their two houses immediately. By the end of the summer, and by dint of intensive activity and the help of several local crofters, they were in. One house was habitable, and triumphantly they occupied it.

Our renovation got off to a slower start. By now we had put down roots in Skye. We had made many friends there, the lease of our house near Portree had still another year to run, and people living in Skye tended to be very disparaging about our proposed island homes.

'You'll be terribly isolated,' they said. 'How will you get

building materials and supplies there, when everything has to come across miles of water? And who can you employ to help you? You can't do all the renovations yourselves. Skilled local labour is very hard to find. Another thing, you'll have to have a boat, but there's no proper anchorage on that shore, it's very exposed. When the south-westers blow up in the winter, you'll be hurled off the hillside.'

In spite of these gloomy prognostications, my sons went ahead with drawing up plans for renovation, applied for an improvement grant and secured an estimate from a Skye firm of builders. A year passed; Diarmaid was now abroad. The responsibility for doing up the crofts had fallen on Iain's shoulders, but he seemed mysteriously reluctant to continue operations. Eventually, he admitted that the island file containing all papers, plans and information had been lost.

The future of the whole project lay in the balance.

'Let's go over to Raasay and see the houses again,' suggested a friend who was staying with us in Skye. It was Easter once more – two years since the first sight of our dream Hebridean homes.

We landed again at the pier.

'I've arranged to meet a man who might work for us,' said Iain. 'I contacted him several months ago. He's an experienced plumber and builder, married to the local schoolmistress.'

We called at the schoolhouse in the village and Iain knocked on the door.

A tall man with a sailor's blue eyes and strong features emerged.

'This is Jock Rutherford,' said Iain.

I noticed that he was carrying something under his arm.

'You see, Jock,' Iain explained, 'we've been delayed in starting work on the houses because, unfortunately, the file containing all the estimates, plans and so on, has been mislaid.'

A slow smile spread over Jock's face. 'The file?' he said, producing the bundle from under his arm. 'Is this what you'd be wanting? You left it behind last time we met. It's been in the back of my wife's car for the last six months!'

So now the way was clear to continue. A sight of the houses

and their superb view rekindled our enthusiasm. We decided to start on the top house, the one nearest the road. Jock Rutherford was engaged, and a plan of work drawn up for the rest of the Easter holiday.

Each morning the work party, consisting of Iain, myself and his friends, caught the 8 am steamer from Portree. We reached the houses about two hours later. Then a hurricane of activity began. One young man dug a sewage pit, sinking lower and lower into the ground until he had disappeared ten feet below it. Another boarded up the broken windows. Another was poised on the roof, removing moss with emery paper. My task was to distemper the discoloured outside walls. One of the girls helped me, and such was our energy that within a week the whole house stood shining white – a great boost to morale. Iain gave himself the enjoyable occupation of demolishing the inside, a destructive process which used up his store of unexpended energy. Piece by piece, the old stove, strips of wallpaper, rotten planks and decayed corpses of furniture were flung outside. Those incapable of being burnt were thrown into the bracken. The others provided fuel for an enormous bonfire. Jock Rutherford kept a watchful eye on the proceedings and dug trenches to and from the sewage pit, the key point in the intended drainage system.

With all this varied activity the spring day passed rapidly. The local inhabitants – sheep, birds and rabbits – scattered at our arrival, but returned from time to time to view with wary eyes these strange intruders. The house itself, neglected for so many years, seemed to awake from a long sleep and respond gratefully to our efforts.

After a week or so, the house party in Skye dispersed. Iain, and the friend who had dug the sewage pit, stayed on. They had begun the job of concreting the pit inside, and were determined to complete it before going south. They camped in the now almost totally dismantled house, and produced a new type of chaos within by making concrete blocks in wooden boxes – their only containers – with which they then lined the walls of the pit. At night they cheered themselves with a huge fire and a bottle of whisky.

Jock assisted by day. 'I'm thinking you've dug the pit too near the house,' he observed, with a disparaging eye. 'The Sanitary-from-Skye will never accept that distance.'

'Too late now,' said Iain. 'Come on, Jock, your job is to see that the pit's exit works properly.' A tinkling burn ran down the hillside; below this our waste products would be absorbed. An efficient sewage system, we reflected, was as important as a beautiful view. The holiday came to an end and Iain returned to Oxford. The completion of the houses still seemed very far off, but at any rate a start had been made.

Plans to continue during succeeding vacations unfortunately failed, and it was not until September 1965, eighteen months later, that the house awakened once more to the sound of hammer and chisel, human voices and human footsteps.

This time the rebuilding was destined to get under way in earnest. Iain, having gained his degree in zoology at Oxford, was on the point of departure for East Africa, to study elephants in the Lake Manyara National Park in Tanzania. Diarmaid had settled in the USA, so the task of renovation was handed over to me. Before leaving, Iain gave me the vital Island file, and told me that plans for the renovation of the house had finally been passed by the Inverness County Council, and that he had engaged Jock Rutherford to be our builder, responsible for carrying out the work.

One blustery day in late September I stood inside the house with Jock. It looked even more dilapidated and depressing than on my first sight of it three years ago. During that time rain, storm and wind had battered the walls, mice had burrowed into woodwork, spiders had strung their webs across ceilings, and the small amount of renovation which we had been able to achieve seemed only to accentuate the general effect of ruin and decay. Try as I might, no comforting picture of a cosy fireside and a warmly lit room would enter my mind. Jock took me round with a businesslike air, the plan of the house in one hand, the Skye builder's estimate in the other.

'This,' he said, indicating a grimy box-like cave which led off the entrance hall, 'will be the kitchen sink area. There's a door here on the left which will make an entrance to the kitchen, then we can extend the back wall there to shut it off from the hall. It'll be an L-shaped room, see, with the sink and work-table compressed on one side, and space by the windows for a dining-table.'

'And the stove?'

'Here against the outer wall, so I'll have an exit for the flue. Then it'll warm the bedroom upstairs and be in the right place to heat the hot-water tank.'

I looked doubtfully at the gaping hole from which Iain had torn the remnants of the previous rusty stove. We went upstairs.

'A bedroom on each side of the stairs,' continued the indefatigable Jock, 'and the bathroom here in between. You'll have a fine view of the hills as you lie in your bath.'

I stepped warily on rotting floorboards and peered out of a filthy window-pane. Bath, wash-basin, lavatory, hot-water tank, storage tank, kitchen sink, Raeburn stove, boiler; I was beginning to tick off the long list of objects it would be necessary to acquire.

'And I'll tell you where to get a lot of things,' said Jock, as though reading my mind. 'The demolition depot in Edinburgh.' His eyes brightened. 'You'll find acres of sinks and lavatories and tanks, all from demolished houses, and you can just take your pick.'

I left the island a few days later with a notebook stuffed with measurements, and a shopping list from Jock of alarming proportions. The weather was closing in, and a nip of winter already chilled the air. Not the most propitious time for house renovation, I thought.

One of our major problems was a water supply. We had scoured the hillside above the house for a suitable burn, alas none was forthcoming. The previous inhabitants had used a spring, but this was thirty feet or so below the house. How were we to get the water up to a level where it would flow into the reserve tank above the road, and thence into the house?

The problem was solved by a miraculous contraption known as a Blake's Hydram. This pump was able to send the water which flowed downhill through it, back up the hill again, and it did this without the aid of electricity or any mechanics. I could never understand how it worked, but the glowing testimonials from retired admirals and air vice-marshals which decorated the brochure describing its activities, assured me that my life would be irrevocably changed by its installation, and it would continue to make its chug-chugging noise and do its job for thirty years if necessary, aided only by the occasional changing of a washer. In preparation, Jock started to dig eighty feet of trenches in the hillside for pipes which would connect the pump to the water storage tank above the road.

In his weekly letter Jock also told me that he had recruited an island man, Calum Macrae, to help him. The Sanitary Inspector from Skye, who had drawn up the original plans for the house and submitted them to the Inverness County Council, had been over to see what was happening. He found Jock and Calum tearing up floorboards.

'Holes have been made in the walls for vents. The floor has been taken out preparatory to a new floor being laid,' he wrote to me. 'I do not yet notice much progress.'

While Jock reported, 'To see inside the croft just now one would think it had been hit by a bomb.'

'How are the trenches for the pipes getting on, Jock?' I asked, in my weekly telephone call.

'Those dratted sheep have been at them again,' he replied, testily, 'sheltering from the wind.'

'What about your last order of building materials from Skye?'

'I ordered one flue vent, one cupboard vent, one copper cylinder, five hundred and sixty square feet of floorboards, twenty-four of five by two by sixteen and a half feet floor joists, nails, ten gallons liquid asphalt, one gallon creosote, one hundred and twenty Aqualite damp course, two hundred bricks and three bags of cement.'

My head reeled.

'Did they send it all?'

'Not half yet. Probably be the wrong sizes when it does

come. I won't be surprised if most of it has to go back again. Anyway, the road is so icy, the lorry can't get out there just now.'

The winter had set in in earnest. Snow covered the Cuillins. Gales delayed transport of vital commodities. At the best of times, transport was uncertain, as everything had to come by steamer across six miles of sea and thence from the pier by lorry over four miles of indifferent road. Finally the materials were carried by hand down a steep slope to the house itself, to be stored in the corrugated-iron porch, already bursting with planks of wood, pots of paint and bags of nails. Jock and Calum, with a talent for improvization, made use of everything that came their way. (I soon learned that in island life nothing is ever thrown away.)

In spite of these difficulties, by Christmas the new floor was laid, and Jock and Calum were immersed in installing the water system. My bathroom suite, bought at the demolition depot for an absurd price, had arrived.

'We had one heck of a job getting the bath upstairs,' Jock wrote. 'But we managed. It's in.'

The water supply was connected up, the heavy Raeburn cooker manhandled down the hill without mishap, and the walls of the kitchen lined.

At Easter I decided to pay a visit. The transformation which greeted my eyes seemed miraculous. Not only were the outside walls still shining white, but now three rooms inside – the kitchen, one bedroom and the bathroom – were finished, except for a coat of paint. The murky 'Black Hole of Calcutta' which had led off the hall, had become the working end of the kitchen, with a sink, draining-board, cupboards, larder and space for a Calor-gas refrigerator. The bathroom was complete. The hot-water tank, installed in a cupboard in the bedroom, dispersed the chill of the March air, while the stove itself burned merrily in the kitchen, a kettle steaming on its shiny top.

At that stage I did not know either Jock or Calum well. They responded warily to my Niagara of enthusiasm.

'Och, yes, it's getting on,' said Calum. 'But I'm thinking

we've a long way to go yet.'

Jock produced another immense shopping list, and a string of complaints about the difficulties of getting supplies from Skye. But later, over a glass of whisky in the evening, they allowed their satisfaction to show through. We decided on a work plan for the ten days that I would be there, and I undertook to paint the kitchen, the hall and the stairs.

The day before I left, I was standing on the top rung of a ladder, scraping moss off the back of the roof. Shafts of yellow light filtering from a cloud-filled sky irradiated the crest of a wave, the corner of a field, the shape of a far hill. Sheep browsed peacefully before the house, and a chaffinch, poised in the rowan tree, trilled its morning song. I heard the sound of a petrol engine and looked up. The red post-van had drawn up in the road. Norman-the-Post emerged, and trudged down the slope to the house. Silently he handed me up a couple of letters, and then stood back, took a short pipe from his pocket, filled it, and looked impassively at the view. After a couple of puffs, 'You'll be busy,' he said. 'Have you come to stay?'

To receive a letter addressed to the house set the final seal on our occupation. I replied with a panegyric of praise for the place, the view, the island. Norman looked at me without speaking, turning over my words in his mind like a cow chewing its cud.

'Aye,' he replied, at last. 'It's quite nice.'

Two years before, in May 1964, I had remarried. My husband, Brian Power, an Irishman whose family came from the wild coast of County Clare in western Ireland, was as interested as I in moving into our island home as soon as possible. We gave Jock and Calum a deadline, sent up a vanload of furniture beforehand, and finally we arrived in the last week of July 1966, with thirty-six packages, a bull-terrier and a Siamese cat.

Things were far from finished. One bedroom was virtually untouched, and the living-room still required painting. But the house was habitable and comfortable.

Every morning Jock and Calum arrived at 9 am to start the day's work. They walked the three miles from the village, as they had done all winter, except when they could hitch a lift in the lorry bringing supplies from the pier; and they would return home the same way.

Calum was an engaging figure, an Island man in his early thirties, who had been at sea for many years and had all but achieved his ticket as a ship's carpenter. He had returned to the island several years ago to look after his ageing parents, who owned a small croft near the village. Calum knew most of the world's big ports and had sailed to most of its continents; but he seemed quite contented now to settle on the island indefinitely. One day, he said, he would go back to sea and get his carpenter's ticket. One day . . .

His attitude was typical of the West Highland genius for procrastination. 'Ach, well, tomorrow will do.' During the years we have known Calum, that one day has never come. Sometimes this dilatoriness made Jock's Lowland blood boil. He and his wife, the island's schoolmistress, are natives of Galloway, in the south of Scotland, but they, too, have no wish to live anywhere but on Raasay.

Jock's initiative and conscientiousness stood us in good stead in the construction of the house, while Calum had a craftsman's eye for detail and decoration. Neither of them worked fast; in fact there were innumerable delays while they argued, smoked, or chatted to us. But they took the work to their hearts and were as interested in the renovation of the house as if it had been their own. This enthusiasm was their most valuable quality. Neither of them had built a house before, so they proceeded by a process of trial and error. But Jock was an experienced plumber and Calum a good carpenter; together they made an excellent team.

By mid-August all the furniture was in place, curtains up, rush matting on the kitchen floor, and Diarmaid's dictum – 'rustic luxury' – well on the way to being achieved.

Each day we woke with the sun, when it peeped over the eastern horizon about 6 am. At that time the sea was usually still, disturbed only by long ribbons of currents which wove between drowsy gulls. Rabbits, hiding in the brushwood near the house, woke up and scuttled away over the short-cropped turf. The clicking of wrens and chirping of chaffinches sounded from the rowan tree, and small birds darted from bush to bush, their wings vibrating in the early morning air. The splash of the burn, rushing down its waterfall to the sea, was always with us, and if we listened carefully we could hear the chug-chug of our trusty Hydram pump.

Each day was a day of discovery. There were many tiresome details to be attended to; long walks to the village for telephone calls to chase up missing supplies; problems of priorities to be solved with Jock and Calum; the occasional failure of some vital piece of mechanism in the house; the non-appearance of some promised piece of equipment. But somehow these disappointments and delays were never permanently frustrating. Fired by the excitement of occupation, we took them in our stride. Even the necessary household chores of cooking, cleaning and washing-up could be enjoyed when rugs were shaken out to a firmament filled with sun and birdsong, and washing-up done with a view of heather slope and hill. Fresh mackerel, Jersey milk (from the Raasay House home farm) and Orkney cheese were our staple diet. They were eaten thankfully with great hunger after a day of exercise in the open air.

We explored the beach, the hills, the coast. The house became littered with shells, fossils and wild flowers. Bird identification books and field-glasses lay on the kitchen table, mixed with water-colour sketches and drafts of poems. It was a honeymoon period. We, and the house, never quite reached it again, but it carried us brilliantly over the teething troubles and problems of settling in.

We lived and ate in the kitchen. Two easy chairs, on either side of the stove, made a comfortable corner; and at night, when the Aladdin lamp was lit and the fire glowed, a cosy atmosphere spread throughout the room.

One evening, as we sat there, we heard a loud knock on the porch door. We opened it to disclose our nearest neighbour, Roddy MacLeod, the shepherd who lived in the croft by the lighthouse at Eyre Point, two miles away. He was accompanied by two of his cousins, also MacLeods.

'We called to bid you welcome,' said Roddy.

The three large figures, dimly seen in the lamplight, loomed against the night sky. A froth of collie dogs brushed against their knees.

'Come in,' said Brian. 'Do come in, we're very glad to see you.'

The dogs were whistled to a sitting posture outside, and, with a polite demur about muddy boots, Roddy and his cousins entered the kitchen. They sat themselves on the edge of three hard wooden chairs and looked around.

'Will you have a dram?'

'Well, that's very kind of you. Yes, indeed.'

I had met these men several times on the hill, but we had never exchanged more than a few brief words. Now I hoped for a longer conversation. Their weather-beaten faces glowed in the dimly-lit kitchen, as each large hand resolutely grasped its tumbler of whisky.

Roddy, the oldest of the three, is a giant of a man, six feet four in height and correspondingly broad, the uncrowned king of the island crofters. He has bright blue eyes and an expressive face on which emotions have carved deep lines. Roddy's wife died some years ago, and his sister now lives with him and his son and daughter in a house which is a replica of ours, erected at the same time. He and his two MacLeod cousins own most of the sheep on our neighbouring hillsides. They are a tightly-knit trio, looking after their stock well, which often wins the highest prices at the Inverness yearly sheep sales.

The three raised their glasses in a toast.

'*Slainte!* And how do you like Fearns?' said Roddy.

I restrained my enthusiasm, which I had found from experience tended to be overwhelming, and Brian replied that he liked it very much; it reminded him of the west of Ireland.

'It's the same kind of life,' he said, 'and the people are much the same, too.'

Brisco, the Don Juan of the trio, winked one long-lashed

violet-coloured eye. 'There now, Roddy, that's a place you should go,' he said. 'You might find yourself a wife there.'

The three exchanged glances, pondering this suggestion.

'Will I bring you one back next time I go?' asked Brian.

A huge smile spread over Roddy's face.

'And what would she be able to do?' he enquired.

'Well, she could cook you nice meals.'

'And what else?'

'She could plant vegetables for you and tend them.'

'And what else?'

Brian cast around desperately for wifely duties other than the fundamental one uppermost in Roddy's mind.

'She could bring up your children.'

'And what else? Would she be a good ewe to my ram?'

'Ach, Roddy. You're going too far,' said Brisco, a deprecatory smirk on his mobile features.

Roddy let out a gargantuan peal of laughter, leaned back in his chair, slapped his thigh, and then thumped Brian's knee.

'I had you there, didn't I, Mr Power?' he roared. 'Ach, well, well, I'll depend on you now to keep your word next time you go to Ireland.'

Two or three whiskies and more than an hour later, the three decided it was time to leave. Rising heavily, they tramped to the door. It was a clear night with the last of the Hebridean light fading slowly away. The dogs moved to meet their masters, padding quietly on soft turf, brushing themselves against stalwart legs.

'We're very glad to see the houses occupied again,' said Calum – Calum Bàn, the Fair One – turning to us before departing. He was the third of the trio, and had in fact owned one of the houses, haggling with the Department of Agriculture for some time about its selling price before letting it go. 'It's great to see lights here when we come up over the hill. You'll enjoy yourselves, no doubt of it. It's a fine place you've got.'

'We think so, too,' said Brian. 'And we hope you'll come and see us any time you're passing.'

'We will so. Goodbye now, and thanks.'

Their footsteps and voices faded away into the night.

We remained outside, staring across the water at Scalpay, the large black island which lay ahead. A crescent of silver light was appearing above the slope of its dark hill. Soon a shining thread ran across the water, extending as we watched into a glittering path strewn with innumerable points of light. The full moon rose in splendour and sailed into the night sky.

I turned. The house behind us, renovated, immaculate, stood outlined in the pure silver rays. How often had the moon risen unseen to shine on these walls? How often had it been watched by other eyes? The night, now dark and unfathomable, held its own secrets. So did the house. Some we might discover. Many, for all our interest and love, we would never share.

7

Raasay House

On my initial visit to the island Raasay House had been a hotel. Its charm and mystery had captivated me and once we had moved into our house at Fearns I took the first opportunity to visit it again.

Jock and Calum told me that the hotel had closed soon after I had taken tea there. The building had then passed back into the hands of the Department of Agriculture who sold it in 1962 to a new owner, an Englishman who lived in Sussex. Raasay House had since been unoccupied, and its condition was deteriorating. Rumours about the new owner's intentions for the house were circulating freely round the island. No one knew what its fate would be, but everyone was anxious, for Raasay House was the island's natural centre and its most prized possession.

I approached the house across the stretch of green which had once been a lawn but was now a rough field on which cattle were allowed to graze. From afar its grace and dignity were unimpaired; however as I drew nearer I was saddened by what I saw. The building was obviously empty and neglected. It had acquired that indefinable sadness which unoccupied houses bear. Through the dusty windows I could see furniture piled in careless heaps. The library's books were scattered over floor, tables and chairs. Curtains and chair-covers were rolled up haphazardly among pictures and ornaments. The whole interior gave an impression of accumulating neglect and decay. How had this come to pass? My sense of foreboding for the house, felt six years ago, deepened. I determined to find out more about its past, and, if possible, its present situation.

Several of the older people on the island remembered the house's history, and talked to me of its previous owners and the glories of former days. The Raasay House Record Books had been preserved and gave accounts of Victorian days. The story of the Raasay MacLeods had been recorded. From these and other sources I was able to piece together a picture of the history of Raasay House and of the island.

Viewed from the sea, the house is a dominant feature of Raasay's south-west shore. It stands in a romantic setting among trees above a grassy slope. Behind it rises a wooded hill. Below it curves a wide bay, bounded on the northern side by a rocky promontory, beyond which lies a small tidal harbour contained by an old stone pier.

The site of the house is well chosen, for it looks on a magnificent view of the Skye mountains, yet is protected by its own hillside and its abundant trees. The faded grey limestone façade merges into the landscape, and the surroundings – meadows, fields, trees and a scattering of small cottages – give the house a pastoral air. This green fertility is at variance with the slopes of moor and heather which lie beyond, culminating in the rocky summit of Dun Caan – wild, untamed country where man has made no impression. Yet the rough landscape does not intrude. It serves only as a background to the charmingly placed house with its civilized appearance, its mantle of trees, and the green meadows and fields which radiate from it.

Above the pebble shore, to one side of the house, stands a steep knoll called the Battery, first fortified in Napoleonic times. It is topped by two small cannon and two large stone mermaids. These objects were placed there early in the nineteenth century by the laird of the time: the cannon (four-and-a-half-pounders, cast at Falkirk) because of the Napoleonic War scare, the mermaids as a temporary resting place before their final destination – the newly-built porch of the mansion. Unfortunately, they proved too heavy to reach it. Instead, they remained on their knoll for a hundred and fifty years, gazing mournfully across the Sound; their beauty, in the course

Our croft house in Raasay

and its view

Raasay House and its view

of time, becoming marred by two broken noses, and their backs straddled by generations of island children. Their faintly Grecian air provides a bizarre contrast to the Ruritanian cannon, now rusted with disuse, and the workmanlike, eighteenth-century stone wall which encircles the top of the little fortress.

Living on Raasay, I soon found that such unlikely juxtapositions were typical of the island, where, with a mixture of providence and Highland laissez-faire, nothing is ever thrown away. Objects remain in their last resting place, acquiring a patina of moss or rust until they finally disintegrate into the landscape.

The first Lairds of Raasay were the MacLeods of Lewis – the Siol Thorcuil – whose founder, Ljot, died in 1280. Raasay was part of their lands, and it is probable that they erected Brochel Castle (the ruined fortress on the north-east shore which I had seen from the summit of Dun Caan), placing it strategically on the route from the mainland to Lewis and maintaining it as one of the strongest fortresses in the Western Isles. The castle dates from the fifteenth century, but it was not until the early sixteenth century that the line of Raasay MacLeods was founded. Malcolm, the ninth MacLeod of Lewis, gave Raasay and Rona to his second son, Calum Garbh (Malcolm the Rough or Rugged) and he became the first of the Raasay MacLeods – Mac Gillichaluim of Clan ic ille Rarsaidh. This line continued unbroken for over four hundred years.

In accordance with the clan system, every MacLeod on the island was bound to serve his chief in time of war. In return each clansman was regarded as part of the chief's extended family, kinsmen with the right of familial possession, who could call on their chief's patriarchal protection, and to whom his bounty and his justice were due.

The MacLeods lived first at Brochel Castle. Then about 1549 they erected a three-storied tower at Clachan on the present site of Raasay House. This tower, to which they moved around 1648, was built as a fortification, for Raasay had its share of clan warfare and feuds raged with the neighbouring chiefs across the water. During the troubled years of the fifteenth and sixteenth centuries, the islands also became a refuge for 'broken men' – outcasts who belonged to no clan but occupied dens in the thick woods of Raasay and its neighbouring islands, Pabay and Rona. From there these renegades plundered shipping and smuggled stolen goods. Their harbour in Rona was named Port nan Robaireann (Port of the Robbers) and they roved far and wide. The chiefs themselves were not above similar enterprises and they probably welcomed these outlaws as supporters in clan reiving, an activity for which Brochel Castle with its easy access to the sea was ideally placed.

In spite of such forays the Raasay MacLeods were renowned as one of the best and kindliest of the chieftain families during the four hundred years of their rule. Their deeds of valour were celebrated in Gaelic poems and songs and cherished in the island's lore. Throughout the Gaelic-speaking West, Raasay was known for its gaiety, its poetry and its music. One of the most romantic figures was Iain Garbh, who became chief in 1648. His strength and beauty were celebrated in a famous *piobaireachd* composed by Patrick Mor MacCrimmon of Skye. Tradition has it that he died at the age of twenty-one, and though this is now considered unlikely, the story provided a theme for many poems and songs. It was said that Iain Garbh was returning by boat from a visit to his uncle, the Lord of Kintail, on the Isle of Lewis. The weather was rough and the crew reluctant to sail, but Iain insisted. Off Trotternish in Skye, the storm increased. Iain's boat was seen and recognized from the shore, but then concealed by a heavy shower. When the shower cleared, the boat had disappeared. The grief of the MacLeod family was shared by everyone in Raasay and beyond, many believing that witchcraft had been responsible for the young man's death. Numerous witches, it was asserted, in the shape of cats had entered the boat and upset it. Iain's sister composed a poem in Gaelic, literally translated thus:

O stout Iain, son of Gillichalluim
Strong art thou without pretension,

When you would propel by the strength of your elbow
It would not be the throw of a stripling.

Thou great man of the race of Thorcuil
In thy body was strength –
When they would stand together
To thee was the respect of the Gael.

The eighteenth century brought varying fortunes to the Raasay MacLeods. In the late '30s or early '40s a new house was built by the laird at Clachan on the site of the old tower. Its lack of fortification signified the hope of more peaceful times. But this hope was to be short-lived. In 1745 Prince Charles landed on Scottish soil and the Jacobite Rising split the Highlands in two.

Malcolm MacLeod of Raasay, then an ageing man, came out for the Prince, and supplied a hundred fighting men for his army. In neighbouring Skye neither the MacLeod nor the MacDonald chiefs supported the Jacobite cause, although Sir Alexander MacDonald, because of an ancient league between Skye MacDonald and Raasay MacLeod families, promised old Raasay help should the Prince's hopes fail. Boswell tells us that Sir Alexander declared, 'Don't be afraid, Raasay . . . I'll use all my interest to keep you safe; and if your estate should be taken, I'll buy it for the family.' Old Raasay 'prudently guarded against a forfeiture, by previously conveying his estate to his eldest son'. But this action did not save him. After Culloden, he was forced to take to the heather with a price on his head. His new house was razed to the ground and even his family silver, hid in 'the cave of the oars' (a cleft in the rocks below Raasay House), was found and commandeered. In spite of his father's caution, young Raasay was also involved. When he heard that the Prince needed help to escape to Raasay from his enemies in Skye he declared, 'I'll go, though at the risk of life and fortune.' The flight to Raasay may indeed have saved Prince Charles, for, as we know, the British militia in Skye thereafter lost track of his movements for a vital few days.

Both Raasay and its neighbouring island Rona suffered grievously for their loyal support of the Prince's cause. Captain Scott, a notoriously cruel officer, and Captain Hay, raided Rona. They caused all the cattle to be killed, all the houses to be set on fire, and all the crops to be destroyed. In addition, a blind girl was raped. Later, Captain Fergussone of the Royal Navy ship *Furnace*, made a punitive visit to Raasay. As well as the laird's new house, more than three hundred cottages were burned. All the animals on the island were slaughtered and left to rot, and thirty-two boats were destroyed. People were robbed of their clothing, two women were raped, and everything of value was taken. Such was the price paid for support of the Jacobite cause.

A number of years elapsed before Raasay House and the fortunes of the MacLeod family could be restored. But, as is well known:

> The heroes and their heroism fade,
> Nature refurbishes the ravished glade,
> Old wounds and enmities the years repair
> And passion dies upon the morning air.*

When Johnson and Boswell visited the island a few decades later, in 1773, they found a rebuilt house which they could describe as 'a good family mansion'. They were halfway through their celebrated tour of the Hebrides, a unique journey which took them to regions virtually unknown to the rest of Britain. They came to the island from Skye, the laird having sent to fetch them, 'a good strong open boat made in Norway'. It was rowed by 'four stout rowers, particularly a MacLeod, a robust, black-haired fellow, half-naked and bare-headed, something between a wild Indian and an English tar. Dr Johnson sat high in the stern, like a magnificent Triton.'

Their pilot to the island, wrote Boswell, was 'a gentleman whom I had a great desire to see, Mr Malcolm MacLeod . . . celebrated in the year 1745-6. He was now sixty-two years of

* Verse by the author.

age, hale, and well-proportioned – with a manly countenance, tanned by the weather, yet having a ruddiness in his cheeks, over a great part of which his rough beard extended. His eye was quick and lively, yet his look was not fierce, but he appeared at once firm and good humoured . . . I never saw a figure that gave a more perfect representation of a Highland gentleman.' This was the same Malcolm who had conducted the Prince to Raasay, and later to Elgol in Skye.

Under Malcolm's direction the journey, though the wind 'had now risen pretty high', was accomplished without mishap.

Four sturdy oarsmen and a boisterous sail
Brought Dr Johnson to the island's hail.
Boreas' zephyrs blew with playful zest
To speed him o'er the waters of the west.
His spurs, untimely carried overboard,
Sank to adorn a Celtic mermaid's hoard,
While from the stern this portly London sage
Calmed with his wisdom the Atlantic rage.
The gallant Captain Malcolm sang in Erse
M'Queen and oarsmen joining in the verse,
While Boswell, whom the elements displeased
Exclaimed – 'We are contending with the seas.'*

A cordial welcome awaited the travellers, the laird himself coming down to the shore to greet them. He was the tenth chief, the same John MacLeod who as a young man helped Prince Charles escape to Raasay. His lady, surrounded by her family of three sons and ten daughters, was equally hospitable, and her guests were impressed by the civilized air of the house and its inhabitants. The laird owned Rona and a considerable extent of land in Skye. Little revenue, however, came from these properties, 'and yet,' Boswell observed, 'he lives in great splendour; and so far is he from distressing his people, that, in the present rage for emigration, not a man has left his estate'.

* Verse by the author.

On the first evening, after the guests had refreshed themselves, 'a fiddler appeared and a little ball began'. All the company danced, the laird 'with as much spirit as anyone, and Malcolm bounded like a roe'. Dr Johnson, sitting slightly apart, watched with interest, sometimes lost in meditation, sometimes talking to the minister, Donald McQueen, who had accompanied him from Skye, sometimes reading, sometimes smiling. 'I know not how we shall get away,' he said, delighted with what he saw. The belle of the ball was 'the eldest Miss MacLeod . . . an elegant well-bred woman, and celebrated for her beauty over all these regions, by the name of Miss Flora . . . There seemed to be no jealousy, no discontentment among them; and the gaiety of the scene was such, that for a moment I doubted whether unhappiness had any place in Raasay.'

The next day Boswell explored the island, climbing to the top of Dun Caan and dancing a reel on its flat summit. He walked to the northern end to see the ruined Brochel Castle, but was not impressed by its romance, remarking only, 'In this remnant of antiquity I found nothing worthy of being noticed, except a certain accommodation rarely to be found at the modern houses of Scotland, and which Dr Johnson and I sought for in vain at the laird's new-built mansion, where nothing else was wanting.' Malcolm MacLeod was his guide, telling him a 'strange fabulous' fairy story on the mountain, and showing him the place where 'in 1745 a hundred fighting men were reviewed . . . Malcolm . . . was one of the officers that led them to the field. They returned home all but fourteen . . . What a princely thing to be able to furnish such a band! The laird has the true spirit of a chief. He is, without exaggeration, a father to his people.' Evidently Johnson shared Boswell's opinion, declaring that he was 'much pleased with the laird of MacLeod, who is indeed a most promising youth, and with a noble spirit struggles with difficulties and endeavours to preserve his people.' Johnson, a High Tory, and a Jacobite in 1745, had only finally accepted the Hanoverian monarchs with the ascension to the throne of George III, whom he respected. If, as many suspect, his Jacobitism was a motive for his Highland tour, he must have felt much at home in Raasay among a company that had so gallantly supported the Prince.

After a few days, however, he wished to move on. 'There was so numerous a company, mostly young people, there was such a flow of familiar talk, so much noise, and so much singing and dancing, that little opportunity was left for his energetic conversation.' He had been royally welcomed, but 'there was not enough of intellectual entertainment for him, after he had satisfied his curiosity, which he did, by asking questions, till he had exhausted the island'. So on Sunday, 12 September, 'a beautiful day', he and Boswell departed.

His pearls of wisdom dropped, his blessing spent,
Johnson on leaving now becomes intent.
Embarked for Skye, he spices his farewell
With Sunday discoursing on death and hell.
The eight-oared boat, skimming across the sea
Holds a devoutly listening company,
His words, 'So die contented, trusting God,'
Serve to increase their deferential mood.
'Though happiness may not be found in life
So various are the ways to combat strife,'
Boswell and Johnson savoured it, the while
They shared the daily living of this isle.
Unlikely travellers, many a Fleet Street quip
Later devalued the romantic trip,
Yet they bequeathed, wherever they had been
A lasting image to the Highland scene.*

The old rooms where Boswell and Johnson slept, ate and danced now lie at the back of the house. But much of the original walls, about three feet thick, and some of the original deep-set narrow windows still remain. So do echoes of the Gaelic music and language, and memories of the house's heyday, when its occupants 'danced every night of the year' and its candles sent out beams of light to the surrounding countryside.

* Verse by the author.

The ten daughters of the house all married and their progeny spread far and wide, so that many Highland families still carry some of the Raasay MacLeod blood in their veins. The eldest son, James, born in 1761, received a special welcome, for six daughters had preceded him. Roy MacKay, piper to Mackenzie of Gairloch, composed a fine tune in his honour entitled 'MacLeod of Raasay's Salute', thus expressing his own joy and the joy of the clan at the advent of an heir.

Six years later, in 1767, another MacKay – John MacKay – was born in Raasay. Starting life as a herd-laddie he raised the island's piping tradition to undreamed-of heights, and became the most knowledgeable piper of his day. He served his apprenticeship with the MacCrimmons, then had a long spell with the MacKays of Gairloch, and finally left Raasay to become piper at Drummond Castle in Perth. His four sons were all notable players, but the third, Angus, was unique. He possessed the particular genius required to link the traditional past of piping to the changing future, and he brought the art out of its hitherto restricted environment into the modern world.

With Angus we come to the nineteenth century, a critical time for the Raasay MacLeods, and the people of the island. This century brought them their most fateful decision and changed irrevocably their way of life. But it started auspiciously enough, and the success of Angus seemed a pointer to greater opportunity for all.

Angus MacKay was born in Raasay about 1812. By his early twenties his playing was outstanding. He became piper to Campbell of Islay and won the gold medal of piping in Edinburgh in 1835. By the age of twenty-six he had produced 'the piper's bible' – his book setting down on paper most of the pipe music of the eighteenth century. Until then tunes had been relayed orally, and many of the old players scorned Angus's efforts to produce a staff notation, and prophesied that no good would come of it. But Angus persevered and after a further sixteen years of continued work his vision was rewarded. He succeeded in recording in its entirety the heritage of the MacCrimmons and the other great pipers in a form which succeeding generations could understand and preserve.

Angus became piper to Queen Victoria in 1843, and, together with Hugh S. MacKay, invented the 'competition march', a form (and the tunes he composed for it) still greatly popular today. But his last five years were clouded with mental illness; brought on, it was thought, by the immense effort needed to remember and record accurately his great repertoire. In Angus MacKay the piping tradition of Raasay reached its finest fulfilment.

James MacLeod, who was chief when Angus was born, was the eleventh of his line. He lived until 1824, and much improved the estate, planting trees, and building the present Regency front to Raasay House. Two spacious ground-floor rooms, with a hall between them, were added, and several bedrooms were built above, all with large sashed windows opening on to the superb view. James meant the projecting columned porch in front of the hall to be decorated by the mermaids, but, as we know, they never got farther than the adjacent hill.

The first half of the nineteenth century was a critical time for Highland lairds and their estates. The greater chiefs survived by sheep farming, commercial investments in Britain and, subsequently, sporting lets. The majority were educated in England, and many turned their eyes to the South. The lesser chiefs, who remained at home and improved their properties, ran into greater and greater debt, and by the middle of the century a large number were forced to sell up their lands and homes.

One such was John, James MacLeod's son, and the last of the Raasay MacLeods to live on the island. He succeeded his father in 1824, and for twenty years struggled to maintain his estate. But the odds were too great. In 1843 he finally sold the house and island to George Rainy of Edinburgh and in 1846 emigrated to Tasmania.

Overpopulation on the island meant that families were living under desperately poor conditions. Nevertheless, only the strongest possible inducements could persuade them to leave their homes. A number of his people followed John MacLeod to seek a new fortune in a new land. But many more remained. They fared badly. The new owner converted much of the island into a sheep-run and deer forest. The best arable land was taken from the people and they were forced to leave.

One of those who went was the son of a crofter, emigrating to New Zealand. Recently a diary written by this man in Gaelic has come to light. It tells the story of an eviction. The crofter's son remembers how his aunt, hearing that the factor and estate clerk were coming to evict her family and burn their dwelling, tied herself to her bedpost and refused to move. She had to be loosened from it and dragged outside by main force, there to witness her home going up in flames. As she lay weeping on the ground the factor pushed her with his foot and admonished her, 'If ye canna eat the grass you'd better crawl under it!'

On one day alone – 6 June 1854 – one hundred and twenty-nine emigrants sailed for Australia. They danced a farewell reel on the old stone pier below Raasay House before boarding the ship which would carry them, amid pestilence, hunger and filth, far from their island homes. 'By far the greater number of these were sent away against their will.' So testified the Reverend Galbraith, Free Kirk minister in Raasay, to the Napier Commission in 1883. Irony of ironies, they were forced, as their last act ashore, to pay the cost of the summons for eviction served on them by the Sheriff. During these years at least ninety-eight families (about one thousand people) left, and around twenty square miles out of a total twenty-seven on the island were cleared for sheep and game. The rich pasturage the crofters had tilled and cultivated was overrun with rushes, bracken and heather, and the melancholy sight of deserted and decaying hamlets, hitherto unknown, became commonplace.

There is never enough time for calamity
Sudden or late, it is always premature.
The sun rises as any other day
But by the evening everything is changed.

The ship rides at anchor in the bay
Families gather slowly on the pier.
Awkward bundles pass from hand to hand –
Clothing, food, tools for the new land.

Children play or cry, women in shawls
Cling to one another without words,
Men, their tempers short, curse and heave,
A life's possessions lie among the stones.

The gulls cry, the ship's siren calls,
A wail lifts and breaks along the shore
'*Cha till mi tuille*, we shall return no more.'
Grief etches this moment on the heart.

There is never enough time for calamity
But after, time stretches and stands still.
The empty houses wait, no smoke, no sound.
The rain falls on the deserted hill.*

In the seventies, Raasay's fortunes rose again. The island was bought by an Englishman, E. K. Wood, who, with his successors, owned it from 1876 to 1912. At this time, the Highlands were being discovered by rich Englishmen, a fashion set by Queen Victoria at Balmoral. New lairds, industriously prosperous, acquired Highland estates and with them the apparent, if dubious, glamour of a feudal and sporting life. Most were absentee landlords, arriving only for the shooting and stalking seasons in August and September each year. But the Woods fell in love with Raasay, and added considerably to its amenities. They cared about the island's beauty and did much to preserve it, planting beeches and sycamores around the house, and laying out a belt of mixed forest beyond. They lined the roads with fuchsia and massed rhododendrons in the grounds. They also enlarged the house itself, building on a long wing which included a library well stocked with a

* Poem by the author.

selection of Victorian memoirs, the works of several Scottish divines, and leather-bound editions of Milton, Spenser and Pope. The policies contained a beautiful walled garden, eighteenth-century stables, farm outbuildings, and cottages which housed the workers on the estate. Keen sportsmen, the Woods stocked the moors with grouse, and some of the lochs with trout. Two thousand pheasants were reared annually, and the southern part of the island was turned into a deer-forest. The roads built to facilitate this sport, as well as the upkeep of the house, garden and farm, brought a welcome source of employment to a portion of Raasay's inhabitants.

For the crofters, however, not many benefits accrued. Rents were high and holdings small. From a total of 19,000 acres, the Woods devoted 11,000 to sheep and game, land which could have been used for pasture. Laws were harsh. Damage to crops from rabbits (preserved by the Woods for sport) was a grievance repeatedly reported to the Napier Commission by crofters, but at the turn of the nineteenth century, a crofter's son was fined ten shillings (then a month's wages for an agricultural labourer) for shooting a rabbit that was grazing on his father's croft. The division between the inhabitants of the big house and the inhabitants of the rest of the island was still immense; a division typical of Victorian, though not of Celtic, mores.

A glance at the Raasay House Record Books, a record kept of the weather and of each day's events in Raasay House, is revealing. The gentlemen shot and fished. The ladies took walks within a radius of five miles of the house (the milestones marked RH, each telling the number of miles to the house, still exist on the island roads). Two hundred trout were caught on the loch below Dun Caan. Seals were shot on Rona. Four yachts anchored in the bay for the start of the grouse season. Every Church minister in Skye came for the presbytery.

Old people in Raasay still remember this period, when the house reached its height of luxury, and the four-fold chime of the clock-tower above the eighteenth-century stables rang each quarter across the island. 'A lovely sound it was,' they say.

To the Woods, as they watched the sun set over the Cuillins, with the graceful mansion at their backs, a yacht moored in the bay below, guns and fishing-rods stacked in the well-kept gun-room, fruit from the walled garden on the dining-table, servants, retainers and ghillies on call, their idyllic life must have seemed impregnable. In fact, it was doomed. The 1914-18 War broke it, as irrevocably as the defeat at Culloden broke the clans. The morning the men of Raasay marched off to the War the stable clock stopped at ten o'clock and could never afterwards be mended. Out of the thirty-six who went, twenty-two were killed.

Two souvenirs remain from this pre-War era. The name of the hill behind the house – Temptation Hill – so called because when the first of the Woods climbed it, pondering his purchase, he was tempted by the magnificent view from the summit to become the owner of house and island. And a stone which still lies on the hill's crest, half buried in moss and heather, commemorating a young girl, a friend of the Woods, who loved the island so much that she wished to be buried there.

In the same sentimental tradition is a row of small moss-covered dogs' graves, lying near the wing which the Woods added to the house. They commemorate Racket, Sheilagh, Dan, Jack, Paddy, Rodil, Chow and Sailor who served their masters between the years 1870 and 1899.

It was as axiomatic then that a trusted sporting dog should end his life in a well-tended grave, as that the avenue of lime trees planted nearby should grow up to shade a future laird. But times changed.

The dramatic twentieth century broke upon the world. In 1912 the Woods sold the house and left the island. It was bought for its iron-ore deposit by a firm called Baird & Co., who built a mine and worked it from 1913. This ownership left a legacy of some hideous mine buildings, now obsolete and in ruins, a massive pier, ugly but useful for the visiting steamer, several rows of cottages in the village, and three sizeable houses. The iron-ore was of inferior quality, nevertheless it was worked intensively from 1916 to 1919, with the help of two hundred and fifty German prisoners. When the national emergency ended, it proved uneconomic to continue working it. The mine closed.

Like all Hebridean islands, Raasay sent many of its men to the First World War. When the survivors returned, it was to face hard conditions. Boats and fishing gear had decayed, homes and crofting land had deteriorated, and no resources were available to make good losses, to repair or to replace. No assistance was forthcoming to help the islanders build new roads, houses or boats. Instead, they were encouraged to emigrate. Some of them went to Canada ('The Land of Opportunity' as it was called in posters prominently displayed on the island which depicted a burly Canadian farmer on a fertile sunny prairie), only to find when they arrived that they had been directed to an area within the Canadian Arctic Circle, where conditions were even more extreme than at home. Those who stayed in Raasay endured a hard livelihood, gradually building up their crofts, livestock and fishing gear; others left to find work and opportunity on the mainland.

In 1922 the island changed hands again. This time a Government department bought it: the Scottish Department of Agriculture and Fisheries, which owns it still. Raasay House was let for shooting from time to time, but no one lived there permanently, or gave it the care and attention needed by a large mansion. Once more the island was bereft of its natural centre. Finally, in 1937, the house was leased again and re-opened as a hotel.

This series of events is typical of many Highland mansions, whose fortunes have mirrored the history of their time. Sporting lairds – usually absentee landlords – have taken the place of the old clan chiefs, and they, in their turn, have given way to tourists. Through it all, the old houses have retained much of their romantic charm, as long as they have been lived in, cared for, and not disfigured by brash additions. The alternative – a slow decay and final death – is a sadder fate.

This is the fate which now threatens Raasay House.

When it was sold in 1962 to Dr John R. W. Green of

Cooden, Sussex, the islanders hoped that the new owner would soon re-open it as a hotel. The property had been advertised but was purchased for considerably less than its real value. (The sale included Raasay House, Borodale House nearby, a gardener's cottage, boat-house, fort-site, walled garden with greenhouse, kennels and twelve acres of policies.) As far as the islanders know, Dr Green has visited his property only twice since buying it, each time for no more than a day. He later acquired several other smaller houses on the island but these have also remained unoccupied; a cause for concern among the population as there is a real need for homes for some of Raasay's inhabitants.

During the first few years of his tenure Dr Green carried out repairs to the roof of Raasay House, and bought equipment and cattle for the home farm. But by 1966, when I came to live on Raasay, all work on the house had ceased. Its contents were gradually deteriorating. Mouldering books remained piled on dusty tables. Panels of walls and cupboards ripped up in search of dry rot were never replaced. Pictures lay on the floor beside broken crockery and glass. Outside, pipes began to leak down walls and cracks appeared. It was as though Raasay House and its policies lay under a malign spell.

The reaction of the islanders was one of impotent fury. With its long and distinguished history, its function as the island's focal point, and its uniquely beautiful site, they felt that their mansion (although they have never owned it, they regard it with a proprietary pride) deserved a better fate.

I soon shared the island's concern about Raasay House. I wrote to Russell Johnson, the Liberal Member of Parliament for Inverness-shire, and subsequently saw him at the House of Commons.

During the years Russell Johnson, the Highlands and Islands Development Board and the Inverness County Council have all tried to influence and negotiate with Dr Green about Raasay House. The adamant doctor has been given by the Press the title of 'Dr No'. In 1977 he at last parted with one of his other properties – Borodale House – and sold it to the Highlands and Islands Development Board, who plan to convert it into a small hotel. But none can guess what his ultimate plans for Raasay House may be. Meantime the beautiful building sinks further and further into decline.

All this I could not know when I stood outside Raasay House in 1966. The fact that it would be allowed to fall into ruin seemed inconceivable. The sense of its past glory was so strong that I felt sure its present plight would somehow be redeemed. And indeed, in the intervening years there have been requests for action.

One came in 1974 from the Scottish Georgian Society who, in a letter to the Inverness County Council, expressed their serious concern over the rapidly deteriorating condition of Raasay House, now in an 'appalling state of neglect'. If it were to be saved, they stated, work must be carried out with extreme urgency.

Another protest was issued from the Clan MacLeod Society who, after a visit to Raasay in September 1974 during their 'MacLeod Parliament' at Dunvegan, set one hundred and fifty signatures to a petition to the Secretary of State for Scotland, citing the state of Raasay House and the 'continuing difficult situation in which Raasay inhabitants find themselves'. But much time has passed since these protests and still nothing has been done.

The latest twist in the tale comes from the owner himself. In 1977 Dr Green applied to the Highland Council for planning permission for a £400,000 restoration and extension programme to Raasay House. And in December of that year permission for this programme was granted. It remains to be seen whether these plans will be carried out. The islanders would agree that there is scope for a hotel which would attract the kind of visitors who treasure Raasay's unique peace. In view of past experience they await future developments with interest.

8

Building Again

Island living brings an entirely new awareness of the dimension which surrounds one – the sea. This governs arrivals, departures, visits to neighbouring islands, and communications between places along the coastline.

In the Hebrides storms can blow up very quickly and a stretch of shining calm water be suddenly transformed into an alarmingly rough passage. The sea decides one's travel plans.

It took time to learn this lesson, and we had not yet learned it when, in December 1966, Brian and I boarded the *Loch Arkaig* at Kyle, bound for Christmas in our new Hebridean home. As I watched our luggage being lashed down under a tarpaulin, I wondered if what we had brought was not rather excessive: several large suitcases, a crate of provisions, my little Irish harp, Christmas tree decorations in a fragile cardboard box, Brian's painting easel, a bag full of books, a dog's basket, and a cat's box . . . Already loose objects were beginning to slide about the deck in an ominous manner. It was pouring with rain. The brief northern day was almost over. At about 3.30 pm night would fall. We steamed out of Kyle in the fading light, and the groans and creaks which herald a rough passage started their depressing chorus.

Animal-lovers will know that the experience their pets most abhor is a rough sea voyage. Ours were no exception. As the ship began to roll Cleo, the dog, took on the expression of extreme ill-use which only bull-terriers know how to exploit to the full; while Chaka, the cat, used his strident Siamese voice in its fullest range to howl his displeasure. Our fellow-passengers, crowded into the stuffy saloon, began to look at us askance.

'Never mind,' said Brian, an enviably good sailor, 'we've only an hour's journey to go.'

Lurch, groan, crack, heave, the *Loch Arkaig* ploughed her way through the darkness. Rain and drifts of spray soaked anyone who ventured on deck. Nevertheless, after a while we went up to search for the lights of our house. As the ship steered directly for the island, the beam of the Eyre lighthouse winked into view, and then we saw two or three bright pin-points gleaming out of the dark hillside. Our lights, our home. Looking much nearer than they really were, they welcomed us from across the water.

I hoped that Jock would have a big fire and a kettle on the stove, thoughts of hot tea and hot baps beginning to seep through my wet consciousness.

The *Loch Arkaig* changed course to the west and steamed up the narrow Sound. The beam of the lighthouse and some sparks of light from Roddy's house near the shore were swiftly left behind. Passengers struggled on deck and lurched to the rail.

'It seems rougher. The wind's up, and it's a bad tide for landing,' said Brian, gazing towards the lights of the long wooden pier jutting out into the Sound. The ship laboured on as the roar of the wind and the lash of the waves increased. We peered through the darkness, rain beating against our faces and water trickling down the backs of our necks. Hebridean wetness, long experienced and long familiar, soaked through to the skin. The wind gave a derisive howl. At that moment the *Loch Arkaig* seemed to increase speed, and suddenly the pier loomed up, large, black and very close. Waves flung themselves against its iron stanchions with a lash of spray. My heart contracted. How could we land? The ship shuddered for a moment, then wrenched herself on to a new course. As swiftly as it had appeared, the pier vanished. The stretch of rough water between ourselves and its lights rapidly widened. We had steamed straight past! Pier, island and lights disappeared. Next stop – Skye.

In the first fury of disappointment our instinct was to blame the Captain – 'Of course he could have landed.' Then, as our frustration abated, we realized that this was one of the things which might often happen, part of island living. For us, it involved spending the weekend in Portree because the storm was too severe for the *Loch Arkaig* to attempt the journey back the following day; and the day after was the Sabbath, when neither man, beast nor vehicle must move on the Islands. Our tempers were strained, our animals bedraggled, and our luggage, which had remained on board, soaking wet by the time we set sail again. But we had learned our first island lesson: be elastic about times of arrival and departure.

After two days snow fell, whirled by a north wind to cover hill and moorland. Vivid tufts of bracken were stained white and trees, bunched together in the burn's cleft, fumed like brown smoke. The opaque water lay calm and still and each peak of the Cuillins, tranced by cold, stood pure and clear. Tones of white, grey and brown infused the landscape. Drained of all bright colour, it seemed in this winter clothing to be most itself.

It was Christmas Eve. Peter and Victoria, our neighbours, had arranged a gathering at their house. We walked across in the early evening, under a full moon of extraordinary radiance. The dark spaces of sky receded beyond gleaming snow and cloud, and the mountains, deeply shadowed, flowed in noble curves to the shore. The silence was profound. Wrapped in its mantle of snow, all life seemed arrested, transfixed in the beauty of moon, winter and night.

Peter's living-room, in contrast, was warm and festive. A fire blazed at either end and the children's Christmas tree sparkled in the light of candles. People laughed, talked and exchanged presents. The isolation of the house and the austerity beyond its windows diminished, and a circle of human companionship grew, much like the circle formed by the island's first inhabitants when they too had assembled round their driftwood fires.

The evening started with a Christmas tableau acted by Peter's family. His young wife, dressed in a long white robe, walked downstairs carrying her small baby in her arms. Behind her came her three-year-old son, a gold paper crown poised precariously on his head, followed by the eldest daughter, aged five, a guardian angel with golden wings.

'Leo is a Wise Man, but his crown keeps slipping off,' she whispered.

This Holy Family grouped themselves before us, and the readings began.

'Christmas: Cristes mæsse, the mass of Christ. The festival of the nativity of Christ, kept on the twenty-fifth of December . . . "Christmasse comes but once a yeare." ' Diarmaid declaimed his piece from the *Oxford Dictionary* with scientific precision.

Iain followed with T. S. Eliot's poem, *The Journey of the Magi*:

> A cold coming we had of it
> Just the worst time of the year
> For a journey, and such a long journey:
> The ways deep and the weather sharp,
> The very dead of winter . . .

Then Brian read the Gospel account, 'Now when Jesus was born in Bethlehem of Judea in the days of Herod the King, behold there came wise men from the East to Jerusalem . . . and, lo, the star which they saw in the East, went before them. till it came and stood over where the young child was . . .'

A small upright piano, which Peter had succeeded in bringing across the sea and into his house, stood in one corner of the room. He sat down at it and played for the carols which everyone sang, and the familiar tunes and words were reinforced with glasses of hot punch. More readings followed, one for each guest, then Peter ended with a passage from Plato's *Symposium*:

'He who has been instructed thus far in the science of Love, and has been led to see beautiful things in their due order and rank, when he comes toward the end of his discipline, will suddenly catch sight of a wondrous thing, beautiful with the absolute Beauty . . . he will see a Beauty eternal, not growing or decaying, not waxing or waning . . . but Beauty, absolute, separate, simple and everlasting; which lending its virtue to all beautiful things that we see born to decay, itself suffers neither increase nor diminution, nor any other change. When a man proceeding onwards from terrestrial things by the right way of loving, once comes to sight of that Beauty he is not far from his goal.'

Pagan and Christian thought fused in the poetry of the words, and as we emerged into the chilly night air, 'beautiful things in their due order' stood before us. The snow, fallen thickly on bracken, path and moor, blurred outlines, making familiar shapes mysterious and imposing a deep silence. Even the lap of water and rush of burn were muted into a white peace. All seemed newly made, expectant as though at the first Christmas. If the Magi, a Bethlehem shepherd, or a mystic star had suddenly appeared, it would not have seemed surprising. But not even an island shepherd was out on this winter evening. Turning up our coat collars, we strode home through the snow, cold and warmth finely balanced between our outer and inner sensations.

This Christmas Eve celebration was not typical of that season of the year on Raasay. The Free Presbyterian Church, to which the islanders belong, keeps no feast at Christmas. On the contrary, it deplores such popish practices. Its service of dedication takes place at New Year when the congregation are warned against contamination by the evils of this world, and reminded that they are born in guilt and sin. The majority of them attend this service, held on New Year's Day, even though some of them have spent New Year's Eve in quite a different fashion.

During this bitter winter weather sheep and cattle grazed the hillside, finding what sustenance they could beneath the snow. The hardy black-faced sheep stay out on the hill all the year round, even at lambing time. The cows are brought in to calve, otherwise they, too, remain on the hill, sometimes wandering on to the beach in search of salt, but more often grazing on slopes below a wide track, now grassed over, which winds across the foot of Beinn na Leac and leads to the rocky point of Rubha na Leac, two miles beyond our house. This path became one of our favourite walks and we soon knew all the rough-coated black, tan and brown cattle who frequented it.

The ratio of cattle to sheep is low in Raasay. One reason for the deterioration of grazing land on the island, for sheep are wasteful feeders, taking only the best grass and allowing coarser grazing, which cattle could use, to be overrun by bracken and moorland. The grass surrounds of our unfenced houses provided good grazing. Sheep were nearly always there; often I would wake in the night to hear the heavy breathing of cattle also, and be reminded next morning of their nocturnal presence by the large liquid puddles which they had left.

A few days before New Year, Iain found a stranded calf in one of the small woods on the track to Rubha na Leac. It had slipped down the precipitous hillside and become lodged in a birch tree. Iain extricated it and returned it to its mother, who was browsing on the slopes below. He also reported its injured condition to Roddy, who promised to let its owner know.

The next day the calf was weaker and by the third day its condition was critical. No one had appeared to attend to it, and it could hardly stand. The iced-up condition of the road made it impossible to use a vehicle to take the calf to its owner, and the situation was complicated by the fact that it was New Year's Eve.

By New Year's Day the calf had disappeared. As we had foreseen, it had fallen over the edge of the cliff on to the shore 500 feet below. Action could no longer be delayed. Iain, taking a gun, walked over to Roddy's house. Then with Roddy and several others, he made his way along the beach to where the calf had fallen. It was still alive, lying on the stones above the tide-line. Iain shot it as the brief winter day closed in.

'Why didn't the owner attend to it four days ago?' he demanded.

'Ach, well,' said Roddy, 'he's careless, you know. He has a lot of trouble with an ailing mother at home. That has distressed him.'

'We couldn't interfere,' Brisco explained. 'It's his calf, you see.' He paused, then added, 'Sure, it would never have been any good to anyone, the way it was.'

'It should have been shot at once,' said Iain. 'Or saved.'

'What's the difference? The owner'll get his fourteen pounds subsidy for it, whatever he did or didn't do.'

The realism of this casual cruelty was a new slant on our islanders' outlook.

The next day a small dinghy with an outboard motor set out from Roddy's house along the shore. Watching through my binoculars I saw that it was heading for the place where the calf lay. When it returned an hour or so later, I guessed what cargo it carried; rightly, as it turned out, for that evening Peter and Victoria were presented with a cut of succulent veal. To my relief none came our way.

Throughout that year we had gazed down the hillside at our second house, still standing in a state of disrepair and decay 200 or so feet below. The experience of sharing a small cottage with a number of exuberant young men and their girlfriends made my husband look at it with increasingly longing eyes.

'I'd like to buy it from the boys, and do it up for ourselves,' he said. 'Then we could create our own atmosphere of peace and quiet.'

Diarmaid and Iain, now both based abroad, willingly agreed. But Jock Rutherford and Calum Macrae expressed doubts.

'It's in very bad condition,' said Jock. 'Much worse than the top house was. You'd have to re-roof it for a start.'

'Well, Jock, that could easily be done,' Calum replied.

They had now reached the state of long-standing workmates or a long-married couple, where each on principle flatly contradicts whatever the other says.

'What worries me is that crack in the back wall. It's a big one, it may mean the foundations are shifting. I don't like it at all.'

'Aye, you'll need to get an opinion on that right enough,' said Jock, agreeing for once. 'I doubt the Sanitary-from-Skye would ever pass that crack for a grant.'

Both Jack and Calum were obviously disturbed.

'Let's consult MacKay, the road-builder,' Brian suggested. 'He used to live there. He'd know all about the construction of the house.'

So several evenings later MacKay paid us a visit. A large man, with keen blue eyes, sunburned face and slow speech, he surveyed the ominous crack.

'Sure, I remember my father building this wall, I remember it very well indeed,' he said, reaching his hand along the stones and sliding his fingers into the crack. 'The wall hadn't a proper corner-stone, that's why it broke. Ach, well, the foundations may have settled a wee bit, that could cause it, too. But there's nothing wrong with the house, nothing at all. That crack couldn't have widened more than half an inch in thirty years.' He turned to regard us with the full force of his blue eyes. 'Half an inch in thirty years,' he reiterated. 'That's good enough for you, isn't it? What more do you want?'

His verdict given, he walked slowly round the house, looking carefully at each wall in turn, then sat down on the grass beneath the broken window-ledges and gazed out to sea. I, curious to know about conditions here thirty years ago, sat beside him.

'How many people lived here when you were a boy?' I asked him.

'There were four families living at Fearns in those days,' he replied. 'One in each house. Ten of us children walked to school every day – three miles into the village and three miles back. In the winter we'd start in the dark and the cold.' MacKay's eyes twinkled. 'And in the summer we'd be playing truant on the way, and sometimes not get to the school at all.'

'Were the families self-supporting?'

'We had cows and sheep and some fowls. Our own milk and eggs. The children's job was to look after the fowls. We farmed this land, and grew crops and potatoes.' MacKay cast his eyes down the grass and sedge covering the slope below us. 'Look, you can see the marks of the fields there yet. Those are the piles of stones where the land was cleared, and there are the remains of the walls that divided the fields.'

'Was it a hard life?'

'It was. But happy. We all helped each other.'

'And you fished a bit, too, I suppose?'

'We did. Mackerel, lithe, saithe. Lobster – sometimes a salmon.'

'And when did you leave?'

'When I was twenty. Ach, there was nothing for a young man to do here. The old people stayed as long as they could. Then they went too and the houses were empty for many years.' MacKay's strong brown face grew wistful. 'Aye, the old life's gone, right enough. And I doubt it'll ever come back.'

He was silent for a few moments, lost in a private reverie. Then he pulled himself to his feet and prepared to leave.

'Well now, the crack.' He turned his blue gaze on us once more. 'You'd be wanting to know if it's safe? Ach, just plaster it up and forget all about it. No one will be any the wiser.'

If the top house (now named Nefarnin, after its place name on an eighteenth-century map) had presented problems, the lower house doubled them. Jock had been right. It was in infinitely worse condition. It had been pirated to provide building material for Nefarnin, so that nothing now remained but bare stone walls. The roof had leaked for many years, making a hole through the floors. All windows were broken, and the treads on the steep staircase so narrow that a balancing feat of some skill was needed to climb them. On the other hand, the experience we had already acquired helped greatly in planning our design and forestalling some problems.

The house was 200 feet below the road. Its only access was a sheep track, which wound to it from Nefarnin, or a sharp drop direct from the road down the perpendicular, bracken-covered hillside. A way must be made for the transport of heavy building materials. Jock and Calum cast around to see who could help.

In Oskaig lived a determined young man called Angus Gillies. He owned a tractor, the only one on the island. Jock approached him and asked if he would be prepared to drive his tractor down the hillside to the house, taking whichever route he thought best.

'It'll be easy after the first time,' said the persuasive Calum. 'You've only got to open up the trail.'

Angus agreed.

The next day his tractor rumbled up the road above our house. It was painted black and snorted impressively. Angus and his vehicle made a dashing combination.

'Maybe we'd better try without a load the first time,' said Angus doubtfully, eyeing the steep slopes below him.

'Never! What a waste!' Calum replied. 'Come on now, you'll be all right.'

The tractor ground into four-wheel gear and set off down the hillside. Lurching and bumping, it ploughed its way through the bracken, then came to a patch of mud. The wheels skidded, it began to slide, and suddenly it was out of control thundering down at 30 m.p.h. Calum and Jock scattered, taking shelter in front of the house. Angus kept his nerve, grasped the wheel with all his strength, wrenched it round, and managed to turn the vehicle to the right. It lurched wildly, then careered along the grass before the house, and finally came to a stop a few feet short of a bog. Silence descended on the hillside. Angus got out, moving gingerly.

'Well, we're down,' he said. 'But it's the last time I come that way.'

The three men then explored the terrain to find an alternative route. After a while they discovered a half-buried old stone track, which led across the bracken slopes, over a burn and thence at a gentle angle to the road above.

'This must be the old road,' said Jock. 'We can cut back the bracken and lay some stones over the burn, and it'll do fine.'

Angus viewed it with some doubt.

'Well, we'll give it a go,' he said.

At the next trial the slope to the burn was negotiated successfully, but crossing it the tractor bogged down in deep mud and the engine refused to start again. There was no crank.

Efforts to borrow one failed. The island cranks were all too small for Angus's tractor. Eventually Angus took out the petrol injectors, and he, Jock and Calum cranked the vehicle by hand out of the bog. They then replaced the injectors, Angus put the tractor into high gear, and Calum and Jock pushed with all their might. The engine caught on just before the vehicle reached a shed. Not daring to stop, Angus plunged through it.

'And what do I do now?' he called. Half the tractor was in the shed, the other half and the trailer outside. The three dismantled the shed.

By now the hillside was taking on the appearance of a battlefield.

'Third time lucky,' said the optimistic Calum.

A few days later the tractor chugged once more along the top road and turned towards the track. Angus, riding it like a cowboy, put it into four-wheel gear and set off down the slope. Swaying, jerking, crashing through bracken and heather, Angus and the tractor thundered on, somehow miraculously holding to the invisible track. They splashed across the burn and entered the final stretch. On the buried stone road at last and within sight of the house, Angus gave the tractor its head. It leapt forward, and roared along, sounding like an aeroplane. But Angus had reckoned without a sudden sharp corner, encountered just before journey's end. Unable to take this, man and machine bounded off the track and went plummeting down the hillside, missing trees by inches and scattering birds, sheep and rabbits in their wild descent. Jock and Calum watched transfixed, expecting both Angus and his tractor to end up in the sea. On they charged, until suddenly a pile of stones loomed up before Angus. He wrenched round the wheel, the tractor hit the stones side-on, their bulk stopped it short, and the vehicle came to a halt.

Angus emerged undismayed.

'Well, that's it,' he called back to Jock and Calum. 'I reckon that track will be OK if we take it slowly. Next time we can bring down a full load.'

From then on Angus delivered all the building materials to the house. His enterprise had made the whole operation possible, for if he had not managed to open up the track, work could not have proceeded.

A year or so later he left the island. He now works for a Glasgow insurance firm. His talents are employed on a safer activity than plummeting down a hillside at Fearns, but I doubt if his daring has as much scope.

It was eighteen months before the house was finally completed. Benefiting from our experience at Nefarnin, we decided to put in a damp-course, cut back the steep bank behind the house by two feet or so, and dig a drain-trench above it across the hillside, which would collect the water that cascaded down on stormy days. With a completely new roof and pine walls throughout, these precautions should keep us snug and dry.

We had installed Calor gas at Nefarnin to light the rooms, but decided to rely on lamps and candles in the new house – 'Very suitable for your medieval outlook,' as Diarmaid remarked – and to use Calor gas only for the refrigerator and the small two-ring cooker.

The entire first floor had to be replaced, and all cross-beams and window-lintels renewed. At one point the house looked like a church, with only the stone walls and the new roof rafters standing intact. Jock and Calum, poised on a transverse beam, argued amicably about their next step, while I wandered around below, trying to site the positions for the larder and the kitchen sink.

We had decided to make the whole ground floor into one large room. This necessitated a ladder-like staircase which rose against the back wall to the second storey. I took careful measurements of a staircase in London which I thought we could copy and handed them to Jock, who in turn sent them to the builders in Skye, asking them to construct the staircase complete and ship it to the island.

The day came when it arrived at the pier. Jock and Calum met it and, amid the assembled company's interested gaze, loaded it on to the tractor.

'I see the Powers have got their staircase at last,' said the harbour-master. 'Be careful with it, now, down the hill.'

The staircase arrived at the house intact, and triumphantly Jock and Calum proceeded to erect it. It would add the final touch to the downstairs room, newly floored and lined by now with glowing Oregon pine walls. They set the staircase in place, then stood back to survey it. The dreadful truth broke upon Jock.

'Calum, it's *warped,*' he said. 'Look! It's curving away right out of its proper line. It looks terrible.'

Efforts to straighten it proved of no avail. There was nothing to be done but heave it up the hill again and send it back to Skye.

Heads shook, and indrawn breaths of commiseration sounded on every side from the watchers at the pier. 'Indeed, it's too bad,' they said, a certain measure of *schadenfreude* mixed with their sympathy. Indeed it was. Another three months passed before a new staircase was constructed and could be installed.

In the early summer of 1968, I paid a visit to the house to place the furniture which had recently arrived from London, and to see what else was needed. It was now perfect June weather, the trees newly green, and each ewe followed by her accompanying lamb. Staying alone at Nefarnin I made no chatter to disturb the birds and beasts around me, and when Jock and Calum left the lower house at about 5 pm I had the hillside entirely to myself. The long Highland evening with its gradual twilight stretched ahead of me. By 11.30 pm it would be dark, but even then seldom completely so. Leaning out of my bedroom window at midnight I could still see the outline of trees and the shimmer of water. The last of the light lingered in the sky, soon to be suffused by the rising of the sun.

The silence was so intense that it lay like a cloak on the landscape, sounds of waves, birds and sheep serving only to deepen it. It was the silence of nature, undisturbed by any man-made noise. At first it was tempting to break it with music from a gramophone or radio. Later, when my ears became attuned, I found myself listening intently and hearing sounds which at first had eluded me, and which only an undisturbed peace could disclose.

One evening, as I stood just outside the door in the fading light, I became aware of a curious vibrant hum – *whish*, through the still air; silence; then *whish* again. The noise seemed to follow a semi-circular pattern, and was repeated at very short intervals. I strained my eyes to see what could be causing it, but could observe nothing. Attentive in every sense, I peered into the twilight. Then I realized what it was; the 'drumming' of a snipe performing its ritual mating display. Its incredibly fast wing-beat produced the whistling hum as it hurled itself down a shaft of air, sped upwards, and then plummeted down again.

Most evenings I strolled along the path to Rubha na Leac, binoculars slung round my neck, my only concern to observe what lay about me. All other anxieties had receded into a dim past. At that hour the sea was usually still, the gulls homing with a last chuckle, and the sheep browsing peacefully towards their night's resting place. I reached the first clump of trees, where the hill drops sharply to a small bay, just visible between the branches of birch and rowan. Then I heard a strange noise. It sounded like the sucking withdrawal of a strong wave on a pebble beach, but at shorter intervals than a wave could break and withdraw. It was coming from the sea, but the sea was calm with no waves. What could it be?

I searched the wide stretch of water with my binoculars. Nothing there. Then I brought them in to the little bay just below where I stood. And I saw what was making the noise. A huge dark triangular fin, a yard high and as long at its base, was sticking up out of the water. Twenty feet behind it a notched tail-fluke swung slowly from side to side, its pressure against the water making the sound I had heard. Between the two stretched a giant brown form, culminating in a snout-like upper jaw above a wide-open mouth. This I could see only indistinctly, but I felt sure it contained a number of ferocious teeth. The beast circled slowly and purposefully through the clear water of the small bay, round and round, and its size and deliberate motion conveyed an air of infinite menace.

Even at my safe distance of 400 feet or so above the bay, I felt a shudder run down my spine.

I watched enthralled, until the light failed, and I could no longer see. Then I hurried home, lit the lamp, ransacked the bookshelf, and found a book of Iain's, called *Stranded Whales and Turtles*. I identified what I had seen as a killer whale. 'Back fin situated midway in body length,' I read. 'In adult males very high (up to six feet), triangular, acutely pointed. Teeth : ten to thirteen on each side of upper and lower jaws. Diameter in adult one to two inches . . . As its name implies the killer whale is distinguished by its great ferocity, being the only cetacean which habitually preys on other warm-blooded animals.'

When Jock and Calum arrived next morning, I burst out my news – 'I've seen a killer whale.'

'Never!' said Calum. 'Where did you see it?'

I related my story. An amused twinkle came into Calum's eyes and he shook his head.

'Yon wasn't a killer whale at all,' he said. 'It'll be a basking shark you saw. It's the same size right enough, but quite harmless. We call them muldoan or sailfish – *cearbhan* is the Gaelic name. They're immensely powerful but they'd never attack you.'

He explained that killer whales, on the contrary, are very ferocious, hunting in packs of nine to twelve, usually with one old bull in attendance. 'They're terrible. Sometimes you'd see as many as forty at a time. The wolf of the ocean they're called. Nothing is safe from them, not even great whales.'

The big bulls can be up to thirty feet in length, with a dorsal fin nine feet high. They are reputed, in Arctic regions, to use these great fins to smash ice-floes on which young seals have taken refuge. Thirteen porpoises and fourteen seals were found in the stomach of one twenty-foot killer whale.

'Well, I wouldn't go near a pack in a small boat,' was Calum's verdict.

Basking sharks, in contrast, come close inshore. In warm weather and still water they cruise along at a speed of two knots, filtering, in the course of an hour, over 2000 tons of sea-water through their wide open mouths. This contains the plankton on which they exist. The weight of a thirty-foot shark is about seven tons, and all this bulk is manipulated by a minute brain.

I saw basking sharks eight times that summer, finally rowing so close to one in a small dinghy with Calum that I could have touched its brown, snake-like skin. The monster, longer than the boat, lay just below the clear water, motionless but for its faintly expanding and contracting gills. Calum, his hunter's instincts aroused, fingered his knife. I knew that one slap of that seven-foot-wide tail, weighing approximately half a ton, could demolish us. But a knife plunged to the hilt in such a side would count less than a fly brushed off a man's nose.

Both killer whales and basking sharks have been hunted in Hebridean waters at various times for their oil, blubber and skins. From 1946 to 1949 Gavin Maxwell based an ill-fated basking shark factory on the Isle of Soay, south of Skye, and chased his prey throughout the surrounding waters, writing about it in his book *Harpoon At A Venture*. But transport costs from such a remote site, coupled with Norwegian competition, doomed the exploit to failure. Nevertheless he discovered many hitherto unknown and interesting facts about the species.

Islesmen used to harpoon basking sharks from massed formations of small boats, and an early nineteenth-century Daniell print in my possession shows this happening in the harbour of Isle Ornsay in Skye. More than two dozen fins are protruding from the sheltered rippling water, but only three small boats are involved. However, the determined attitudes of the harpooners standing in their bows promise a good supply of oil for the next winter's lamps.

I needed some kitchen articles and a few more pieces of furniture for the new house, so Calum suggested running me across in his small dinghy with its outboard motor to the nearest landing-point in Skye. From there I could make my way to Portree. We set off about mid-morning on a clear fine

Roddy MacLeod clipping a sheep

Mara and Prunella watch Calum Bàn tying a fleece

Calum Macrae

Jock Rutherford

day. The sun sparkled on the sea, sprinkling it with dazzling points of light, while I lounged in the stern of Calum's small boat idly watching a couple of dolphins who were playing round a fishing boat nearby. They leaped sheer out of the water, almost to the height of the ship's bows, then fell back again with a twist and a splash, to turn and twirl through her wake.

'They're wonderfully tame,' said Calum. 'I've watched these two following that ship for several mornings past.'

'Is it true that there was a dolphin who used to meet the steamer each time it came in at Kyle, and followed it up the Sound past the lighthouse?' I asked.

'It is indeed. The Captain told me so himself. Seemingly, he'd look out for it every day, and throw it food, and he'd be really put out if it didn't turn up.'

Calum was an ardent fisherman and spent every moment he could on the sea.

'Did I tell you about the dolphin I caught myself the other day?' he continued. 'There was a net out in the sea a week or so ago near Fearns. What should I hear all of a sudden, but a great splash. So I looked down, and there was a dolphin struggling in the net. I rowed out to it, and heaved dolphin and net and all into the boat. Poor thing, it was almost strangled. You'd think it would be wild with fear. But it lay there as quiet as a mouse, just looking at me, while I undid all the knots it had tied round itself. Never a cheep out of it. It seemed to know I was helping it. And the moment it was free – whist, away over the side it went, back into the sea. It's wonderful sense they've got.'

Calum leant his sunburned face towards me, and opened his blue eyes wide.

'Now I'll tell you something else,' he said. 'The dolphins did *me* a good turn one time. Indeed they did. It was when I lost my outboard engine in the Sound. A wild rough day it was. I was lifting the engine off the boat when she gave a lurch, I lost my balance, and out of my hands the engine flew. Right down to the bottom of the sea. Well! What a thing! "That's gone for good," I thought. I put out three buoys on a long rope to mark the place, and rowed ashore. As luck would have it, it was stormy for over a week afterwards. No chance of going out in my small boat. And Alastair, with his ferry, was getting annoyed because my buoys were on his line of travel and might be fouling up his propeller.'

Calum shook his head ruefully, lips pursed, eyes downcast.

'What a plight! A boat I had, but no engine. Well, at last, I borrowed another man's boat, and went out to collect the buoys. It was still rough and stormy. "Will we ever have a chance of finding the engine, do you think?" I asked him. "Not a chance. Not a chance in a million. Never a chance, not at all," he replied. We got the buoys into the boat, and we started pulling in the long rope attached to them. "It's mighty heavy," I thought. "Must be clogged up with seaweed." We pulled and pulled and it got heavier and heavier, and we went on pulling and at last what should we pull on board but my engine!'

'I don't believe it!'

'It's true. I swear it's as true as I'm sitting here. I dried the engine out for a week or so and then I took it to sea again and it was as good as new. Now – ' Calum fixed me with an impressive glance, from which he had banished all merriment. 'What was it, do you think, that tied the engine on to the end of the rope at the bottom of the sea?' He paused. 'You don't know? What but the dolphins?'

He reflected for a moment, then grinned. 'Unless it was the mermaids.'

The house was completed soon after my June visit, and one evening in late July, Brian and I stood at the doorway, looking inside. The large ground-floor room was empty (we had been cleaning and sealing the wooden floor for the past week) and the bare walls glowed in the light of the setting sun. The stone hearth, with its massive lintel, was swept and clean, ready for its first fire, while at the other end of the room stood the Rayburn stove, practical and workmanlike, flanked by wooden kitchen cupboards and kitchen sink. The staircase, now remade, sloped gracefully upwards to the next storey, the new windows shone. All was ready for occupation, we were the owners, and tomorrow we would move in.

It was a moment for rejoicing. Why, then, did I feel an indefinable reluctance to disturb the house's solitude, a hesitation as momentary as a gleam of fading light? The air seemed full of ghosts, the silence palpable.

The house grew more remote and mysterious with each slowly passing moment. In the past, I reflected, it had been the abode of people whose lives were hard and poor. It had provided for them a family centre, a refuge from rain, wind and storm, later a magnet for nostalgic memories. What would it give us? Perhaps no more than the opportunity to stand like this in silence, to feel, to be aware. That would be enough. Here, I thought, between these walls; here, among the grass and bracken, the bird and sea sounds, the rain, sun and wind; here, if anywhere on this earth, we will find peace.

9

Life on Raasay

Time does strange things on Raasay. It elongates – a week seems like a month – and yet it flies past so swiftly that the years merge imperceptibly, and suddenly one realizes one has known the island for over a decade.

At first, we explored it minutely. With the aid of an Ordnance Survey map, we discovered traces of ancient inhabitants: a burial cairn at Eyre Point, a dun or broch above Raasay House. We pinpointed the cairn and walked along the beach to Eyre lighthouse to find it.

The stones have disappeared but the grave which they covered lies on a green slope above the shore, looking from afar like any one of the boulders scattered there. A large rectangular stone slab about four feet long and two feet wide is supported at each corner by four upright stones. Two have sunk, so that the slab leans at an angle. Algae has grown on its surface and it is pitted with weather-marks. Below, scooped out of the earth, is a dusty hole large enough to contain a body curled up in the foetal position. Rabbit dung scatters the earth floor. Any other remains disappeared millennia ago. Who had been buried there? A powerful Bronze Age chief, laid to rest with his hunting spear, his drinking vessel, his knife? Whoever it was, their eyes would have seen the same view, their ears heard the same sounds.

The broch – marked Dun Borodale on the map – we found by climbing through the forestry plantation at Inverarish.

It stands on a rocky knoll in a clearing of the forest. The site is strewn with large boulders through which ragwort and willow-herb grow, but the circular shape of the broch is still discernible, and in some places five feet or so of dry-stone wall still exist. At the turn of the century the walls were over seventeen feet high. Later they were dismantled to build an extension to the schoolhouse at Clachan.

Like all Hebridean brochs, this one is built on an excellent vantage point three hundred feet above the sea, looking across the Narrows of Raasay and up the Sound. When invaders threatened, the island's women, children and cattle would have crowded here for refuge in the space enclosed by strong walls, while a beacon fire signalling danger would have been lit on the hill above: a warning to other brochs similarly placed along the coastline. Probably Pictish in origin, it may have stood for eight or nine centuries of vigilance, overcome at last by fierce Viking invaders, its ultimate foe.

Another fortress stands in the north of the island – Brochel Castle built by the MacLeods in the late fifteenth century. Rising from a precipitous rock of volcanic origin about a hundred feet above the sea, it is now a romantic ruin, the masonry hardly distinguishable from the conglomerate rock on which it stands. Originally a three-storied tower it was described by a sixteenth-century writer as 'ane strange littel castle . . . bigget on the heid of ane heich crag . . . callet Prokill'. Impregnable from the sea, its only entrance faced the landward side and was approached, as it is now, by a steep slope of slippery grass and scree. It was abandoned in 1610, but in its day it served as a strong fortress for the MacLeods and was envied and admired throughout the Western Isles. Below the castle curves a wide and beautiful bay, and beyond lies the sea, spreading in a stretch of blue to the hazy mainland shore.

The tarmac road stops at the castle, but seven or eight miles of land continue to the northernmost tip of the island; rough heathery moor pitted with slabs of grey rock sweeping up into craggy hills; wild broken country now used only for sheep.

Until very recently, the one path through this area was a grassy track which served a number of crofters and their families, and the two little townships of the north end, Arnish, and Torran which contained a church and a school. Still farther north lies Fladday, the tidal island off Raasay's north-western shore, which used to be inhabited by four crofting families, self-supporting with their own livestock and their own school.

In the first two or three decades of this century the resident population of this north end of the island numbered over ninety people. Now it is reduced to two. One by one the families have left, and though, in some cases, their sheep still graze the land, their houses are abandoned. An important reason for this decline lies in the lack of an access road to connect the area to the main road, ending at Brochel. For over fifty years a succession of appeals for such a road to the Inverness County Council have met with no response. Finally, one of the crofters decided to take matters into his own hands.

Calum MacLeod lives at Arnish, about three miles north of Brochel. He set himself the task of extending the road from the castle to his home. A beginning had been made in 1965 when a stony track had been laid for half a mile or so. Calum MacLeod decided to complete it, following plans for a road which the Army had made. Single-handed, he rolled boulders down the hillside to build up the borders of the track and widen it. To avoid a steep drop into the valley, he cut a swathe across the side of a hill and round a corner so that his road could rejoin the path in the glen below. He built viaducts, lay-bys, and culverts and his road traversed steep gradients and peat bogs. He broke stones, hacked away at turf and heather, carted loads of earth, and rolled the surfaces smooth. The Department of Agriculture helped with rock blasting and fellow crofters gave their aid from time to time (notably John Park, who owns a croft opposite Calum's and lives there part of the year), but the majority of the work Calum achieved alone, and his was the driving spirit and determination which carried the project forward against odds which would have defeated most men.

The creation of Calum MacLeod's road became a legend. Each time we walked up to the north end we observed its progress with astonishment. Finally, as the *West Highland Free Press* reported, after about eight years' labour 'the two-and-a-quarter miles of road which one man had built with a pick, wheelbarrow and his bare hands' was finished. But now that it is completed, whom will it serve? A resident population of two people – the indomitable Calum and his wife.

Calum is elderly now, with ruddy cheeks, white hair, clear eyes and slow reflective speech. Until recently, he still served his turn as lighthouseman in Rona, one week in each month. We have talked to him many times as we walked along his road, and his hospitable wife has given us tea in their house at Arnish, tucked into a hollow below the hill and flanked by fertile fields. His achievement is in the best tradition of Highland independence.

The western seaboard of Raasay is more fertile than the precipitous east coast. Here, we discovered, are the crofting townships of Oskaig, and farther inland, Balachuirn and Balmeanach. Other crofters have houses on the hill above the new pier and at Eyre Point.

The island's oldest hamlet is Clachan, the small number of dwellings around Raasay House. Martin Martin, in his *History of the Western Isles*, published in 1695, recalls that 'the proprietor of the isle is a Mr MacLeod, a cadet of the family of that name: his seat is in the village of Clachan. The inhabitants have a great veneration for him as any subjects can have for their king. They preserve the memory of the deceased ladies of the place by erecting a little pyramid of stone for each of them with the lady's name. These pyramids are called crosses . . . There are eight such crosses about the village, which is adorned with a little tower, and lesser houses, and an orchard with several sorts of berries, pot herbs, etc.' But Dr Johnson, on his visit to Raasay in 1773, heard a different tale: that the stone crosses marked the church's sanctuary or consecrated ground.

For the oldest church in the island is also at Clachan. It is dedicated to St Moluag, the early Irish saint who founded a monastery on Lismore, off Mull, between 561 and 564. This foundation became a bishopric with Moluag as its first Bishop.

Tradition says that St Moluag visited Raasay, and though this cannot be proved, it may well account for the ancient incised cross on the rock above the old landing place below Raasay House.

The church at Clachan and its 'vicarage of Kilmolowok (Kilmoluag) in Raasay' formed part of the parish of Snizort and Kilmuir in Skye, and in 1501 Nichol Berchame was appointed vicar by the Scots King James IV. His successor, Donald Munro, received the vacant see in 1526, and thereafter the island and its church came under the jurisdiction of the Bishop of the Isles. But the turbulent MacLeod chiefs were constantly remiss in their payments of dues to the See of Iona, and actions were brought against them by the Bishop in 1532 and again in 1580.

Boswell and Johnson visited the church at Clachan in 1773, and though it was then roofless, Johnson said, 'I look with reverence on every place that has been set apart for religion.' Boswell noticed the head carved on one of the chapel walls, which he took to be 'a small bust or image of the Virgin Mary'.

Today the church is in ruins. Mounds of half-buried stones are heaped against its walls and in the churchyard headstones lean amongst rank grass. One of them bears a poignant inscription:

In Memory of
MURDOCH MACLEOD
Aged 26 years
And his Brother
RODERICH, Aged 24
Drowned off Rona
13th December 1880

MacLeods, Gillies, and Nicholsons lie beside one another in their last sleep. And on one of the most recent graves, dated 1973, a Gaelic inscription shows the old tongue's survival on the island, '*Cha léid sibh air di-chuimhne*' – you will not be forgotten – it says.

From the churchyard a road bends round the high stone

wall of Raasay House gardens and then runs northwards. The Raasay House woods border its western flank, giving glimpses of sea and rocky shore between foliage of chestnut, oak and lime. On the other side of the road a fir plantation ends in a fuchsia hedge which in summer spills blood-red blossom on to the tarmac. And there, tucked away between the fuchsia and the firs, stands an ancient symbol stone, bearing Pictish symbols of the V-rod and crescent, and the tuning-fork, as well as an incised Christian cross. It is thought to date from the late seventh century. The style of the cross is unique; it is so deeply incised that the spaces between its arms are thrown up in relief like the four petals of a flower. The combination of Pictish and Christian symbols on one stone indicates the existence of a church founded by an Irish saint among a Pictish population.

Old and worn, the stone leans at an angle above the grass, half-sinking into the ground. But it still bears witness to the message which St Moluag and St Columba brought to the Isles; a new concept of peace and compassion preserved since that day and lingering yet in the pure Hebridean air.

About a mile from Clachan is Inverarish, the island's main village. It possesses a post office, a district nurse, a shop and two telephone kiosks. If you walk down the hill of the only road, you will find these things in that order. There are also two rows of houses – built in 1913 for Baird & Co.'s tin miners; a scattering of cottages along the burn, and a war memorial.

Most of Raasay's population of about one hundred and fifty residents live in Inverarish. The community is a close-knit one, yet each family values its privacy. Each keeps its own distance from the rest. The two churches, the school and the shop provide a certain focus, but since Raasay House has stood empty there is a sad lack of any real social life.

The population of the island is largely elderly. One hundred are pensionable, and only half a dozen are children under school age. With young people leaving and not being replaced, the community is reaching the critical stage where it may no longer be viable.

No one is more conscious of this sober fact than Alastair Nicholson, who for ten years represented Raasay's interests on the District Council of Portree East in Skye. Alastair was born and brought up in Raasay and after a spell as a forestry officer in Kenya returned to live and work on the island, operating his own ferry service to Skye seven months of the year and running, with his wife, the only guest house on Raasay. Alastair constantly pressed the Skye District Council, the Inverness County Council, the Highlands and Islands Development Board and the Department of Agriculture to take some action on the island's problems. The chief of these was the lack of an adequate ferry service.

Early in 1973 the Inverness County Council at last took steps to secure the small area of land at Churchton Bay near Raasay House needed for a ferry terminal. But Dr Green's objection to the compulsory purchase of the land forced a public enquiry. Its outcome was a confirmation in November 1974, by the Secretary of State for Scotland, of the Inverness County Council's action. 'The best news for ten years,' said Alastair Nicholson, when he heard this verdict. He hoped that the building of the ferry terminal would now get under way. But he and his fellow islanders were to be disappointed, for there was no swift implementation of the compulsory purchase. The owner of Raasay House immediately exercised his option of appeal to the Court of Session, and this procedure held up the starting of work on the ferry terminal for another indefinite period.

Russell Johnson, the Liberal Member of Parliament for Inverness-shire, was also concerned about the island's plight. In a debate on Raasay which he instigated in Parliament in December 1973, he said: 'Nothing in nine years' experience of representing the constituency of Inverness remotely compares with the bitter frustration I have had in trying to get something done in the Island of Raasay; and what I feel can only be a pale shadow of what the islanders themselves feel.' On this occasion he also referred to Dr Green's 'actions, which have been evasive, delaying or downright obstructive of anything proposed for the island's benefit'. He stated that he could not understand the inexplicable inactivity of the Highlands and Islands Development Board, and recommended that the Board should use its compulsory powers forthwith to aid the island.

In September 1974 a BBC programme on Radio 4 exposed the problems of life on Raasay. Called 'Raasay: A Forgotten Community', it gave an opportunity for the people of the island to state their views. They stressed the isolation experienced because of lack of daily contact with the mainland or Skye, felt especially keenly in winter when Alastair Nicholson's launch service to Skye could not operate. Anyone then needing medical attention had to travel by steamer to Portree or Kyle and spend a night there. Crofters had no adequate means of getting their stock to market, and the lack of a cheap and efficient daily ferry stopped new settlers or tourists from coming to the island. 'Whatever it was before, the history of Raasay since the '45 has been a very tragic history,' commented Sorley MacLean, the distinguished Gaelic poet, born in Raasay, who opened the BBC programme.

Another source of anxiety was the Naval activity in the Sound of Raasay, where a torpedo testing range had been set up. This had already led to a restricted use of these waters for fishing, and Raasay inhabitants feared that restrictions would increase.

'What's the latest news on the Navy?' we asked one of the islanders, as Alastair Nicholson ferried us across to Raasay.

'Och, they're spending a mint of money on their war games,' he replied. 'Their torpedoes cost more than twenty thousand pounds each. And not content with that they can't even find them when they've fired them off. The other day they lost two.'

'And then?'

'Well, they searched up and down the Sound. They even brought up a midget submarine to help. Eventually they found one torpedo. But the other was still missing. So they went on searching. A few days later, two boats were fishing off the coast, well within the fishing limit. Along comes the Navy and tells them to clear off. "Clear off? And why?" says the skipper of one. "The midget submarine is beneath you," was the answer he got. Well, that skipper told the Navy what they could do with their midget submarine and where they could take it. "I'm well within the fishing limit," he said, "and I'll not move." He stayed where he was, and in the end it was the midget submarine that had to clear off.'

However, in spite of fishing restrictions, the Naval activity in the Inner Sound of Raasay has meant the reprieve of the Highland Railway Line from Inverness to Kyle, a line threatened with closure before the Navy came. And for tourists or visitors travelling to Skye or Raasay this line is of great importance.

No account of Raasay would be complete without mention of the Church. Raasay is the home of a dissenting section of the Free Church, which itself broke away from the main Presbyterian Church of Scotland in 1843. The issue of the disruption was the determination of congregations to have a say in the selection of their own ministers, and to resist ministers being presented to livings by the landowners. But disillusionment with the established Church had already gone deeper than this one issue. It was embodied in the spiritual despair which followed the failure of the Jacobite rising, and its aftermath of suppression, eviction and emigration.

During this traumatic period for the people of the Highlands and Islands, the clergy for the most part sided with the landlords and tacksmen. With a few exceptions (one of whom was a Raasay minister, the Reverend MacDougall, who resigned his charge in 1855 in protest against George Rainy's ruthless evictions), they did little to relieve injustice beyond exhorting their congregations to accept and bear it. Consequently, when the Disruption came in 1843 and four hundred and seventy-four rebellious ministers seceded from the established Church, many of the people gave them fervent support. At last a focus for religious feeling had come into being, and ministers were once more in touch with their congregations.

Unfortunately, as the power of the ministers increased, so did their denunciatory zeal. It took a negative form. All pleasure was suspect, and in pleasure was included each of the former delights of the Gael – story-telling, dancing, piping, poetry and song.

In Skye, an evangelical preacher in 1805 caused bagpipes and fiddles to be burnt on a great bonfire at Loch Snizort. In Raasay, music and dance were banned. The fervour spread to all the Protestant islands. Only the Catholic ones escaped. South Uist became the centre of piping instead of Skye, and, with Barra and Eigg, continued to preserve the sources of folk songs and sagas.

In Raasay, the puritanism of the dissenting 'Wee Frees' – (wee, because they claimed to be more humble, more pure, and 'poorer in spirit' than any others) took an even more extreme form. A yet more uncompromising sect arose on the island and seceded from the seceders.

In 1893, the minister in Raasay, Mr MacFarlane, gave notice of his withdrawal from the 'Wee Frees'. He was swiftly followed by the minister at Shieldaig, on the mainland near Applecross. The dissenting ministers and others formed a new sect, and its doctrines (one of which was the rejection of Darwin's theory of evolution) spread to the mainland and other islands.

The original 'Wee Free' Church still survives on Raasay, situated near Inverarish on the forestry road leading to the Youth Hostel. Services are held there whenever a 'missionary' from Skye is available. A few families support it, but the majority of the islanders attend the church of the breakaway sect, originally unique to Raasay, still called the Free Presbyterian Church. It stands in a prominent position on a hill above the village, its manse beside it. This church has a resident minister and holds two services every Sunday, one in the morning in English, the other in the afternoon in Gaelic. Each service lasts for one and three-quarter hours, and further devotions are held during the week, on Wednesday evenings. Their religion means much to the islanders and attendances at the church are regularly maintained.

We soon learned that the Sabbath is sacrosanct in Raasay. Any form of work or sport is forbidden. People do not emerge from their houses, except to go to church. Any backsliding during the week is severely reprimanded from the pulpit.

In 1960 a group of islanders and their friends gathered one Saturday evening in front of Raasay House for an impromptu ceilidh. Singing, dancing and piping got under way. But the minister happened to be crossing over to the island from Skye. Next morning he gave his opinion of the celebration: 'Last evening as I crossed the waters of the Narrows I thought the gates of hell had opened on Raasay.'

Inside the church every Sunday morning, one hundred and thirty or so of the islanders assemble, the majority elderly, the men all dressed in suits, the women all wearing hats. The children are attired in their Sabbath best and are very well behaved, except for the surreptitious eating of sweets, an activity which the adults share.

The minister dressed in black, sits at a high dais, like a judge. He delivers his prayers extemporarily, repeating key phrases. The congregation is not expected to respond, only to listen.

Three psalms are intoned during the service, an elder giving the first note and the congregation then joining in. The psalms are paraphrased in rhymed verse and produced with a curious wail. No lessons are read, and no liturgy follows. The minister, with his extempore prayers, carries the full load of the service.

The sermon, undoubtedly the climax, is delivered with zeal, the minister thumping the pulpit to emphasize his points. First, there is a long theological discourse. Then the congregation are reminded that they are born in guilt and sin, and that they must consider their eternal souls. Evolution, they are told, is an idea from the bottomless pit – 'What a doctrine to teach a child! Very few can understand spiritual things,' the minister continues. 'Their minds are occupied with filthy things of this world, like many of this generation. But blessed are they which hunger and thirst after righteousness. Without this blessing, a sinner is vain and empty, cursed for all eternity. And only the elect can be blessed.'

The congregation listen intently. Only the rustling of sweet-papers relieves the concentrated gloom.

'Everyone who lived here formerly is now in heaven or hell,' concludes the minister. 'A short while and the worms will eat your body. You will turn up in another world as sure as you are sitting in this church.'

The hour-long sermon comes to an end with a prayer for

the Royal Family, 'that the fear of God may be put into their hearts', and then the congregation files out. The minister has gone next door for lunch. There is no mixing with the people as they emerge.

How seriously his exhortations are taken is difficult to determine. Those outside the church accuse those within it of hypocrisy. Some indulge in theological disputes in the columns of the *West Highland Free Press.* (Closing one such correspondence, the Editor remarked, 'Few communities the size of Raasay can contain so many articulate letter-writers.') But the attitude of the majority is probably best summed up by the islander who spoke in the BBC programme, 'Raasay: A Forgotten Community'.

'There are a lot of do's and don't's on Raasay,' she said. 'Sunday observance for example. No one would dream of doing anything on a Sunday apart from going to church, staying at home, or perhaps looking after the animals. There's nothing recreational on a Sunday.' Nor are there any youth fellowships. Young people returning to the island must conform to the Church's strict doctrine. But the Raasay community is not an uncaring one. The old and ill are looked after, burdens are shared, and so are sorrows and loss through death, now all too frequent in the winter months.

Certainly the virtues of fidelity, probity and loyalty which the Free Church encourages have been an integral part of the Highland character. But now a positive outlook embodied in the gentler aspects of hope and compassion seems essential if the islanders are to move into the modern world. Without it, the disillusions and licence experienced when controls are inevitably relaxed, become harmful and self-destructive.

Opposite the Free Presbyterian Church is the school, built on a site many town children would envy, standing in the shelter of the hillside beside the sea. The day I visited the school fifteen neatly dressed children sat at desks graded according to size, their eyes resting dutifully on their teacher Mrs Rutherford (Jock's wife) and occasionally straying towards me, the visitor who knew them all by sight. Primary I, the five-year-olds, fidgeted in the front row, while Primary VII sat at the back – three pretty girls who would soon leave Raasay to go to Portree where they could reach A-level or University entrance standard if they wished.

Mrs Rutherford was discussing with her charges her recent trip to the mainland.

'So I crossed the ferry at Kyle,' she said, 'and then drove twenty miles to Kishorn. Now what would I have seen there?'

'A huge big hole, miss.'

'And what would that be for?'

'The oil platform, miss.'

'Would any of you know how high the platform will be when it's completed?'

Several boys' hands shot into the air.

'Yes, Hamish?'

'Six hundred feet, miss.'

'That's very high, isn't it? It'll be the largest platform ever constructed.'

'When will it be finished, miss?'

'Soon, I hope. Well, there's a big labour force working on it now. And why was Kishorn chosen to build it?'

Silence. The idea of the towering platform was more appealing than reasons for its site.

'Something to do with the launching,' prompted Mrs Rutherford.

Hamish's hand shot up again.

'I know, miss. Because Raasay Sound has the deepest water off the coast of Britain.'

'Right. So it will be launched there, and then towed out to the oil-fields in the North Sea.'

Primary I were showing signs of boredom at the turn the conversation was taking.

'Well, now, that's enough for the moment. Would the wee ones like to give us a song?' Mrs Rutherford suggested.

At the back of the classroom was an old upright piano wedged between shelves containing a good selection of well-worn books. The children clustered round the piano, the youngest lifting expectant faces.

North Raasay

Calum MacLeod on the road he built

Prunella and Brian

Mara, Saba and Calum Macrae

'What will it be, then?' asked Mrs Rutherford, preparing to accompany them.

'*Tha mi sgith*, please, miss,' they piped.

The reed-like voices, eager, if a little out of tune, embarked on the old Gaelic song, and continued manfully to the end.

'Good,' said their teacher. 'Now, will the older ones try the fairies' song from "The Immortal Hour"?'

This was a more ambitious piece, taxing both singers and accompanist. They brought it to a close breathlessly, with heightened colour.

'Well done,' I said. 'That's a difficult one. I know, I've tried those arpeggios myself on the clarsach.'

Smiles ran round the group.

'Now, something for all of us,' said Mrs Rutherford. ' "Mairi's Wedding".'

The clear voices rose, boys and girls trilling out the lively tune, and the sound streamed through the windows and echoed over the water to where sun and wisps of cloud touched the hills of Skye.

Later, Mrs Rutherford took me round the school building. Though old-fashioned, it is well equipped, with a second classroom which acts as a canteen, a gym and dining-room; a staffroom; and a kitchen producing a hot dinner for all the children each day. Thirty years ago the school had sixty pupils and three teachers. The island's children received their whole education there, leaving at the age of fourteen. Some of Raasay's older inhabitants feel that they were better served by this system.

'The slow ones certainly got more attention,' they say.

'In the big secondary schools there's no time for them. Classes are too crowded, only the brightest get on.'

Calum MacLeod of Arnish (builder of the famous road) felt strongly enough on the subject to write about it in the *West Highland Free Press*. He castigated 'the tyrannous system of centralized education pursued by the Scottish Education Department during the last two decades. In practice, this form of education compels every pupil on attaining 11½ years of age to leave home and be boarded elsewhere for the rest of their education – about 4½ years. The result is that homes in rural areas are systematically emptied. In fact, all rural areas and especially the islands are reduced to a skeleton of ageing population, while villages and towns are crammed by youngsters without parental supervision, growing up urbanized to such an extent that they become practically alien to the home environment or to participating in agriculture or fishing. Industrial or manual work is frowned on, while delinquency, especially immorality, vandalism and drinking has increased to an unprecedented scale.'

But even if this uncompromising view is correct, the educational clock cannot be turned backwards. Parents will opt for the highest qualifications their children can get and these are found in the large secondary schools, although the children's early formative years will still be spent on the island.

In Raasay the scholars, as they are called, are held in high esteem and the school is considered particularly important in the island's life. The intake of new pupils at the start of the academic year in September, is a ceremony for which both parents and children are duly spruced up. The well-groomed youngsters arrive and are delivered to Mrs Rutherford, who has run the school for twenty-one years. She receives her new charges with zest, and proceeds to integrate them into the widely varied age-group – five to twelve – which she handles with the confidence and success born of long experience. Her rule is firm, insisting, among other things, on a clean and tidy appearance (skirts not trousers for the little girls) and a recreational quarter-of-an-hour outside for everyone at midmorning, whatever the weather.

As well as the usual academic subjects, the curriculum includes games, gym, nature outings, Gaelic and singing. Mrs Rutherford deals with every subject. (Jock assists by retrieving 'no balls' from the school's roof gutters when rounders is played in the yard.) She can skip with the six-year-olds, point out the island's plants and trees on nature rambles, supervise carols for Christmas, and insist on the modicum of homework necessary for progress. The boys and girls in her charge are a happy and energetic group. I guess that memories of their

Raasay schooldays will colour their imaginations and be preserved in their dreams for years to come.

We soon realized that Raasay is predominantly a crofting island, and the majority of its inhabitants are crofters and their families – either active or retired. There are twenty-six crofters in all, and for crofting purposes the island is divided into the North end and the South end. The grazing in these areas is held and used by several Crofters' Clubs, each with its own fank for sheep shearing and dipping, and its own hereditary members. Croft ownership is handed down from father to son (or near kin), a practice which makes it difficult for any outsider to croft land on Raasay. Crofters' shares can be sub-let, but only with the general consensus of the club and 'if the face fits'. The quota of sheep and cattle allowed to each member on club grazing ground is limited, but the rule is not always strictly observed.

In South Raasay five crofters graze their sheep on the hill, each holding individual sheep stocks. In addition, there are several more living near Inverarish with small crofts who have shares in the South Raasay Common Grazing, but not the right to keep sheep on the hill. In the North Raasay club there are nine tenants with a common financial owning of sheep, and several of these also have stock on their own crofts. A few of the North Raasay club are absentee crofters domiciled in Skye and elsewhere.

Calum MacLeod at Arnish is the only resident crofter in the extreme north of the island. He remembers the area when it was well populated, and is incensed by what he regards as its neglect. Much good agricultural land has reverted, and absentee crofters, who come over only to gather their sheep for dipping or shearing, or for the autumn sales, are unable to undertake the necessary draining and cultivation. With enlightened outside help much of the former fertile land could be restored. But attitudes would have to change. The old crofting tradition of cattle rearing has been superseded by sheep, so crops are no longer needed to feed cattle. Sheep damage the good land but they bring in a more profitable return and require less attention. In the case of absentee crofters it is cheaper to lose a sheep than to pay a shepherd. Not one young couple, Calum says, has set up home in a croft in Raasay during the last twenty years, and now over eighteen square miles of the island are practically uninhabited.

One of the chief problems facing the Raasay crofters is the transport of their stock to the sheep and cattle sales in Inverness. For many years this was done by steamer. I watched the process, one late August afternoon in the summer of 1974. Four hundred lambs, frightened and shivering, flooded along the wooden pier, the sheep dogs yapping at their heels to keep them moving. They surged towards the steamer's narrow gangway and then pushed up it in spurts, sometimes jamming in a tight jostling pack before they could struggle on to the crowded deck.

Two of our MacLeod shepherds stood near me, also watching, and we started to talk.

'The sheep are very scared getting on to the boat,' said Brisco. 'Sometimes they even have to be beaten on. It's bad for them, you know. They lose so much appearance and weight. Pressed together like this their coats shrink.'

Calum Bàn, his brother, agreed. 'I've known some of them panic and fall over the side,' he said. 'Aye, last year we had to fish one up out of the water.'

At that time about 1,500 sheep and 50 cattle were exported from the island each year, and the steamer was their only means of transport.

'Mind you, what happens here isn't the worst,' Calum continued. 'When they get to Kyle they're herded into floats – huge lorries with three floors – and then driven to Inverness. They arrive late, and they probably aren't put out to grass until tomorrow morning. That's twenty-four hours without food and they're still milk-feeding. They were taken from their mothers this morning for the first time. It's a hard experience for them, right enough.'

'If only we had a car ferry we could load them straight into a lorry this side and they'd be at Inverness hours sooner,' said Brisco. 'It's terrible the way they lose condition on the journey. This year they're selling for four to six pounds a lamb, depending on their condition, but I've known some of them lose pounds or even die on the way.'

'When will they be sold?' I asked.

'In four days' time. After that they'll be fattened up for six weeks or so and then killed. Well, I hope they'll fetch a good price. But island shepherds like us are at a great disadvantage. We *have* to sell. We can't bring the sheep back home again.'

The last stragglers had insinuated themselves into the heaving mass of animals on board. They foamed against the deck-rails, and as the steamer drew away we heard their bleats diminish in a falling scale of anguish. Calum Bàn looked after them thoughtfully.

'Man,' he said, 'he does everything to his own advantage. Upsets nature. Increases the breeding of the beasts, then eats them.' He turned away. 'Of course, they don't know what's coming to them. Sheep have a great instinct right enough, but not as great as that.'

He and Brisco strode off the pier. Their own sheep would be loaded in a few days' time, and they would accompany them to Inverness.

Later that evening a waning moon rose. Under it the ewes bleated for their lost lambs. They bleated all night. Only when the new day dawned were they silent, wandering disconsolately from place to place, bereft of the shadows which had followed them from the day of their birth. A national taste for tender lamb had led to this early severance. Given a few more months the lambs would have gradually grown away from their mothers and left them without pain.

In Raasay, such a violation of nature seemed more harmful than elsewhere. Yet the shepherds have to live, the markets have to be stocked, and the island must respond to demand. Raasay, I reflected, was not an enchanted citadel immune from change. It was a small community battling for its life. To survive, it must take its place as part of a wider structure, and be influenced by the activities and growing-points of the outside world. It could do this, given the chance. But would that chance be forthcoming?

10

Rona

North of Raasay lies her sister island South Rona, six miles in length and three miles broad, separated from Raasay by Kyle Rona, a deep channel of water about half a mile wide.

'To an ordinary observer Rona's aspect is quite repulsive; presenting no picturesque features, and but little verdure to chequer its grey and sterile surface, and hiding most of even its patches of brown mountain-pasture amid a profusion of dull and naked rocks.' So the island was described in the *1844 Gazetteer*. But modern eyes, searching in wild and unspoilt places for a different aspect of beauty, see it in another light.

During the sixteenth century Rona, then thickly wooded, became a refuge for desperate men; pirates and victims of clan feuds who operated from the island's Port nan Robaireann (the Port of Robbers) and harassed shipping in the surrounding seas. At that time Rona belonged to the MacLeods of Raasay whose eldest son took its name as his title. When later, during the Clearances it passed from MacLeod hands, the Raasay crofters who were forced to leave their own good land sailed north to Rona. There they struggled to make a living among the island's rocks, breaking the ground with axes before it could be planted. There were settlements on the west coast at Acarseid Thioram (Dry Harbour), and Acarseid Mhor (Big Harbour); and also at Doire-na-Guaile in the east. The island possessed its own church and two schools, and before the First World War eighteen families lived at Acarseid Thioram alone. These included the schoolteacher and the 'missionary' (as the minister was known), Alexander MacLennan, now buried in Raasay.

After 1918 conditions became increasingly difficult. Land promised by the Board of Agriculture in north Raasay nearby never materialized. The young men and women left. The elderly were no longer able to cultivate the rocky ground. By the late '20s all the families but one at Acarseid Mhor had gone. Most of them settled in Raasay, some occupying the same sites their forefathers had left several generations before.

Today Rona is uninhabited except for a NATO signalling station manned by the Navy in the far north, and a lighthouse on the north-east tip. Sheep still graze the land, tended by crofters from Skye who come over to dip, shear and gather them for the sheep sales. Apart from these, the island has lapsed back to its pristine state. Once more it is the 'rocky isle', the 'isle of seals'.

I had often looked at Rona from Skye, where I had seen its long low outline emerge from the water, desolate and mysterious, insubstantial in the changing light, a vision summoned by marine deities and likely to disappear on closer inspection. I longed to visit it, and this longing was reinforced when we came to live on Raasay. But how to get there? We consulted Alastair Nicholson, hoping to go on his launch.

'I'll take you, sure,' said Alastair. 'But let's wait for a fine day. You want to see the place at its best.'

The launch could hold up to a dozen people. Besides friends staying with us, Brian asked Roddy MacLeod, the big shepherd, who had lived on Rona until he was fourteen years old, and Calum Gillies, a burly seaman who now resided in Inverarish, but who was born and brought up on Fladday.

The *Dignity* awaited us at the old stone pier below Raasay House. Painted white, with a capacious well, lined with wooden benches, a small cabin, and a powerful engine, she accommodated everyone with ease. Alastair manoeuvred her out into the Narrows, steamed past the village, long pier and Eyre lighthouse, and headed north for the open sea.

It was a fine day for the Highlands. Cumulus cloud moved across a high blue sky casting chequers of shadow on the hill slopes. Sun and shade washed the sea with alternate dazzle and dark while the wild eastern coastline, roadless and uninhabited, unfolded itself on our port flank.

Alastair, Calum and Roddy, ensconced in the stern of the boat behind a protective Perspex screen, kept up a hum of Gaelic conversation broken every now and then by a head which emerged round the screen to talk to us.

'D'you see yon rock?' said Roddy, as we steamed towards Rubha na Leac. 'The big one with the flat top by the water? Well, a wee baby was exposed there once. It belonged to the young wife of a crofter who lived on the hill above. When her time came she crept down to the shore and delivered the baby there all alone, then left it out on that rock for the sea to take it. It wasn't her husband's, you see. She had it from another man. Well, what should happen but that very evening, the crofter took a stroll down to the shore. And what should he hear but a wee mew like a lamb. And what what should he see but a new-born baby! He was a good man and an unsuspecting man. He lifted it up and carried it back to his wife.

' "See Morag," said he, "what I found on the shore. We must keep the babe and bring it up as our own."

'Well, she never let on, and he never let on, and what they felt in their hearts I don't know, but that's what they did. There's the rock and that's the story. I'm thinking she was a lucky girl it turned out the way it did.'

Roddy withdrew to his lair, and the boat skirted Rubha na Leac's ragged point, with its string of half-submerged rocks and perching cormorants, then swept across a wide bay bounded by Hallaig waterfall, cascading a sheer hundred feet to the shore. Dun Caan's cirque of rocks rose above steep slopes, broken by boulders which had accumulated a growth of lichen, moss and heather as the years passed. A rock face of four hundred feet, broken into extraordinary shapes of tower and bastion came in sight: Screapadal, haunt of golden eagles. Below, near the water, stretched a patch of brilliant green. Here many families had lived. Evicted nearly a hundred years ago, the dry stone walls of their houses still stand. Protected by the crags, tucked into the side of the hill, the ruined township in its emerald setting draws to it a strange peace.

The agony of desertion is long past; in its place lies a mystery of isolation and of lonely vigil long sustained.

We were reaching the north of the island. Brochel Castle and its bay were past, and grey granite gave way to red Torridonian sandstone, the rocky bones of the landscape pushing ever more strongly through the scant covering of grass.

Calum Gillies heaved his bulky form round the protective screen and came forward to sit beside me. Brought up on this coastline, he knew every inch of it and returned to it now like a bird homing to its nest.

'You see yon ruin up on the hillside?' he said. 'That one, near the skyline? Alastair's mother lived there. There's not much left of it now, but in those days it held a whole family. Strong and tough they were, too, I tell you. One day two of the women decided to visit some friends on the mainland. They had a big boat – well, it would take a couple of men to row it now. They set off early in the morning and they rowed six miles across the Sound. Look!' Calum pointed over the glancing water to the faint shore-line below the mainland hills. 'All the way there they rowed and all the way back again. I doubt many of us would do that now in one day, but they thought nothing of it.'

The ruined house and the north coastline passed by. Rona lay ahead. 'This little isle . . . the most unequal rocky piece of ground to be seen anywhere . . .' as Martin Martin had written of it in 1695. The *Dignity* crossed the half-mile of choppy sea between the two islands and then Alastair steered her to a small channel off the Rona coastline where the tide ran strongly.

'Be quiet, now,' he said, shutting off the engine.

The boat glided slowly down the shallow inlet, passing between low rocks, half-submerged in the lapping tide. Dark forms slipped silently into the water.

'Seals!'

They were all round us, surfacing nose uppermost, turning curious heads on supple necks, staring fixedly with expressive eyes, then submerging again with hardly a ripple to roll and swim in the clear depths. No noise accompanied their watchful play.

On a rock a white seal pup basked beside its mother. As we approached they slipped together into the water. Then the youngster, swimming below the surface, made straight for the boat. It emerged within five yards of us and swam alongside as we sailed slowly onwards; then dived, rolled, turned, sped underneath and reappeared on the other side while its mother kept anxious guard.

'Yon's a common seal,' said Calum. 'They bear their young in June and the calves go to sea almost at once and are suckled there.'

'Do they breed on Rona?' I asked him.

'I think some must,' he replied. 'I've seen seal pups here so small that they must have been born nearby – probably up on the northern shore.'

The common seal abounds in the Southern Hebrides. The seal of the North is the grey Atlantic seal which is larger – six to eight feet long – and more rare. Uninhabited islands as far apart as North Rona and St Kilda, and rocks and skerries along the west coasts of the Inner and Outer Isles attract them in large numbers from October until the end of the year. They mate and calve on flat rocks above the water, and the young remain ashore for two or three weeks after birth, shedding their first white coat before going to sea. Some are swept off the rock ledges by winter storms but the majority survive to range over a wide area from Iceland to Ireland.

Rona, long known as the 'isle of seals', remote and uninhabited, most likely harbours a few such families.

I watched the seals, enthralled. So beautiful they were, so perfectly attuned to their environment, so vulnerable. Silently they disclosed to us another world: timeless, legend-haunted, the domain of mermaids and seal-women. For a fleeting moment I entered this dimension, shared their sun-dappled watery ways.

Out in the open sea again, Alastair switched on the engine.

'Now I'll show you a contrast,' he said. 'The cormorants' nesting place.'

We rounded a headland and pulled into a narrow fjord.

Cliffs, deeply chimneyed, and scarred by inlays of rock writhing like a van Gogh painting, towered above the still water. The clamour of hundreds of wing-beats and bird-calls filled the air. Dark clouds of cormorants spiralled away as we approached, then returned, singly or in couples, to perch beside their nests, made of dried seaweed and sticks hung precariously on ledges all the way up the rock face. Earlier in the year the nestlings had pecked impatiently at the parent's beak until the catch of fish was regurgitated, then jostled for position to poke their bills down their parent's gullet.

These fierce birds, with their long yellow beaks and black feathers shot with a green gloss, guard their youngsters with the same care, if not the same charm, as the anxious seal mothers.

'They have to,' said Alastair. 'The black-backed gulls take a dreadful toll. They eat the eggs and even the young birds.'

'How long do the fledglings stay in the nest?' I asked.

'About four weeks. Both parents feed the youngsters and guard them. Then they fly, after about eight weeks. Imagine taking off from that cliff for the first time! That is, if you'd survived the black-backs and the hoodies. Aye, it's a hazardous life.'

Roddy's keen eyes were searching the coastline for remembered landmarks.

'We're nearing the harbour,' he said. 'You see yon white arrow painted on the cliff? That's the entrance.'

Alastair eased the boat between steep banks, and the narrow channel opened out into a splendid bay – Acarseid Mhor. Part of its northern shore is the original Port nan Robaireann, but the thick woods which formerly existed have given way to heathery slopes, broken only by one plantation of small birches and alders. The harbour, swelling out from its narrow opening like a Cretan jar, could house a fleet of small ships. Seaweed is collected from Acarseid Mhor and carried away on a Stornoway boat. Shepherds land from Skye, and cruising yachts find shelter. Otherwise the harbour is deserted, the cottage at its head (occupied until the '40s by the one remaining Rona family, an old Macrae man and his two sisters) giving a false impression of habitation.

'Aye, it's a wonderful harbour,' said Roddy. 'I wish we had one like it in Raasay. Now, who's coming ashore with me?'

The party split into two, some to land with Roddy, others to cruise on up the coast with Alastair and Calum.

Roddy gathered his group together and then led the way at a slow pace, off the small stone pier, across the shore rocks, past the dilapidated cottage and into a spacious glen. Here he stopped and looked around him, his bowed shoulders straightening as he sniffed once more the island breeze. Tufts of heather hung from grey boulders. Blue scabious starred the grass on each side of the path. A honey scent filled the air. The silence, palpable and complete, enfolded each stone and flower. It seemed as though, just behind the visible surface, unseen eyes and ears awaited Roddy's return. He walked slowly on, then stopped once more. A small sheep track had crossed the narrow path we trod.

'This is the cross-roads,' he said. 'Here's the path that leads to Doire-na-Guaile, over the hill on the other side. Och, I remember every inch of this place.'

'When were you last here, Roddy?'

'About fifty years ago, when I was fourteen years old.'

'And you never came back to the island since?'

'Aye, once I did. In 1944. The Department of Agriculture asked me to take a large wild bull across the Kyle. Well, what a time I had with it! I roped it in an old stone building near the shore – another man was helping me. It bellowed and kicked, och, it was wild! We led it down to the shore and into the sea, and it struggled all the way. But when we pushed off, it put its head over the stern of the boat, gentle as a lamb, and two men held it with ropes, one on either side, and that's how we crossed. I suppose it would be a surprise for the beast, finding itself in the cold water being pulled over the Kyle. So it was quiet. But would you believe it?' Roddy paused, and gazed impressively round his audience. 'When we came to land on the other side, it was as wild as ever!'

The path to Acarseid Thioram – the tidal harbour farther north – crossed a narrow neck of land and then wound through rocks above the shore-line, giving glimpses of pools fringed with anemones and yellow lichen-covered stones. We reached the edge of the bay with its cluster of deserted buildings, and looked out over the open sea. The tide was in, flooding the harbour, and the water, flecked with particles of light, stretched away in an unbroken blue to the Skye hills, faint on the horizon.

'Aye,' said Roddy, 'that's the view. That's what I saw every day from my desk in the school.' The building still stood, with walls but no roof. Roddy searched inside, finally locating the exact spot where he had sat.

'Many's the weary hour I spent here,' he said. 'Och, I often longed to be away out over that sea. I wasn't much of a scholar, you see.' He chuckled to himself. 'But we children worked harder out of school than in it. We all helped with the harvest and when the time came for manuring the fields with seaweed, every one of us would be carrying creels of seaweed on our backs over the stones from the shore to the be at it. We had no horses and no machinery. Everything was cultivated patches on the hill. Ten or twelve days we would done by hand.'

'Show us where you lived, Roddy.'

We climbed over heather and bracken to a group of houses farther up the hill. Only the foundations and a few dry-stone walls remained. Roddy pointed to a hollow square of stones. 'That was my home,' he said. 'Aye, we were all brought up there, six of us. And that was my cousins' house, Calum and Brisco MacLeod. And the one near – over there – was Donald's, and this one was MacKay's. Well, well, just look at them now!'

Ragwort and nettles sprouted among the ruins. In some houses rowan and alder bushes had seeded themselves, and pushed branches through the decaying walls. Looked at carefully, the empty hillside disclosed further forlorn groups of buildings.

Roddy stared at them, pain in his eyes.

'So many people were here,' he said. 'I remember, when the missionary held his weekly prayer meeting every Thursday at twelve noon, eighteen families attended. People from Doire-na-Guaile and Acarseid Mhor, too. Everyone stopped work and came to the church. It was a hard life, right enough, but we all helped each other, and we were happy.'

'Why did the crofters leave the island, Roddy?'

'Too many people for too little land. The men came back from the 1914 War. Everything had deteriorated. The old people who were left hadn't been able to manage at all. There was no help from the Government and no further land, and even what there was had been parcelled out into such small pieces you couldn't work it properly. No proper boats, either. Sometimes in the winter the island would be cut off for a month at a time. Ach no, there was nothing to do but go.'

Roddy stood remembering, reading again the freshly written pages of his childhood, while the broken walls before him scarred with poignancy the deserted glen.

He came back to the present with a visible effort. 'Well, well. It's sad, right enough, to see it like this. But that's it, then, that's it. Now, you'll be wanting to visit the Church Cave? Yes, you must see that. It's on the east coast. I hope I can find the way after all these years.'

Casting about like a pointer, Roddy followed first one sheep track then another through knee-high heather. We walked for two miles or so until the eastern sea shone below us, then dropped down a steep hill and turned to face a cliff wall about thirty feet above the shore. Cut into the rock, extending backwards for a full fifty yards, was a magnificent cave arched like a Gothic cathedral. Huge slabs of stone formed its ceiling while steep walls on each side gleamed with moss and fern. Rows of stone seats had been hewn out of the centre aisle. Here the congregation had sat, a large rectangular boulder before them serving as an altar. Down one wall coursed a trickle of water which ran into a hollow stone beneath – the font. Roddy explained the uses of these stones in a reverent whisper, and then told us that families had come from all over the island to attend services here.

'When, Roddy?'

'Not in my father's time. But my grandfather would have

worshipped here as a boy, sat perhaps in that very seat.'

And heard the kirk psalms reverberate around these walls before they drifted out over the water, I thought.

Framed by the cave opening, the sea sparkled gaily. But often it must have raged, matching the stern sermons delivered within. And sometimes it would have wrapped itself in a white mist, so that the worshippers, hidden from the world, intoned their prayers on the edge of an unseen abyss.

The day was waning. Roddy led us back across the island and we rejoined our boat on the other shore.

Turning homewards, spectacular views of Skye to the west, and the whole Cuillin range to the south, unfolded themselves against a darkening sky. But the weather was changing. Temperamental as a beautiful woman, the island we had left withdrew into a veil of mist and fine rain.

Roddy knew how to make himself comfortable under such conditions. Ensconced in the small cabin, he stretched out full length on one of the bunks, took a pile of oilskins for a pillow, and closed his eyes. The less hardy amongst us followed his example and for a while silence reigned. Then Roddy awoke and prepared to hold court once more.

'So now you've seen the island the Raiders came from,' he said.

'The Raiders, Roddy?' I knew the story but wanted to hear Roddy tell it.

'Aye, the Rona Raiders. As I told you, in 1921 seven families decided to leave the island and find better conditions somewhere else. They looked around them and they selected Fearns, your area, and Eyre, a little farther south down the coast. Both places seemed to have good fertile land, and that's what they wanted. So they set off, my own family among them, to land there. The people and household belongings travelled in big rowing boats, each with four oars. The cattle and sheep were ferried across the Kyle. The sheep were no problem, if the first one went into the boat all the rest followed. But the big milking cows – about three to each family – what a fuss they made! They had to be tied and ferried across in the bottom of the boat, one or two cows on each trip. Once they got over, they were all gathered together – about twenty head of cattle – and driven south by hand. That was my job.' Roddy paused and chuckled. 'And a fine time I had of it. I didn't hurry, I tell you. It took me all of two days to get to Fearns.'

He turned, settling himself comfortably, and prepared to lapse back into childhood memories.

'But why were the people called Raiders?' I reminded him.

'Because they raided the land. It didn't belong to them. The whole island belonged then to Baird & Co. who'd been getting iron-ore out of it during the First World War. The Raiders didn't ask Baird's permission. They just landed and lived in the ruins of the houses they found there, building up the dry-stone walls and thatching the roofs. Well, not long after they landed, a man from Baird came along one day and told them to leave. They refused. "We've nowhere to go," they said. "You can go back where you came from," said he. "We will not," they said. "We'll stay where we are."

'At that, Baird prosecuted them and set the police on them. The head of each family was arrested and taken away to Inverness to be put in prison, awaiting trial. Och, that was an anxious time,' Roddy shook his head. 'There were the women and children all alone, wondering would their men be returned to them, or would they have to serve a long prison sentence.'

'What a disgraceful thing!'

'It was. Seemingly, the country thought so, too. When it was reported in the press there was a public outcry. All the newspapers took it up. I believe even a question was asked about it in Parliament. It was just after the War, you see, and people remembered the slogans about "Homes for Heroes". And many of these men had fought in the War.

'Well, we had several anxious weeks to wait for the verdict. But at last we heard that our men were coming home. Under what conditions we didn't know. We went down to the shore below Fearns to watch for the steamer. She came in sight. And as she drew near what should we hear but a skirl of pipes coming across the water. Och, those pipes! Never will I forget their sound! So then we knew it was all right. We knew our men had been pardoned and they were coming back to us for good. The piper played them off the boat and right round Raasay House before he led them out along the road to Fearns, piping all the way. And the women met them with tears of joy running down their cheeks. And we children were wild with excitement. What a day! What a day!'

'And then they settled for good?'

'Aye. After a while they built the houses you are in now, and three others like them at Eyre. Well, they had a better living there than on their own island. I don't believe they ever regretted the change. Later on, when the Department of Agriculture took over from Baird, the private ownership of the south end of Raasay was broken, and crofters were allowed holdings there. Now a number of crofters own land there. But the Rona Raiders were the pioneers, indeed they were. They opened it up for all the others.'

The story had taken some time. Emerging on to the deck again I found the evening closing in. The rest of the party were crowding excitedly to one side of the boat. I just had time to observe, some distance away, a huge shape heave itself leisurely out of the sea, then submerge again sending up a spout of water.

'A whale!'

Field-glasses raised, I stared tensely at the patch of choppy water where it had disappeared.

'It's a sperm whale, I think,' said Alastair. 'They migrate regularly through these waters on their way to and from the Arctic, but you don't often see them.'

'Once more, *please*, once more,' I whispered to myself, the day's accolade seeming to depend on the whale's reappearance. Nothing happened. The sea looked grey and formless, the sky had become leaden and rain fell with chilling persistency. At last, after interminable moments, the dark shape emerged once more. Like an enormous porpoise, it surfaced, rolled, humped above the waves, and then slid slowly back, this time with an air of finality. 'Good night,' it seemed to say. With this last wonder of the deep our day came to an end.

PART III

The Sea

11

Sea Experiences

The longer we lived on Raasay the more we became aware of the sea which surrounded us. Its beauty was unending, continually changing in colour and texture. It could whip itself into white-flecked waves or bask in limpid calm, stretch vast and mysterious to the horizon or contract to ripples idly caressing the shore. Unaided it succoured its fishes and birds, upheld its ships, linked its islands. To us it was a source of continual wonder and though it limited our environment at the same time it challenged us to further adventure.

During our second summer we acquired a small dinghy with an outboard motor, painted blue and white and called the *Victoria*. In her we could visit Brochel Castle up the coast, or chug over to Skye. We could fish for mackerel before lunch or dinner, or row quietly out from the shore when the day waned and evening shadows striped the hills. Seen from the water, with its added space and peace, the four houses on the hillside looked idyllic, each eased at a slightly different angle into its surrounding slope; the lowest one – ours – protected by four trees which gave it a virginal air and which Brian refused to cut down, preferring to see the distant hills through a foreground of foliage.

In this house the sound of the sea was always with us. We went to sleep listening to the lap of water on stones, heard the cries of oystercatchers and gulls through the night, and awoke to an immediate awareness of calm or storm. When gales blew, waves pounded the beach and rocked our small boat anchored to a buoy offshore. Open to the North Sea the

Sound could be rough, while on the other side of the island the Narrows between it and Skye acted as a funnel for wind and tide, making the crossing hazardous when the fierce north-easter blew.

We became practised at adapting ourselves to the climate. In a storm, like birds and animals, we would go to ground, lighting the log fire and settling ourselves to a day of reading and writing indoors, with only brief excursions outside. But often the weather took us by surprise. On a clear day, suddenly dark clouds would mass over Skye and then roll across the water to disgorge themselves in a shower of sharp hail. And a rough sea could blow up just as swiftly – something to remember when out in a small boat.

Our second Christmas on the island was one of bright cold days and starlit nights. A north wind brought snow which piled up in soft masses on the hillsides and hardened into ice on the road. The brief hours of sunlight struck diamonds from frozen surfaces but did little to melt them; the surrounding air was too cold. Soon no vehicle could traverse the road, not even the heavy lorry trying to lay sand, and walking into the village for supplies entailed sliding over icy patches and more than once coming a hard cropper on the frozen surface.

We were due to leave the island two days after this freeze-up began. It was obvious that we would not get to the pier by road. Calum Macrae came to our rescue and provided an alternative. 'I'll take you by sea in the *Victoria,*' he said. 'The steamer docks at half-eight. If you don't mind an early start, we'll easily manage it to the pier in time.'

We packed up our heavy luggage early next morning and then strode out of the house into an azure and white world. The snow, still frozen, crunched under our thick boots. The sun cast long violet shadows. The red-tipped silver birches flamed, their colour echoed in patches of bracken, and the crisp keen air tingled fingers and toes and brought icy drops to the ends of our noses.

We walked swiftly over the frosty moor, starting up one or two mountain hares in their white winter coats. We were on the lookout for golden eagles and the few deer who live on the island, elusive animals more likely to be seen in winter when hunger drives them down from the crests.

At the coast, high on the hillside above Roddy's house, we stopped and scanned the water for divers and eider duck, frequent winter visitors. The sea was dead calm, winking in the brilliant light, innocent, inviting.

Calum was waiting at the house on our return. He helped us shoulder the luggage down to the shore. 'A wonderful day right enough,' he said. 'The weather's set fair. It should be fine for you tomorrow morning. I'll be back at half-six.'

The little *Victoria* chugged out on to the smiling water with Calum at the stern, our suitcases stacked at odd angles providing the only discordant note in the peaceful scene.

In the night the wind changed. I awoke to hear a south-wester whistling round the house. It tore through the branches of the trees, and flung handfuls of hail against the windows. From the shore came the crunch of angry waves. I listened uneasily, half awake, half asleep, until the alarm shrilled at 6 am, forcing me out of bed.

The house was bitterly cold, all heat having evaporated during the night. We dressed, as though for an Arctic expedition, and peered through the dark windows. Nothing could be seen outside but driving rain. We switched on our torches, blew out the Aladdin lamp, and emerged into the winter night.

I was carrying a small dressing-case in one hand, and my torch and the lead of our obstreperous bull-terrier in the other. Bull-terriers hate rain and Cleo alternately shook a miniature shower all over me, or strained at her leash, pulling me off balance in her efforts to be somewhere else. Far down the hillside two lights appeared on the shore, wavering in our direction. I followed Brian towards them.

The path was steep and slippery. At one point a burn, invisible in the blackness, had overflowed its banks becoming a sheet of ice. With no warning at all my feet shot from under me and I sat down heavily. Cleo, her lead released, bounded down the hillside to be caught by Calum and his friend, Calum Gillies, waiting on the beach. I picked myself up painfully and followed. At last, friendly hands grasped mine.

'How are you? Wet already? Aye, it's a fearful morning.' The *Victoria* was pulled up just above the white line of breaking surf.

'Get the dog and the luggage into the boat first.'

Cleo, shivering with apprehension, was deposited under a seat, and the two Calums and Brian manhandled the heavy little *Victoria* down the pebble slope. I followed, slipping on stones covered with seaweed until I could take a leap into the boat as she rocked between surf and shore. Calum Macrae, thigh-deep in the swell, pushed her off, then sprang aboard and made his way aft to the engine. Two strong pulls on the rope and it started, its sputter sending a reassuring man-made noise across the night's clamour.

I looked around. The boat was fully loaded. The dark shapes of Brian and the two Calums filled the stern and the centre, while I sat in the bows, the wretched Cleo shivering beneath me. The four-horsepower engine drove us forward at an erratic pace into waves which slapped the bows sharply then broke in a shower of spray. Water sluiced around our feet and streamed off the gunwales. Rain pock-marked a heaving black sea. Out of the gloom an oilskin was flung over my shoulders, and I looked up to see Calum Gillies' rugged face.

'It's very wet ye are,' he said. 'Here, shelter a bit under this.'

The spray, breaking on the oilskin, sounded like small shot. I fixed my eyes on Calum's dim form, from which emerged an encouraging Highland voice.

'Did ye hear about the wreck in Stornoway harbour the other night?' it enquired, by way of conversation. 'Ye didn't? Och, it was a terrible thing. A fishing boat went down at the mouth of the harbour by the lighthouse. Pitch black night it was – rather like this. Seemingly, a sailor lying in his bunk saw a hole at the side of him and the sea pouring through. Splinters of wood he had in his jersey from the break in the side of the boat. He made to get out of the hatch – he could as well have got out of the hole.'

A whistle of commiseration came from the other Calum sitting at the stern. I listened bleakly.

'Well, the ship was heavy,' continued Calum Gillies. 'She had one hundred and forty crans of herring aboard. She went down in no time.'

'Was no one saved?' I shouted above the wind.

'Och, yes, they all were. Only the ship was lost. Another boat had hit her, you see, so fortunately this second boat picked up all the crew and got them back to the pier, although she was listing badly herself. But imagine – that good fishing boat going down and in weather no rougher than this.'

Gaelic comments flowed between the two Calums, punctuated by laughter a shade derisive, while I thought my own thoughts.

The sky was lightening. Shafts of grey showed between racing clouds, and the outline of Beinn na Leac began to loom above the shore. No rose and pearl dawn this, but a cheerless revelation of stormy sea and sky. It showed us Eyre lighthouse gradually approaching in spite of our slow progress in the heavily laden boat. The pier lay a good two miles beyond the lighthouse.

'Will we make it, do you think?' shouted Brian.

'Best see when we're round the headland,' Calum Macrae answered. 'It should be calmer there.'

He was steering close to the shore, now disclosing itself as a line of jagged boulders and pounding surf. We changed course to round the Eyre headland and Brian leaned over the side and peered into the sea. 'Hell of a lot of rocks here,' he muttered. 'Only just under the surface. We're missing them by inches.'

The cross-currents of the Sound threw the boat from side to side. She creaked and strained as we laboured on. Once round the headland the wind's full force struck. Far from being calmer it increased in strength, and, funnelled between the two shores of the Narrows, attacked with fury. The whole sea-surface between Raasay and Skye was broken by storm-tossed waves. Calum Macrae took a long look at sea and sky and made a decision. 'We'll come in to land,' he cried.

He turned the *Victoria* towards the beach, and at that moment the engine stuttered. The heavy swell slewed us sideways on to the shore and suddenly the engine ceased. Helpless, we rocked on the tide, in danger of being driven on to the rocks or capsizing where we lay. Calum Gillies dived into the bottom of the boat. 'The oars!' he shouted, groping in the gloom. Seizing them he pushed them through the rowlocks and wrenched the boat round to face the shore. Then, breasting the waves, he rowed in with strong though uneven strokes. Tide and swell took us to where the surf broke, and the boat began to grind on boulders. All three men tumbled out. I stood up, lifted Cleo from under my feet, threw her into the waves and leapt out myself. Two on each side, we pulled with all our might to get the boat out of the water. She was ricocheting from rock to rock but with a mighty heave we lifted her up and on to the beach, not stopping until she was well above the surf-line. Then we stood back in the dawn light and regarded the scene.

We were breathless and dripping wet, water streaming off our oilskins and down our wellington boots. Cleo, frightened and frozen, whimpered at our feet. My dressing-case, awash in the bottom of the *Victoria* reminded us of the purpose of the trip. We looked at one another, and dissolved into helpless laughter. Brian consulted his watch: 'We can still make it,' he said, 'if we walk fast. How far is it to the pier along the shore road?'

'About two miles,' Calum Macrae replied. 'You'd better get going. We'll pull the boat above the tide-line, then follow you.'

It was a long wet walk. The Skye hills slowly emerged on the farther shore as Cleo skidded over the ice in a vain chase of early morning rabbits, and my fingers and toes burned back to life, blood flowing once more to their frozen extremities. Brian strode ahead until he reached the top of the last hill where the pier came into view.

'It's all right,' he called back to me. 'The steamer's not in sight yet.'

We trotted down the hill, warm at last, and took shelter by the wall of the corrugated iron-roofed storehouse. There were still fifteen minutes to go before sailing time. When the two Calums joined us, flasks were produced and the dram that we drank then coursed like elixir through our veins.

We dried off on the steamer and fortified ourselves by thoughts of a hot breakfast and a hot bath at Kyle. But when we reached the only hotel open, it was to be told, 'Breakfast's off. And there's no hot water. The boiler's out.'

Thus ended our baptism by sea.

After this trip Calum Gillies became a friend and taught us much about the sea. Like most Hebrideans, he had a spell at sea and then decided to live on Raasay with his family for as long as he could find work there, no easy task.

Calum has the sea in his blood. His twelve years on a fishing boat among the Northern Hebrides, gave him an intimate knowledge of their waters, winds and coastlines. In his garden stands the shell of one of the old rowing boats which brought the Rona Raiders to Raasay, and on the beach below his house is a small dinghy, blown across the Sound to him from Skye. But a boat capable of going out in all weathers and fishing in open waters had been beyond his means to procure.

As time passed, we got to know Calum well and discovered that one of his chief anxieties was the absence from home of his two sons, John Alan and Alastair Iain. Like all other children of secondary school age, these boys had to leave the island once they were over eleven years old, to go to the High School in Portree. They stayed at the School hostel during the week and often were unable to return home at weekends because there was no boat to bring them. Many Raasay parents shared Calum's disquiet at this enforced separation from their children.

They appreciated the obvious advantages of a good secondary education, which the Portree High School provided, but resented the lack of proper ferry facilities to return the children to the island at weekends. Alastair Nicholson ferried them across in spring and summer, but in the winter his launch was laid up.

'If only I had a seaworthy boat which could cross in bad weather, I could bring my own two and the others back myself,' said Calum.

We also wanted a larger boat than the *Victoria*, so Brian discussed sharing a vessel with Calum. He would use and maintain it while we were away from Raasay (particularly for ferrying the scholars across in the winter months), while we would have its use during the spring and summer holidays. Calum was enthusiastic about this idea and we asked him to look out for a suitable craft. One evening an excited Calum telephoned us:

'I've found the boat we want,' he said. 'The very thing. She's a ship's lifeboat which has recently been converted. She's in Stornoway just now but I could go across and see her, and if I like her, buy her and sail her back across the Minch.'

The vision of a graceful yacht skimming across Hebridean seas floated before my eyes.

'She's got a sound engine and a wee cabin and she's splendid value for the money,' Calum continued.

'How much?' I asked.

Calum named a price.

'And will she be fit to go out in rough weather and ferry the scholars across in winter?'

'She will. And she'll take you some fine trips in the summer.'

A decision had to be made immediately. We contacted my two sons, persuaded them to share in the venture, and telephoned 'yes' to Calum.

A week later a radiant Calum spoke to us again.

'Well, I've got the boat,' he said. 'Aye, she's anchored in the bay just below the house. Och, she's a beauty. She came over the Minch as steady as steady. Nothing but a wee roll . . . Aye, it was quite stormy. The journey took all night. She went like a dream. She's a *safe* boat right enough, really safe . . .'

A dreadful thought struck me.

'Calum, has she got a sail?'

'A sail? What would she want a sail for? Who heard of a converted lifeboat with a sail? She's got a fine Diesel engine – well, the oil leak is making some fumes just now . . . and the cabin's not waterproof, but . . .' Calum's voice continued its eulogy.

A month or so later we saw the boat for the first time and our worst fears were confirmed.

'Tugboat Annie,' said Brian.

Two men were needed to start the engine – one to tinker with the compression valves while the other wound the ancient crankshaft, a feat requiring unusual strength. Once the engine sprang into life the noise and the fumes were overwhelming. The throttle was controlled by a string which emerged from the depths of the engine to be hung on a nail hammered into a thin screen of two-ply wood. The oil leaks were plugged with two rags. There was no deck-rail and no shelter except for the minute cabin.

'What happens when she rolls?' I asked.

'Och, she won't roll much. She's such a *safe* boat, she'd weather any storm,' Calum replied. 'Of course you could go below if you wanted to.' I peered into the leaking cabin. It had no seats and was shuddering with the engine's throbs.

'Well, the first fine day I'll bring her round for you to try out,' said Calum cheerfully.

A day or so later we heard a noise like a tank reverberating up the Sound. Our craft came into sight, flashes of orange oilskins denoting the presence of Calum and his two sons. They anchored offshore. Brian gazed at the sturdy twenty-foot-long bulk of our new acquisition. 'She's got good lines,' he affirmed.

Her straight prow, curved black sides and small white turret did indeed give a certain air of reliability.

'A carthorse, not a racehorse,' I sadly agreed.

But as the days passed we grew fonder and fonder of the *Samara*. We accompanied Calum and his sons on several trips and the final seal of our approval was forged during an unforgettable voyage to the Crowlin Islands.

This small group of islands lies about a mile off the mainland at the tip of the Applecross peninsula. The day we steamed towards them was one of flat calm. A sea-mist enclosed us in a strange intimacy, as though we were the only living beings abroad. The Cuillins and Dun Caan showed as faint high shapes bordering a silent world, and the few sea-birds that glided across our line of vision seemed mythical – like auguries bearing portentous tidings.

Brian and I leaned on the *Samara*'s engine-house, while

Calum's Highland voice, lowered in response to the sea's mysterious mood, rose and fell.

'Och, it's not often you see a calm like this,' he said. 'I'm more used to storm in these waters. Farther up the coast there, just above Applecross, I was in one of the worst storms I ever remember. It was the night the Irish ferry steamer sank.'

'The *Princess Victoria,* on the Stranraer-Larne crossing?' asked Brian.

'Aye, that was it. A terrible night. We were anchored in the bay at Diabeg at the mouth of Loch Torridon – my fishing boat, the *Johan,* and three others – the *Maigdhean Bhan,* the *Marshalie* and the *Caber Feidh.* Well, the storm was so severe we feared all four ships would be thrown together by the waves. We couldn't remain at anchor, we'd have been blown ashore and the harbour was too small for us all to cruise round together in safety. So two ships had to leave. The *Johan* was one of them. It was pitch dark, and the seas were huge, even in the mouth of the loch. We sailed up the loch towards Shieldaig, not seeing a thing, and then suddenly we picked up a light on the shore. It came from one of the cottages and it belonged to an old woman from Raasay – aye, Alastair Nicholson's great-aunt, the one who rowed six miles across the Sound and back in a day, d'ye remember me telling you? Well, this old woman had kindled a light for the seamen, and she kept it going all night. Were we glad to see it! We picked it up, steamed towards it, then turned away from the coast, steamed out, lost it, turned, found it again, and so on, all through the night. The waves were enormous – *mountains* – and the visibility nil. What a night! We didn't dare anchor or run for shelter to a harbour, we just had to ride out the storm.'

John Alan and Alastair Iain, crouched on the deck, had been listening intently.

'Was that the worst storm you ever were in, Dad?' asked the younger.

'No, there was one worse.' Calum shifted his bulk into an easier position, gave a tweak to the throttle string and continued.

'It was in the same fishing boat – the *Johan.* We were fully loaded with a big haul of herring aboard – one hundred and forty cran, four boxes to each cran. That's a lot of fish. We put into Gairloch to sell it, but there were many other boats there too, and the price was only one pound a cran. "Not enough," said the skipper, and he decided to cross the Minch to Stornoway and sell his load there.

'We left about 9 am. By the time we got to the Shiants the weather had worsened and there were huge seas. We should have turned back then, but the skipper decided to go on. He was a good man, a good skipper, but he took wrong decisions. And this was one of them. The waves were just mountains, tons of water. Beside the shoulder of the boat there was a great green wave running. Into that and we would be over.

'The tarpaulin across the hold was blowing up, and we had to get it tied down or the sea would be into the hold. I and another man tried to fix three wire ropes on to it, and a terrible job we had. The boat was pitching and tossing, och, it was fearsome, but somehow we managed it, and thank God, the wire ropes held – the only ones which did. All the others gave way.

'Down in the bunks between watches the water was dripping through the ceiling. The forward bunks were soaked. I was all right aft, but suddenly the ship heaved and a wave came running in there too. Then, halfway across the Minch, the skipper decided to make for Tarbert, due west, sailing into the teeth of the storm. I objected.

' "It's suicidal," I said. "On that course we'll be over the first big wave, into the next and under the third."

'The skipper thought. Then he asked me to take the wheel while he went below to chart the course.

' "You take over," he said.

'I steered for Stornoway – nor'-west – putting the ship diagonally against the gale. And after that I steered all the way until at last we made harbour. It was about six pm, nine hours after we'd left Gairloch. We unloaded and sold the fish for two pounds a cran, one pound more than at Gairloch. So perhaps the skipper thought it was worthwhile. But whatever he thought he made a wrong decision. He should have turned back. We were lucky to come through that storm alive.'

Calum was silent, his memory busy. The *Samara* steamed on through the mist, and ahead rose phantom shapes of islands gradually drawing closer. Off Crowlin's northern point Calum shut off the engine. In the silence the wing-beats of a great grey heron sounded like an omen. Fulmar and tern circled the rocks and two seals surfaced quietly, looking to see who had come to disturb their domain.

'Aye, it was a hard life,' Calum said, his mind several jumps behind. 'When I first went to sea I worked for five months and got nine pounds at the end of it. No fish that summer. Then in the autumn we ran into a shoal and the ship was loaded up and emptied twice. Three days and three nights without sleep. I was shovelling the herring out of the hold asleep on my feet, knees giving way under me at the wheel. Och, I was tired! But at the end of those three days I got sixty pounds.'

Calum shook his head, a rueful smile on his face.

'And now fishermen in Stornoway are making one hundred and fity pounds a week on prawn fishing,' he concluded.

Between Crowlin Mhor and Crowlin Beag runs a narrow sea channel, bordered with orange kelp and flanked by thin grey rocks. As we cruised down it ten seals surfaced and swam towards the *Samara*, leaping like porpoises, and making for the exit to the sea. Brian and I transferred to a small dinghy, the better to observe them, and rowed silently forwards until one cow came up within five yards of us. She blew through her large nostrils and gazed at us steadfastly with mournful eyes. Her whiskers quivered and her long eyelashes blinked. Seal legends raced through my mind, the kinship felt between us seemed so real. Seconds – perhaps minutes – passed while we regarded one another. Then the seal firmly closed her eyes, lifted her snout, and submerged, becoming once more only an evasive shape below water.

We anchored in a small bay on the east of Crowlin Mhor, and lunched at the edge of a green enclosure surrounded by heather slopes. Here, Calum said, the islanders would have kept their milking cows, shutting them in at night with a low wall and a gate, and milking them early next morning before letting them go free.

The ruins of four or five houses were grouped round a patch of grass. Two chimneys and some broken walls survived, but no roofs, although a tree growing through the centre of one house looked from the sea like a green thatch. I walked the length of Crowlin Mhor from east to west, passing Loch nam Leac, a small stretch of water bearing rushes and water-lilies, its shores laden with a pile of mussels and razor shells left by sea-birds. I saw no more than three sheep (although shepherds do graze stock on the Crowlins), and felt for the most part as though my human steps were the first to tread land known only to birds and animals. Calum and his sons explored the shore with its broken rocks and deep caves and Brian sketched the *Samara*.

We met again by the ruined houses.

'I was thinking of the talk and laughter and community life that used to go on here,' said Calum. 'And now – nothing. It's all gone.' He paused. 'And Raasay is going the same way.'

But a different future may lie in store for the Crowlins. They are under consideration as a location for the building of oil construction platforms. It had been suggested in an article in the *West Highland Free Press* that 'deep water close to the southern tip of the islands would allow second and final stage construction, while the first stages of further platforms could be undertaken in a construction dock, thus allowing the simultaneous production of as many as six platforms'. If this fate overtakes the Crowlin Islands then the isolated habitat of their birds and animals will be destroyed for good.

We sailed back to Raasay in late afternoon sunshine. The mist had lifted and the contours of the island stood clear. The sea, still dead calm, seemed incapable of the lashing fury Calum had described.

Near the shore, thick seaweed massed under clear water and a jellyfish drifted lazily past, long tentacles trailing. Calum manoeuvred the *Samara* close to the buoy and untied the small dinghy.

'Aye, it's been a fine day,' he said, as we prepared to row ashore. 'But the sea's like a woman. You never know where you are with her. There's only one thing you can be sure of. If you take too many chances, it's the sea that will win.'

12

The Northern Islands

Muck, Eigg, Rhum, Canna

The Small Isles lie in a scattered group off the south-west coast of Skye. Their exotic names – Muck, Eigg, Rhum and Canna – are mainly of Norse origin, and their appearance, remote and mysterious, embodies the legendary appeal of all far isles.

I first saw them from the high vantage point of the Cuillin ridge on Skye. From there they appeared to sail like enchanted galleons on the wide sea, their colours deepening as the day passed until the evening light gathered them into a roseate sleep. Their setting of water and wave seemed so remote from the arid Cuillin crags that they were invested with a seductive charm.

'Oh, to visit them and to sit on those soft sands,' I thought, as I grasped the rough Cuillin rock and clambered over the hard Cuillin stone.

Each of the islands has a distinctive shape; Eigg with its hogsback rising to a sharp crest of rock; Rhum with its serrated peaks and shadow-filled glens; low-lying Muck, and far Canna with its high platform of hill. Their silhouettes are visible from a wide stretch of the western coast as well as from the southerly Outer Isles. Veiled in storm or luminous in calm, they seemed the epitome of man's ancient longing for an enchanted isle, a place of refuge and retreat.

I longed to visit them, particularly Rhum whose mountains – companions to the Skye Cuillins – drew me like a magnet. But Rhum was difficult to approach. For many years it was a jealously guarded preserve, and although since 1957 it has belonged to the Nature Conservancy, only a pass from that body will allow a visitor to land.

Soon after we had settled in Raasay, my chance came. Our old friend, Evelyn Baring, companion of many climbs in Skye and elsewhere, was Chairman of the Nature Conservancy. He invited Brian and myself to visit Rhum with him. We accepted with delight.

Had we been birds we could have flown south-west in a direct line from our house to the island, crossing the Skye Cuillins and an eight-mile stretch of sea. As it was, we had to undertake a day's journey – by launch from Raasay, car across Skye, ferry to Mallaig and finally steamer to Rhum.

We reached Mallaig halfway through the day. The crossing from Armadale in Skye had been choppy, and the ferry pulled up to the quayside in pouring rain. Evelyn Baring was waiting, his tall figure clad in dripping oilskins. As soon as he saw us an arm shot up in welcome and a broad smile spread across his sunburnt face. The glow of enthusiasm and energy which radiated from him dispelled the weather's damp gloom. He gave me a hearty kiss, grasped Brian's hand and introduced his companion, an elderly botanist named Dr Grant Roger. Together we crossed the slippery cobble-stoned quays to the Rhum steamer. It was none other than our own *Loch Arkaig*, familiar from the Raasay run. This dapper little boat, which until now we had associated only with the comparatively calm waters of the Inner Sound, sets sail twice a week for the Small Isles, carrying mail and freight and often braving heavy seas before reaching Canna, the farthest of the islands, twenty-five miles out from the mainland.

The harbour at Mallaig was crammed with fishing boats, gulls circling their tall masts with raucous cries. The stir of seamen, passengers and tourists proceeded in spite of the downpour to which no one paid any attention. Mallaig habitués were immune in their oilskins, and tourists were already too wet to care any longer. Swiftly the freight was loaded, the last passenger came aboard and the gangway was pulled in. With her familiar toot, the *Loch Arkaig* nosed out of the harbour and set sail for the Sea of the Hebrides.

Our first stop was Eigg. This island, the principal one of the group, lies eight miles from the coast and has the highest population, about seventy people. It also houses the Small Isles parish minister, a priest, a doctor, a post office, a school and a store. Like Muck and Canna it is fertile, though much of the island which measures five miles long by three wide, is high hill moor. The impression it gives as one enters the harbour at Glamisdale on the south-east coast is of wooded slopes, green fields, yellow crops and a pastoral peace. High above the trees on the bare hillside looms the Scuir of Eigg, a tower of rock shaped like a curved horn which thrusts up nearly 300 feet above the 1,000-foot hill on which it stands. This bastion of pitchstone lava gives Eigg its distinctive outline from the sea.

The *Loch Arkaig*, having sailed for an hour and a half from Mallaig, steamed slowly through the harbour's narrow entrance and stopped near a rocky island on which stood a lighthouse and a small tower. The jetty projected from the shore into clear water, too shallow for use by the steamer, although the harbour is a favourite anchorage for yachts.

Most of the *Loch Arkaig*'s passengers were due to alight at Eigg and a launch came alongside to take them off. Several of them had changed colour since embarking and seemed none too sorry to leave. They were bundled into the launch, together with bags of mail and crates of supplies for the island. Then, with a last click of the camera at the Scuir, and a relieved backward glance at the *Loch Arkaig*, they steamed away. Half sorry not to be landing also, for Eigg is an island of many delights, we resumed our journey.

As we sailed south-west along Eigg's shore I had time to reflect on the island's history. It had been a turbulent one, entailing many feuds between MacDonalds and MacLeods, for Eigg was MacDonald territory, having been gifted by Robert the Bruce to MacDonald of Clanranald in 1309.

The most famous of these clan feuds is the story of the MacDonald cave, an occasion when marauding MacLeods suffocated the entire population of Eigg – 395 men, women and children – by lighting a huge bonfire in front of a cave in which they had taken refuge. This happened in 1577. Very soon afterwards the MacDonalds took their revenge by setting fire to a church at Trumpan in Skye in which a number of MacLeods had assembled for protection. Violence did not end on Eigg even when the era of clan feuds ceased. During the Jacobite rising the islesmen were called out by their chief, MacDonald of Clanranald, and forty of them served in the Clanranald Regiment of Prince Charles's Army. This allegiance cost them dear.

After the defeat at Culloden, Eigg was visited by Captain Fergussone and his Navy ship *Furnace*. A hundred men were landed at the harbour. The Captain promised a reprieve to the islanders if they would lay down their arms and deliver up Captain John MacDonald, whom they had tried to conceal. The scene was described in poignant words by Alexander MacDonald, a Jacobite poet, when he testified five years after the event to Bishop Forbes, who included it in *The Lyon in Mourning*.

'The men were seen coming in a body. Immediately Fergussone ordered Captain MacDonald to be seized upon. The men laid down their arms, such of them as had any. The few old people that came among them were picked out and dismist home. Then Captain MacDonald was stript of all his clothes to the skin, brought aboard the *Furnace*, and barisdall'd in a dark dungeon. And to the poor people's misfortune, there was a devilish paper found about him, containing a list of all the Eigg folk that were in the Prince's service. Then that catalogue was read by their patronimicks in the name of giving promised protection, which ilk one answered cheerfully, so that there were no fewer than thirty-eight snatched aboard the man-of-war, were brought to London, and from thence transported to Jamaica where the few that lives of them continue, slaves as yet. Many of them dyed and starved ere they arrove at the Thames. The most of them were marryed men, leaving throng families behind them. They slaughtered their cattle, pillaged all their houses ere they left the isle, and ravished a girl or two.'

The treatment was similar to that suffered by Raasay when Captain Fergussone 'set Raasa Isle afire'. But though both islands shared this misfortune they also shared something more lasting: a tradition of Celtic story and song which spanned many generations. This was wonderfully preserved in Eigg by the Reverend Kenneth MacLeod who was born and brought up on the island. Together with Marjory Kennedy-Fraser he collected some of its most haunting songs and these were published in their famous *Songs of the Hebrides*, the first volume of which appeared in 1913: 'The Rieving Ship', 'To the Cradle of the Lord of the Isles' and 'The Curse of the Aspen Tree', all from Eigg, have since been sung the world over wherever Gaels forgather, and have brought to the singers some touch of Eigg's 'extraordinary mystic charm . . . the charm of a small island bound together by imaginative possessions, stories and poems that have grown out of its own life'.

Alas, in recent times Eigg and Raasay have again been companions in misfortune. Each has known the trial of an unsatisfactory landlord.

Eigg belonged for many years to Lord Runciman, but in 1972 it was sold to an owner who proposed to run a school for handicapped children at Glamisdale House. This laudable objective was accepted by the islanders in good faith until, as the years passed, it became apparent that the school was failing to fulfil its function and, in addition, many of the islanders' traditional rights were being infringed. Finally, at the end of 1974, the Highlands and Islands Development Board felt bound to intervene. They offered the owner a large sum for Eigg but he found another bidder and sold the island to Mr Keith Schellenberg, Vice-Chairman of the Scottish Liberal Party.

I watched Eigg diminish as I thought of these things. The steamer drew away, the small houses were lost to view and the sea widened between me and its isolated people – people who would now have to adapt to modern conditions if they were to survive. Eigg is predominantly a crofting island, but like all Hebridean Islands, it faces the problem of depopulation.

Its new owner is encouraging new activities and some measure of prosperity is being restored. But one hopes that in the process Eigg's 'extraordinary mystic charm' will not be lost. For this it is, which has survived through bad times and good, which draws back its expatriate sons and daughters, and which brings old and new friends year after year to its shores.

The *Loch Arkaig* steamed across the Sound of Eigg and before long the small island of Muck drew near. I and the other members of our party propped ourselves against the ship's rails, raised our field-glasses and viewed its low green slopes with interest.

'I'm told it's exceedingly fertile,' Evelyn Baring observed. 'It gets specially early crops and vegetables, and there's good grazing for sheep, too.'

Muck, I knew, has been owned for many years by one family, the McEwens. I had met one of the sons on the *Loch Arkaig*, on the occasion when she steamed past Raasay in a winter storm. During the subsequent weekend's wait in the Skye hotel, this young man had told me of his island, farmed by his family and some crofters – a population of about twenty in all – living a self-sufficient life on a territory of no more than two miles by one.

A motor boat was approaching, and as it came closer I saw that it contained a crew of teenage children. Their boat drew alongside, a hatch of the *Loch Arkaig* opened, and supplies for Muck poured forth. Barefoot, the youngsters leapt on to the gunwale, torn trousers flapping, hair flying in the wind, and raised capable sunburnt hands. They seized the heavy crates of provisions and stored them swiftly away, working with speed and precision as their boat rocked in the swell. A fusillade of jokes cracked between themselves and the *Loch Arkaig* seamen, while their engine rattled, impatient to be gone. Then, the last package of mail thrown aboard, they turned the boat about and with a cheerful wave, sped back to their island. The whole procedure had taken little more than five minutes, but that five minutes was crammed with such purpose, vitality and gaiety that it spoke well for the inhabitants of Muck.

In fact, to farm such an isolated island takes a special brand of dedication. All the stock has to be ferried out to the steamer and then hoisted aboard in a sling. Winter storms can cut the inhabitants off for days, and transport costs increase the price of every commodity. The owner of Muck overcame these obstacles for many years. Since his death in 1972, his three sons have continued his tradition, running the farm on Muck, in addition to another farm on the mainland. I guessed that island living of this kind becomes a passion. Once experienced, for all its difficulties it cannot easily be forgone.

Our route now led from the comparatively sheltered Sound of Eigg out into the open sea and thence north-west up the Sound of Rhum. The *Loch Arkaig* ploughed through the freshening waves and settled into a long slow roll. The wind rose, a spatter of rain fell, and I went below.

The saloon was stuffy but uncrowded. I found a seat and watched the gyrating horizon through a porthole. The *Loch Arkaig* tipped sideways so steeply that sea filled my porthole with each roll, and it seemed as though the ship must pass the point of no return and capsize. I remembered that she had been converted from a minesweeper after the War and that an iron superstructure had been added to her wooden base so that she would be tall enough to come alongside the high pier at Raasay. This made her alarmingly top-heavy. Suitcases slid rhythmically from wall to wall, china rattled, and the strong cups of tea being drunk by unhappy passengers slopped into their saucers. Seasick though I felt, the fresh air aloft was preferable to this. I climbed on deck again, and was greeted by Brian, 'Evelyn has just slid right across the whole width of the deck,' he said. 'Fortunately the railings stopped him.'

Unperturbed, Evelyn stood where he had come to rest, gazing at a flock of birds flying low over the water.

'Come and see,' he called, 'it's a whole drove of Manx shearwaters.'

The birds flew in a rapid glide, flashing alternately black and white, their frail bodies outlined against the sea, wing-tips shearing the waves. They looked so fragile that it was hard to believe they spend all their lives on the ocean, only coming ashore to breed in the spring.

'They nest on the slopes below the Scuir of Eigg,' said Evelyn, 'and on the mountains of Rhum. They burrow into the ledges up there and the young are reared thousands of feet above the sea.'

Like spume in storm they patterned the air above the waves with wild grace, diving to within inches of the sea then soaring up again on stiff wings, one with the driven clouds, the rain and the sudden shafts of silver light.

If you wanted an embodiment of the Hebrides, I thought, there it is.

Rhum was approaching. Its mountains towered through mist as the *Loch Arkaig* sailed up the island's eastern coast, battling against wind and tide. At last she reached Loch Scresort, a deep inlet leading to the harbour. Once within the mile-long loch, the water became calmer and gentle green slopes undulated to the shore. Kinloch Castle, an imposing building of red sandstone situated at the head of the loch, came into view, and below it emerged a bay with a stone jetty and good anchorage for a steamer. This was our destination. Tired, cold and wet, we were glad to arrive.

Rhum – eight miles by eight between its farthest points – is owned by the Nature Conservancy and is run as a National Nature Reserve. Its geological interest, with a wide variety of different forms of rock; its large herd of red deer which provides opportunity for the study of their ecology and management; and the mountain-top colonies of Manx shearwaters are some of its special features. In addition, its remoteness, which is yet within easy reach of the mainland, makes it an outstanding station for research: 'The most suitable island for this purpose in Scotland,' as the Scottish Wild Life Conservation Committee stated when recommending its use as a Nature Conservation Area in 1949.

On Rhum the natural characteristics of a Hebridean island are encouraged, and experiments are undertaken in the restoration of tree cover, the provision of shelter, and the scientific management of mountain and moorland vegetation. Because of the extreme geological variety and the extensive differences in altitude – the Rhum Cuillins reach the height of 2552 feet above sea-level – there is a remarkable range of soil and vegetation types, and several rare plants are to be found on the island.

For more than a century, from 1845 to 1957, Rhum was a private sporting estate. During these years it acquired the reputation of 'Rhum, the Forbidden Island', and it was thus that I thought of it when I first saw it from the Cuillin ridge in Skye. The Nature Conservancy now allows visitors, provided they respect its rules, and over a thousand people visit the island every year, many on day cruises from Mallaig and Arisaig. But the terrain is devoted first and foremost to the animals, birds and plants which inhabit it. Man (except for the scientists and staff who operate there) has become a secondary species on Rhum.

As guests of the Nature Conservancy we were to stay at Kinloch Castle, and there we went immediately on disembarking. A greater contrast to the heaving deck of the *Loch Arkaig* could hardly be imagined. The castle was built by Sir George Bullough in 1901, and was designed to be the last word in Edwardian luxury. Its turrets of red sandstone (the building material conveyed all the way from the Isle of Arran), its crenellated walls, arched loggia, Italian gardens, lawns, orchard, greenhouses and turtle ponds, were only rivalled by the splendour of its interior. This unique period piece enjoyed a hey-day of less than a dozen years. Then the 1914 War intervened and all was changed.

In the large furnished hall of the castle are two full-length portraits: a young man in the khaki of the First World War, and a young woman in Edwardian evening dress. The young man, Sir George Bullough, stares forth with assured calm, never doubting that his comfortable world would last. His wife, Monica, has a more wistful expression. She was French. Did she miss the civilization of her own country? I guessed that hers was the taste which had decorated the miniature ballroom, where musicians had played from a small gallery and couples had sat out on yellow damask sofas. Only the wind and rain beating on the curtained windows would have sounded a Hebridean note.

When the young man's father, John Bullough, a Lancashire engineer, bought Rhum in 1887 it had been a sporting estate since 1845, owned first by the Marquis of Salisbury and later by the Campbells of Oronsay. The new owner planted eighty thousand trees at Kinloch, and imported a number of stags and hinds from Windsor Great Park to augment and improve the island's herds. His son continued his improvements, building – as well as Kinloch Castle – a road across the island. During the construction of the castle the workmen sent from Lancashire were supplied with kilts to add the authentic flavour. They responded with the complaint, 'If it isn't the midges it's the clegs, and if it isn't the clegs, it's the rain.'

We arrived at the castle, and were conducted to our bedrooms through a gallery containing water-colours of Scottish sporting life, and stuffed eagles with yellow glass eyes who clutched their prey in fearsome talons. The bath before dinner proved to be an adventurous experience. The array of gadgets at the tap end of the bath included one for making waves. In addition there were showers and squirts. If the wrong knobs were pressed, the seven-foot bath turned into a whirlpool.

Outside the castle, the Rhum Cuillins, with their evocative Norse names – Hallival, Barkeval, Trallval and Askival – towered into the night sky. Their presence was haunting and all of us were impatient to be on them.

Next day they lived up to their promise. The walk up Hallival, the nearest to Kinloch and 2,365 feet high, was a revelation. Dr Morton Boyd of the Nature Conservancy joined us; and he, Dr Grant Roger and Evelyn Baring proved admirable guides to the profusion of plant-life which grows on the lower slopes of the mountain.

The excitement of the naturalists in finding a rare flower was infectious. Progress along the path became erratic as the three dived to the ground, the better to observe a minute leaf, and then halted to discuss its characteristics, three tweedy bottoms stuck into the air, three earnest faces communicating at plant level.

Scottish asphodel, plaintain and thrift; goldenrod with its beautiful Latin name, *Solidago virgaurea* (gold for the virgin); club moss, (*Lycopodium clavatum*) the plant which provided the first stage of coal; all these were pointed out to us. And finally, high up, the rare rock bramble whose tomato-coloured berries glowed against grey rock.

Red deer appeared to be the only other inhabitants of this mountain world. There are about 1,500 on the island, and we could see stags and hinds grazing on slopes across the glen. But as we climbed higher even the deer were left behind and we were alone with the craggy rocks. Or so we thought.

Suddenly Morton Boyd signalled us to stop. We had reached one of the colonies of Manx shearwaters. I remembered their vivid flight above the broken water. They nest on the summits of Hallival and Askival, burrowing into the grassy ledges under the rocks and laying one egg inside each tunnel. Many hundreds of them gather at the nesting season, tending their young during the day, flying and feeding only at night.

'I'll try to find a young one for you,' said Dr Boyd. Carefully he searched for the entrance to a burrow, then drew a thick glove on to his right hand, knelt down and plunged his arm inside. A moment later he withdrew it and in his hand sat a small fledgling. Its mauve feathers were bunched round it like a miniature eiderdown, and its bright black eyes surveyed us with an uncomprehending stare.

'The mother wasn't there,' said Dr Boyd. 'I needn't have bothered to protect my hand. She's likely flown back to her ocean habitat and left this young one on its own.'

Until September, he told us, the fledgling would remain in the nest. Then, too hungry to stay any longer, it would start the 2,000-foot descent to the sea. Unable to take off from the ground, it would stagger over the moor and launch itself from the cliffs to reach the water. Then it would live on its reserves of fat until it could feed itself from the sea and eventually migrate. Some of Rhum's Manx shearwaters have now been ringed, and this has shown that the oceans of the southern hemisphere are their destination. These Rhum colonies, situated at such high altitude, are almost unique in Britain.

The summit of Hallival, dark and forbidding, rose above us. We clambered up the last few blocks of stone, stood on the crest and were greeted by a radiant seaward view. The Outer Isles and the Skye Cuillins lay in grape-blue silhouette, the space between them washed by reaches of silver-grey sea. Three miles to the north-west, the little island of Canna gleamed green and fertile, its large Catholic church by the harbour appearing as a distinctive landmark.

We lunched on Hallival's summit, on the lookout for one of the three or four pairs of resident golden eagles which nest on the island. They are indigenous although on average only one eaglet has fledged each year since 1957. But instead of eagles, ominous clouds appeared, and the knife-edge of rock which runs from Hallival to the crest of Askival, the next Cuillin, began to look disconcertingly high and steep. Evelyn Baring, however, was not to be dismayed. He had determined to traverse the main Rhum Cuillin peaks, so with undiminished zest he set out along the ridge accompanied by Morton Boyd and Grant Roger.

Brian and I turned homewards. As we descended, the storm broke. We looked back to see the climbers pinned to the ridge by hail while the sea-view beyond dissolved in shafts of slanting rain. But Evelyn and his friends completed the traverse in spite of the weather and returned to the castle that evening wet but triumphant. By then I had relinquished mountains for history and was in the library searching out records of Rhum's past.

The island was first mentioned, I read, in Ptolemy's *Geographica*, a catalogue of places written at the end of the first century. Tacitus also referred to it in his account of Agricola's expedition against the Picts in AD 83. Before that, in the Bronze Age, Rhum Bloodstone was found in the Rudh an Dunain Cave in Skye, once the centre of a Bronze Age stone-knapping industry.

But Rhum was not permanently inhabited until the Middle Ages and even then, for many generations, it remained remote and little disturbed by man.

At first Clanranald territory, it later passed to John of Islay and then to the MacLeans of Coll. Faced with the population explosion of the early nineteenth century the MacLean who was then laird arranged in 1825 for the island's entire population of four hundred people to emigrate to Canada. This was no forced eviction but a desire of the people, who had found themselves, through overcrowding and poor living conditions, unable to continue their traditional crofting life. The ground was thus cleared for sheep. Soon afterwards eight thousand of them moved in, and, by the end of the nineteenth century, in spite of the subsequent settling of a few Skye families, the last crofter had gone.

John Bullough loved Rhum and wished to be buried on the island. After his death in 1891, his coffin was placed in a chamber hewn out of the rock at Harris on the west coast. Later his son, Sir George, built him a strange memorial – a mausoleum shaped like a Greek temple with a wide flight of supporting steps, eighteen columns and a massive roof. Through the columns the Highlands winds blew. And there, in the course of time, Sir George joined his father. Finally his wife Monica was also buried there. The tombs of the three Bulloughs stand on a grassy promontory near the steep gabbro cliffs of the west coast. Close by, at the mouth of the Glen Duain river are the remains of the largest single crofting settlement in Rhum – thirty black houses and about three hundred acres of former lazybeds. The contrast between the Greek temple and the crumbling dry-stone walls emphasize the differing fates of the owners and crofters of Rhum.

Rhum is for the most part desolate hilly country and its fascination lies in its wildness. But at Kilmory, in the extreme north, a different atmosphere prevails. Here are the ruins of an old hamlet and of a chapel – St Mary's Church. They are surrounded by green turf, on which the Bulloughs' laundry used to be spread to dry. In the white-sanded bay below sea-birds abound. Mallard and shelduck, shag, gannet, oystercatcher, curlew and heron – all rose before our delighted eyes the day we visited Kilmory. Its silence, broken only by their cries, cast a spell. Lying on a grassy headland, gazing seaward while rollers creamed the beach below, all the indefinable magic of the Hebrides seemed suddenly to be made manifest. The contrasts of pasture and mountain, field and rock, sun and storm, so closely related and so swiftly interchanged created a rare mosaic. And the light which washed them seemed to be suffused with a radiance not of this world.

So I thought at Kilmory on the last day of our Rhum visit. So I was to think many times more.

On the summit of Hallival we conceived the ambition to visit Canna. A few years later we set sail for it in the *Western Isles,* a large fishing boat commissioned originally by the Admiralty but taken over half-completed and built to schedule for Bruce Watt, who ran a regular service from Mallaig to the Isles. Much smaller than the *Loch Arkaig,* this gallant craft pitched straight into a heavy sea but her shipshape rig and super-efficient crew, in the person of a marvellous fair-haired and oilskinned girl who seemed ready for any emergency, were well able to handle it. As before, we stopped at Eigg, landing some tourists the worse for weather, and Rhum, where a few initiates, including a sunburnt elderly man in a tattered kilt, a visitor to the Schools' Hebridean Society Camp on the island, disembarked. Only four passengers remained: ourselves; a Canadian priest, Father MacDonell, whose great-great-grandmother came from Eigg; and a young Anglican curate who had just visited Eriskay in the Outer Isles.

We cruised along the north-east coast of Rhum, passing four immense grey Atlantic seals who lay immobile like boulders on the rocks; two red deer standing mysteriously on a tan pebbled shore; and some shearwaters glancing above the waves. The miraculous girl brought us steaming cups of tea while the rain deluged and the sea roughened. In this familiar Hebridean situation Canna came into view, its high contour rising to 690 feet at Carn a' Ghaill on the north-eastern end. The island's excellent harbour has a pier at which steamers can call. We landed on it, dumped our luggage in a waiting Land-Rover, and walked the mile or so to our lodgings with Canna's postmistress, Mary Ann MacLean.

Her house stands on a neck of land between the harbour and the open sea, close to the stone bridge which connects Canna to Sanday, the tidal island forming the southern shore of the harbour. We were wet and cold when we arrived, but a huge fire, a meal and a truly Gaelic welcome awaited us. Mary Ann's sharp tongue soon shared with us gossip of the Small Isles and Skye. She regarded these territories as her parish and from her vantage point, the post office, held long telephone conversations, gathering news from her fellow postmistresses strategically dotted round the Isles. Her habit of repetition in speech gave dramatic emphasis to all her remarks, and her infectious laugh ended most sentences with a delightfully conspiratorial air. During the summer she slept in a caravan while her guests were installed in rose-wallpapered bedrooms with comfortable pink-quilted beds. The only rule, stipulated with impressive force, was that high tea must be eaten at 6 pm.

Canna – five miles long by one mile wide – has been owned since 1938 by John Lorne Campbell, a distinguished scholar in Gaelic and a lepidopterist who has discovered at least one species of moth unique to Canna. He is a friendly laird who cares well for the island and its twenty inhabitants. With tertiary basalt rock Canna has good soil and is the best cultivated of the Small Isles, yielding early crops, and good vegetables and fruit. The ratio of cattle to sheep is high, and the Cheviot sheep themselves are of excellent quality. Everything on the island seems well looked after. Walls are intact, gates open and shut, fences are in good repair, and there is no rubbish – so often a disfigurement of the Hebridean scene. The air of prosperity and friendliness extends to the people. Two brothers, each in their early forties, each with New Zealand wives, work for John Campbell, one as shepherd, one as maintenance man. Another brother, married to a Donegal girl has five children, and there are seven children on the island in all. They attend their own school run by an English schoolmistress.

The whole community is Catholic and John Campbell has built a small chapel for the people in place of the Marquis of Bute's large church (which we had seen from Rhum, but which is never used). Services depend upon a visiting priest, usually from Eigg but sometimes from farther afield. On the Sunday we were in Canna the Canadian Father MacDonell said Mass in Latin and everyone on the island came, including a baby of eighteen months. The austerity of the chapel with its plain stone walls and wooden rafters was lightened by a vase of sweet peas on the altar and a view of sea and hill; and the prayers at the end of Mass, rising and falling in Gaelic, flowed like the sound of waves on the shore outside. Father MacDonell, fifth in the generations of his family living in Canada, spoke Gaelic as fluently as his forebears, and used it for his sermon: a reminder of the living Celtic culture brought to the other side of the Atlantic by emigrants and still cherished there.

After Mass we visited John Campbell and his wife in their home which stands above the harbour, sheltered by a variety of trees. The Campbells have planted the trees, and in Canna House have created a rare atmosphere compounded of love for their environment and scholarly knowledge of it. The remains of several old Celtic crosses found on Canna, and some palaeolithic stones with rubbed ends leaned against the outside walls. A pink Albertine rose in full flower curved below the windows, and indoors its scent mingled with bronze sunbeams lighting the surfaces of old furniture and books. The open piano and small Irish harp were instances of the Campbells' love for music; the old prints of Canna under MacDonald ownership reminders of the island's history; and all the objects, collected with love and care, evidence of a rare perception. Mrs Campbell told us of a splendid Celtic cross to be seen in a field behind the post office, and of an ancient Celtic nunnery on the south coast of the island.

We decided to visit the nunnery that afternoon. Its ruins, named Rudha Sgor nam Ban-naoma (the headland of the holy women), are best reached by sea, but being Sunday no boat was available. We set off along the road and were soon offered a lift in a Land-Rover loaded with laughing children. Squeezed among them, we were told they were on their way to a picnic in Tarbert Bay – a very different way of spending Sunday, I reflected, from the restricted Free Church habits of Raasay's population.

Tarbert, when we reached it, consisted of a deserted farm cottage poised on top of a hillside. (Our Anglican curate friend whom we had met on the journey to Canna and who was sharing our lodgings with Mary Ann MacLean, fell in love with it and wanted to occupy it there and then.) A herd of Highland cattle, tan, black and cream, cropped the short grass above the cliffs, the bull calves as shaggy as huge St Bernard dogs. And beyond them lay a narrow sheep track, our route to the shore.

We were all taken aback by its exposure. Hugging the foot of a steep cliff-face it wound along the top of precipitous grass and rock slopes. The beach was a good 500 feet below. A steady head and a sure foot were needed to traverse it safely.

Brian had recently broken two ribs in a rough sea off Raasay and wished to be treated with care, and our Anglican friend had no experience of heights. Both looked doubtfully at the track. But there was no other way down. Treading cautiously we set off along the dizzy route. It ended in a steep grass slope down which we slid. And then finally, there below, was a grass peninsula, the abode of the holy nuns. We reached it with nothing more amiss than slightly frayed nerves.

The shore around the site was of flat black volcanic lava, pitted with pools. A circle of half-buried stones stood in the grass among scabious, prunella and a few late sea-pinks. Close by was another circle – perhaps an altar – and the ruins of a house foundation. That was all that remained of the dwelling place of the holy women. Inaccessible by land, unless they risked the exposed walk, all their supplies must have come by sea, for it was impossible to imagine anything growing on this rocky shore. Yet the isolated position was typical of the foundations of the early Celtic Church.

After two abortive attempts to find another way back – up the steep grass slope to the cliffs above which proved unclimbable, and along the rocky coast until stopped by a deep inlet of sea – we braved the giddy track once more, and finally arrived safely back on the road.

We turned for home. The evening light, radiant on the water, splashed deep shadows over Rhum. High on the cliffs above the road sat a golden eagle, gazing motionless into the setting sun. Some ravens called, gliding between sea and sky, and their hoarse chuckle drowned for a moment the smaller noises of song-birds twittering to sleep at the day's end.

Mary Ann was waiting for us outside her front door.

'The *sun*set,' she said. 'The *sun*set over Rhum. Colours . . . colours, you'd be watching for hours. For *hours*. You couldn't believe how many. In June, July – early June till late July – that's the best time. It's well you saw the *sun*set. I believe it's more beautiful here than anywhere else in the Isles.'

Before leaving Canna next day, we wanted to see the Celtic Cross and to climb Compass Hill, the island's highest point. We found the cross standing in a rank field. Over six feet high, it is, indeed, a splendid example of Celtic art, and if complete would be superb, but one wing has been defaced and the top arm is missing. On the shaft the Pictish symbol of a man riding a horse is carved, and below are a man and a woman, she carrying a baby, he touching her breast. There are also three animals, one with head curled to flank, another with head bent and a long nose like an elephant, the third (on the right-hand arm of the cross) shaped like a camel.

Mrs Campbell had told me that these invented forms of animals are called zoomorphics and that they date from the earliest period of Celtic art. True representations of animals and of man were hardly ever then executed, perhaps because of a religious taboo which dictated that man must not presume to copy living things whose creation was the prerogative of the deity. But the imagination of these early artists stretched wide enough to conceive forms like elephants and camels, and they are portrayed with great assurance and vitality.

Compass Hill is a volcanic crater now overgrown with grass. Ships are wary of sailing too close to it as the iron in the rock is liable to deflect their compasses, hence its name.

The sea-cliffs which ring it, fall with vertiginous steepness direct into the sea and give Canna its formidable eastern outline. Nearby, north of the harbour, rises an isolated stack of rock, sea on three sides of it. It is called An Coroghan, and the ruined tower on top is said to have been the prison of a Clanranald wife, incarcerated by her jealous chieftain husband where, in Sir Walter Scott's words:

> ... Canna's tower steep and grey
> Like falcon's nest o'erhangs the bay.

Not only falcons, but also Manx shearwaters, puffins and guillemots breed on the island, and on the flatter rocks to the west grey seals have their nurseries.

The view west from Compass Hill haunted me and during our last hours on Canna I climbed the 500-foot spine which runs across the island to see it again. I walked swiftly over ridges of heather, each one higher than the last, until finally a magnificent panorama burst into view.

Across a sheet of sea the Uists, Barra, and its tail of islands shimmered, iridescent pearls strung along the edge of the world. Nearer at hand the Cuillins towered, a dramatic purple wall; while to the south, beyond the heights of Rhum, the far shapes of Coll and Tiree darkened the water. I could see Oisgeach, the low-lying reef six miles distant which is a breeding ground for kittiwakes, eider duck, terns and seals; and away to the far south-west the Ardnamurchan peninsula fading into lilac shadow, its colour diminishing like a minor chord, tone by tone from the sea's deep-blue. From this circle of mountains and water came no sound. All was as still as on the day of creation.

I remembered a question Brian had asked me the evening before: 'If the condition was that you must never again leave the island, would you choose to remain on Canna?'

The archetypal question for the archetypal island! It could not be answered logically; no cerebral weighing-up of pros and cons would avail. The space and silence around invalidated words.

Yet something older than the conscious mind had awakened in this remote place. A memory, a recognition? An awareness of ancient modes of being which perhaps themselves contained the answer? I did not know. I let the question go and it became lost in the blue reaches of sky and sea.

Leaving or staying, I thought, Canna will always now be with me.

13

The Southern Islands

Islay, Jura, Colonsay, Coll, Tiree, Mull, Iona

I had now lived on Raasay for some years. I knew the island well and also many of its inhabitants. I had explored its paths and beaches, fished its waters, watched the sun rise on its horizon and set behind its hills, felt its magic at all seasons. At first I had peopled it in my imagination with figures of the past. Then I had become aware of the controversies and problems of the present. And now the haven of peace and solitude which I had first sought seemed to be receding from me.

Was this island too small, too remote, too cut off from the world? Were its problems insoluble? Must they inevitably lead to internal feuds and enmities? Were the people here facing a slow death? I asked myself these questions and suddenly behind the beauty of the scenery, beyond the cottage gardens and the friendly croft houses I began to sense an anxiety, a hopelessness of inactivity, a numbed waiting for the end. The dead hand of the Church, with its rigid standards; the lack of opportunity for the young; the ageing population. These things depressed me and became ever more apparent to my eyes. There seemed so little evidence of initiative, or resourcefulness. So much laissez-faire.

I'd like to see some other islands, I thought, and compare Raasay with them. I'd like to find out how Raasay's problems are tackled elsewhere, whether conditions differ on different islands, or whether Raasay is unique, what hope there is for Raasay's future . . . I felt restricted and, for the first time, ill at ease.

And so I decided to set off on a trip to the southern Inner Hebrides, those islands which lie along the coast below the Ardnamurchan peninsula, pieces of land which had gleamed so seductively for me across the sea, and which now seemed to beckon me to a different experience.

What would I find in my quest, I wondered, as I leaned over the deck-rail of the Western Ferries steamer, which was taking me to Islay, southern and most historic of the group? The gun-metal sea was restless with unbroken waves and the sky stormy. But as I watched, the sun broke through clouds and cast a pathway of silver light across the water. An omen? Gradually the moving surface calmed and as the sun's orbit increased the sea was transformed to a deep still blue. The legendary hills of Islay and Jura, her sister island, rose into view and the steamer moved quietly towards them, eating up the ocean miles as sailing ships, galleys, and raw-hide coracles had done for centuries past. The weave of the Hebridean Islands was indivisible, I knew, but here might be some trace of the languorous South, some respite from the stern Northern atmosphere of Raasay and Skye.

Later that evening I stood on the old bridge which crosses the River Sorn at Bridgend. Dark brown, with surface flecks of foam, its peaty waters flowed through the little hamlet and divided the few stone houses, the one shop and the bank. Two white ducks were exploring the water, fishing for their supper. The road near Bridgend had run between green fields decorated with small haystacks, each with its own cap. Iris and meadow-sweet spilled on to the tarmac and the grey stone walls of Islay House nearby enclosed wind-bitten sycamores, chestnuts, and lavish rhododendrons.

All seemed fertile, warm and sensuous. Yet the sea, glimpsed across a *machair* of short grass, brought a vivid tang, linking this landscape with my own barren Raasay, and the sky was washed with the same luminous light.

As night fell I wandered over the machair towards the wet sands. From six o'clock onwards birds had been flying into the head of Loch Indaal, and the air was full of their calls. Curlew, oystercatcher and plover sounded, and a drove of herring gull flew past to join the huge black-backed gulls on the beach. Pools in the short-cropped turf reflected the sunset, then darkened under grey and silver clouds.

The vast skyscape changed slowly from rose to indigo, and a waxing moon appeared, half-full, and brightened as the light waned. The blue-black sea was felt rather than seen, its waves just audible. A cow lowed, a surprised rabbit scampered away to freeze on the beach-line, and the lights of Bowmore, the little town across the bay, pricked out one by one.

The sweep of maize-coloured sand held rows and rows of birds, feathers beginning to puff out ready for sleep. Water, spread between the machair and the sand, reflected the fast of the light, while a lone curlew limned in black flew silently home. Last of all came a cloud of lapwings, tossing through the sky like bits of torn paper, one shade darker than the encircling night.

Silence accentuated by bird calls. Space, peace. The sea's throb bringing awareness of the land's isolation. Twenty-three miles from Scotland, twenty-three miles to Ireland, alone in the ocean, her birds, cattle and plants already drowsy, Islay prepared for sleep.

Seen from the air or on a map Islay looks rather like an ungainly bird flying north, with Jura in the east as one enlarged wing, and the jutting peninsula of the Rhinns in the west, as the other. Two sea-lochs cut deeply into the land, Loch Gruinart from the north and Loch Indaal from the south, and at the head of Loch Indaal is Bowmore, the island's capital.

It is a spick-and-span town with administrative buildings, shops, a hospital, police station, and a picturesque harbour on Loch Indaal. The steep main street is crowned by a distinctive circular building – Kilarrow Parish Church, painted white and built with no corners in which the devil might lurk.

Inside, the brown varnished pews enclosed by red-painted columns wait patiently for their Sunday congregation, while outside Atlantic clouds race across clear windows. A Cradle

Roll lists the names of children who have been baptised here: Campbells, Carmichaels, Shaws, Mackenzies and MacLeans. No turbulent MacLeods, and no denunciatory 'Wee Free' minister. This Presbyterian kirk has an atmosphere of ordered calm and peace.

Near the church, also on the hill, is Bowmore's School, housing about five hundred and twenty children, from primary level up to the age of eighteen.

'Do the children speak Gaelic?' I asked the hospitable headmaster.

'They learn it throughout their secondary schooling, and it's compulsory in the first year,' he replied. 'But it's not their natural language, as it used to be. We took a choir to the National Modh a short while back and we heard the Lewis children chatting away in Gaelic. But not ours.'

I thought of the whispered Gaelic conversations of children and their parents in Raasay's shop, an island where Gaelic is still the first language.

A number of the school's pupils leave Islay when they leave school, although there is employment for them in the farms and distilleries at home. But many return for holidays. In Port Charlotte alone there are forty-three holiday homes owned by former Islay citizens.

This village, chief centre of the western peninsula of the Rhinns, has great charm. Rows of double-storey, terraced houses line streets with Gaelic names. Each house is painted white or cream, and each has doors and windows in a bright contrasting colour – blue, red, terra-cotta, brown or black. The houses stand, gay and orderly, above the neat harbour with its sandy bay, stone pier, lobster pots and sailing dinghies.

Island villages often grow casually out of the countryside, formed by the fold of a hill or the curve of a burn, hardly distinguishable from their surroundings. But Port Charlotte asserts its presence with confidence, undismayed by the vast skyscape above or the wide stretch of sea beyond. Here Islay expatriates can enjoy all the benefits of a Hebridean holiday without being committed to living in the Hebrides all the year round.

Islay has the longest recorded history of any of the Isles,

for Irish warriors came here in the first half of the third century and stayed to colonize Argyll and found the kingdom of Dalriada of which Islay and Jura were a part. So Christianity reached these shores from Ireland long before it came to the islands of the wilder north. On the western coast of the Rhinns, near Port Charlotte, is a ruined chapel at Kilchairan, said to be founded by St Columba on his way to Iona in 563, and farther north stands the Kilchoman Cross, one of the most beautiful of Islay's seventeen crosses. It rests in the churchyard of a seventh-century Christian foundation, where the beat of Atlantic rollers mingles with bird-song and the voices of cows and sheep are interrupted by the wind's stir. Slim and tall, it bears on one side the figure of Christ crucified and on the other an intertwining floral design still distinct although the cross was erected in the fourteenth century. John, Lord of the Isles, put it there in memory of his wife Princess Margaret, daughter of the first Stuart king.

In contrast, the Kildalton Cross, in the south of the island, has a pastoral setting in a ruined churchyard, framed by trees. It is much earlier in origin, made from a single block of the local epidiorite stone about AD 800, and erected, not as a monument to a grave, but by a living person to the glory of God. Its massive shape, in a wonderful grey-green colour, is carved into elaborate patterns of spirals and interlacings, scriptural scenes and animals. The Virgin, flanked by two angels, gazes meditatively across the quiet countryside towards Kilchoman and her crucified son.

The Isles' Christianity did little to curtail their bloody clan feuds, but it has left the legacy of a few beautiful objects, such as these two crosses. And more; an indefinable mystery which surrounds them, part of their durability, and a source of spiritual solace to all who seek them out.

A different kind of solace is obtained from Islay's chief export – her smooth, strong whisky, 80% proof. On a rainy day there is no better occupation than to sit in one of the island's cheerful pubs, sampling it. There are six brands to choose from, for six distilleries operate on Islay, each with its own distinctive blend and name. 20,000 gallons of whisky are exported each week, and the distilleries form an important source of employment. What would Raasay's church elders say, I wondered, at this surfeit of whisky and the opportunities which flow from it – not least the opportunity to drink in company in an atmosphere of good fellowship, rather than behind the closed doors necessitated by church disapproval and opposition to an alcohol licence?

Though Islay's history is rich – as the seat of the Lords of the Isles she occupied a position of unique power for over four hundred years – her people do not live in the past. Good transport to the mainland assures markets for their farm products. Tourists come, but have not overrun the island. The large sporting estates and the distilleries provide employment, but in spite of this many of the young leave for the mainland, the boys to join the Merchant Navy, the girls to train as teachers or nurses. Islay has the same problem as all the Hebrides – a falling population. Nevertheless, her ties with her children abroad are strong. Money is sent back from them to the island, and often on retirement they return. They have found nowhere which can truly compare with their own island – 'the Queen of the Hebrides'.

6,000 deer share Jura, the deer island (christened *Dyr Oe* by the Norse), with two hundred people. The people live on the east coast, the deer mainly on the west, a wild region of hills and caves, accessible only by boat or by stalkers on foot. Jura is bleak in comparison to Islay; at first sight like Raasay, long and thin with the same desolate approach, but larger, twenty-eight miles by eight. A mere quarter-mile of sea divides the two islands, but Jura has none of Islay's fertility, no prosperous farms, only one distillery manned mainly by outsiders from Glasgow, and little crofting. Four large sporting estates and six deer forests provide the island's main source of revenue and work.

Once Jura supported many more people. In the eighteenth century the island was a centre for the breeding and transport of Highland cattle and was famous for the quality of its Highland bulls. Donald Budge in his book *Jura* writes of these cattle, 'dignified and stylish . . . endowed with a remarkable degree of intelligence and intuition'. By 1841 the population had risen to 1,320. But then came emigration, the introduction of sheep farming, the impoverishment of good crofting land, and the slow drain of population abroad. A typical island story, I thought, as I drove up Jura's one road. Above me the Paps of Jura, three high hills rising to 2,400 feet, flew pennants of white and gold cloud. Flowers spilled from the cottage gardens of Craighouse, the capital, down to the lochside. And on the loch drifted a family of whooper swans.

I was on my way to dinner at Tarbert Lodge, owned by William Astor, the young grandson of the second Lord Astor who bought the Lodge and its deer forest in 1902. At Tarbert a narrow neck of land only a mile wide joins north and south Jura. The wide inlet of Loch Tarbert winds in from the west, and to the east a small peninsula juts into Tarbert Bay. The Lodge stands at the end of it. I turned off the road and drove along a rough track, bumping over undulating moorland, looking in vain for the house. The wind had risen, bringing mist and rain, and in the failing light it was hard to see. A white building glimmered to the left of the road. I was past it before I realized it must be the Lodge. Late already, I struggled to turn the car. When it was broadside across the narrow road, I backed for a further turn. 'Careful now,' I said to myself, 'ease her round, inch by inch.' Suddenly – *crunch*. My back wheels shuddered. I slammed on the brake, but too late. Slowly, with a dread irrevocability, the whole back of the car subsided, and lurched into a ditch at the side of the road.

I leapt out and started to run back to the dim white building. Hopes of help mingled with my embarrassment. How could I explain my predicament? I reached the house. No lights, no sign of life. I peered through the twilit windows. No people. A dog barked and a spatter of rain dripped from a gutter. The eerie walls rose, shabby and untenanted. No help. I turned back to the car which was still parked slap across the road. No kind fairy had moved it. There was nothing to do but trudge on along the track. How it curved, how it dropped and lifted, and at the crest of each hill how my hopes rose, only to be dashed again! The wind shrieked across the moor, water soaked the hem of my long skirt, rain washed away my party make-up. I was near despair when at last the lights of the Lodge gleamed away to the left of the road. I ran towards them, too cold and wet to care any longer about excuses.

William Astor and his friends welcomed me, heaved my car out of the ditch and then gave me an excellent dinner. After it, we sat round a peat fire and talked about stalking in Jura. William is the third generation of his family to occupy Tarbert Lodge. His young, sensitive Renaissance face lights up as he talks of it, but like most sporting landlords he is in the main an absentee, spending only a few months each year on his estate. Seven men are employed full time – a source of regular income for these islanders – and the stalkers cull carefully when shooting the deer, keeping the welfare of the whole herd in mind. So a few Jura men and beasts benefit from his tenancy. Sporting estates like his help to keep the last wild uninhabited areas of Britain intact. But at an enormous cost. Many of their owners have to sub-let them. Was the lively Texan lady in the sequin poncho whom I met at dinner, and who had slain two beasts on the hill that day, a prospective tenant for next year's summer shoot? Highland estates, like much of the rest of Britain, tend to be in thrall to US money.

As I carefully drove back to the hotel, thinking about this, I reflected that perhaps a quixotic American or Arab who would buy and restore Raasay House, might be one solution for that island. My headlights illuminated the brooding moor, sending a swathe of light across it for an instant, then flinging it back into darkness. There, in that mysterious gloom, lived the true inhabitants of deer island.

The third island in the Islay-Jura group is Colonsay. Like Islay, it lies far out to sea, twenty-five miles from the mainland. Atlantic rollers break on its western shores, but a ring of hills protects its central farmland, and its soil is fertile.

Colonsay is a laird island, owned by Lord Strathcona, whose great-grandfather bought it in 1904. It is a small jewel of an island containing on a miniature scale all the beauties for which the Highlands are famed – heather hills, burns, sandy beaches, caves, mysterious lochs, woods. The population is slightly less than that of Raasay – one hundred and forty people – but, unlike Raasay, Colonsay has had the benefit of four generations of responsible lairdship. Its crofters and farmers consist very largely of original Gaelic-speaking stock, and their way of life has not been influenced by tourism. Caravans and camping are forbidden. Those who visit the island are mostly habitués who stay in the one hotel or rent one of the Strathconas' holiday cottages. Neither they nor the inhabitants wish for change. But change must come.

Colonsay House, where the Strathconas live, is a pleasant eighteenth-century house, painted pink and surrounded by gardens famed for their rare plants. A mile or so away, washed by Atlantic waves, stretches the Traigh Bàn of Kiloran, one of the most beautiful beaches in the Hebrides.

I walked along this beach on a windy sunny autumn day, an experience as near to Paradise as I shall get. The sky's clear colour was reflected at the tide's edge, where tongues of wet sand merged with forgotten pools. Ringed plovers pecked busily among rocks, and the surge of waves, gentle on this calm day as though heard through a shell, sounded like the soft breathing of the sea. At the far end of the beach is the Lady's Cave, a place where many Neolithic remains have been unearthed: flint tools and weapons, Bronze Age brooches, earthenware pottery. I sat on a driftwood tree-stump and gazed at the view, sharing it with long-dead Stone Age men, Picts, Scots, Norsemen and Celts, all of whom used this cave. In the dunes behind the beach a Viking grave was discovered, complete with a Viking warrior interred with weapons and ship. And at Kilchattan village, farther inland, are two standing stones of unknown antiquity.

Colonsay inhabitants, however, are less interested in these relics of the far past than in prospects of the immediate future. The laird tradition is costly and the Strathconas may not be able to maintain it for much longer. They have already sold Oronsay, the tidal island off Colonsay's southern shore.

Colonsay's farmers and crofters virtually own their land and stock, but their island's future is inevitably deeply affected by the character and resources of the laird. Pub conversations tend to veer towards this topic.

The visitors: 'People here are living a sort of feudal existence, largely dependent on the laird.'

'Old Lord Strathcona, this one's father, pumped about £15,000 a year into the island and never refused a request for repairs.'

'That's the tradition they're used to. Yet the average crofter pays only £15 a year in rent.'

The inhabitants: 'The laird makes money on the hotel and his holiday cottages. He should put some of that money back into the island.'

'He should run the home farm.'

'He's trying to make the island self-supporting.'

'He'll pull out if he can't, you wait and see.'

Remembering the fate of Raasay House and its effect on Raasay's inhabitants I could understand the islanders' concern.

Colonsay was first inhabited by the legendary Sith folk, the small people who built the ancient burial mounds found in Colonsay and Oronsay. They were followed by Picts, MacPhees, MacDonalds and MacNeils. MacNeils still occupy the chief Colonsay farms; and the whole island of Oronsay is worked as one large farm by Andrew MacNeil (a fine piper who traces his line of teachers directly back to Angus MacKay of Raasay) and his wife Flora. His thousand acres of grazing land is cut off by the tide from Colonsay twice a day – a formidable mile-wide barrier, as I was to discover when I reached it at 5 pm one evening. Low tide was at 7 pm but I hoped to get across the strand sooner. The water was deep and running fast, uncompromisingly cold. I waded into it from a jutting headland, but it was soon above my knees. Forced to retreat, I stood shivering on a rocky island, only quarter-way across. The tide sank imperceptibly and I resigned myself to a long cold vigil. But after half an hour or so a tractor emerged from the Oronsay shore, drove straight into the flood, churning water above the wheel-hubs, and finally hauled out on the other side.

Taking heart, I plunged in again. The tide had ebbed and the water this time was no higher than my calves. Grinding small hard sea-shells underfoot, I waded to the Oronsay shore.

Like several islands I was to visit, St Columba had landed before me. He named Oronsay after St Oran, his devoted disciple, and founded a monastery on its southern shore. He chose a site of great beauty, remote and within sound of the sea. Today the ruins of a fourteenth-century Augustinian priory stand there.

I reached the priory with numbed feet, after a swift mile-and-a-half walk along the road in a biting North wind. As I rounded the last corner Ben Oronsay's grey cliffs towered up. and below, in their shelter, stood the priory's ancient dry-stone buildings, the same colour as the cliffs but washed by the setting sun with a patina of gold. The wind dropped and the peace of the place took over.

The church was roofless, its floor grass, its walls topped by wild flowers. A mullioned window, a niche with human bones. The arches of the small cloisters enclosed vignettes of hill and sea. By the entrance, a high Celtic cross, slim-shafted like Islay's Kilchoman Cross, bore also a crucified Christ. In the mortuary chapel of the MacPhees, on one of the twenty-seven tombstone slabs, a sword and galley were incised, insignia of the Lords of the Isles.

The silence was absolute, unchanging since the time of Columba. History had fallen away from these stones but the spirit which gave them life remained. A pilgrim coming here in any century would recognize it.

I waded back to Colonsay, with the water now only ankle-deep, listening to the cries of curlew, oystercatcher and plover. In the centre of the strand I met Flora MacNeil, returning from her visit to Colonsay. She told me that my feet would be sore from walking on the sea-shells. She was wearing wellingtons.

'Never mind,' she said, 'you enjoy yourself while you can.'

A warm smile lit up her very blue eyes. We turned away from one another, she to her lonely island, I to my car, a hot bath, dinner, the hotel. It was almost dark. A last ray of light streamed over the wet sand and a few birds flew low above its reflection. The space and silence were like the beginning of time. Six thousand years ago the Mesolithic men who built the conical middens on Oronsay's shores had known the same peace. Christians had given it a name and enshrined it in buildings. Modern man had lost it. Was my quest, I suddenly wondered, a pilgrimage to find it again?

Oronsay's beauty had put me into a trance-like dream. Next morning I shook myself and reminded myself that my quest was not merely a personal one, a search for my own peace and happiness, but rather a means of assessing the differences and resemblances between the Southern Islands and Raasay. If I saw solutions here to some of the Hebridean problems they might be valid for Raasay as well. But Raasay possessed no large farms or distilleries like Islay. No deer (or only very few) like Jura. No conscientious laird like Colonsay. The life-patterns which I had observed in these three islands were based on conditions which did not exist in Raasay and therefore would not be applicable. Where should I go next?

I remembered two small pieces of land which I had first seen from Canna several years before. Dark-blue shapes lying far out to sea, shimmering on the horizon, they had fired my imagination and I had asked their names. Coll and Tiree. Rising only 300 or so feet above sea-level, made of the same ancient gneiss rock as the north of Raasay and Rona, their shores washed by the Atlantic, no land between them and Labrador . . . Yes, I thought, that is where I shall go. And maybe in these remote oceanic islands I will find what I am searching for.

So I boarded a steamer in Oban and set sail for Coll. I had time to reflect during the four-hour journey that on this occasion it was Dr Johnson, not St Columba, who had been there before me. The storm which raged as his ship approached Coll has been vividly described by Boswell: 'A prodigious sea, with immense billows coming upon a vessel, so that it hardly seemed possible to escape. There was something grandly horrible in the sight.'

Dr Johnson, when consulted as to whether or not to take shelter, cried, 'Coll for my money,' and so after 'violent plunging in the rough sea', to Coll's harbour they eventually safely came.

I was more fortunate with the weather, but even so my first sight of Coll was forbidding; a bleak spine of rock thirteen miles long, sparsely covered in moor. No roads, houses, fields or livestock. Not a person to be seen.

The s.s. *Columba* sailed for a while up Coll's coast, then turned into Loch Eatherna and berthed at a good modern pier. And at once the atmosphere changed. The island's main village, Arinagour, disclosed itself; a street of attractive single-storey, white-washed houses, each with a bright garden. The spacious loch caught reflections of the sky, and at its head stood the hotel, well-kept and friendly. Poised on top of a hill, guarding all and completing the picture was a weather-beaten grey kirk.

Living on Coll is like living on the deck of a liner. Ocean winds tear across the moorland, and the skyscapes are vast, great domes of white, purple and blue. When storms rage the whins are bent flat and waves thunder on to the Atlantic beaches. But there are more periods of calm than storm. The climate is mild, and several large farms flourish on Coll.

The largest, Breachacha, is owned by the Stewarts, lairds of Coll. It has 6000 acres of land, 500 breeding cattle and about 1200 sheep. Breachacha means 'speckled field'; the wealth of wild flowers there gave it its name. These provide wonderful grazing for cattle and sheep, as does also the springy green turf which borders the sandy beaches all along Coll's Atlantic coast.

At Breachacha are two castles, an ancient one built as part of the Lords of the Isles' defence system, and a more modern one, in which Dr Johnson stayed, 'a mere tradesman's box' he called it, 'there was nothing becoming a chief about it'. Nevertheless it was the home of the MacLeans of Coll from 1750 until the island was sold in 1856 to Stewart of Glenbuckie, ancestor of the present laird. Now it is being renovated as a holiday home. And the old castle, which still retains many of its medieval features, is also occupied. It has been splendidly restored by Major MacLean Bristol who bought it in 1961, and now lives there with his family.

I saw this pattern of restoration repeated in other parts of Coll. The two castles stand at its apex, so to speak, but when I drove round the island with Janet Stewart, the laird's wife, she pointed out a number of ruined crofts which had been bought as holiday homes and were in the process of renovation.

'Their owners come here regularly for holidays,' she said. 'I think it does a service to the incomers and to the island.'

Not all the renovation has been undertaken by tourists. We passed the little village of Bousd where a young farm worker and his wife have transformed an old ruin into a spacious open-plan dwelling, doing all the work themselves, including the spinning of textiles. Farther on is Scorisdal, a tiny crofting community on the extreme eastern tip of the island. There three old bachelors occupy the last inhabited house. When they die it will pass to a nephew in the Merchant Navy who may decide to live there and transform it into a new home. While close by, another ruin has recently been renovated and occupied by an Edinburgh art master and his family.

This tendency gave me food for thought. I knew that most of Coll's indigenous crofters had emigrated to Canada and Australia in the 1840s. The island was then laid out as farms, and dairy farmers from the mainland settled it. Today not one child on the school-roll comes from a Gaelic-speaking family. So an influx of 'strangers' would be nothing new in Coll's history, and if the incomers show respect for the island and its ways, they would not be unwelcome. Raasay could learn, I thought, from this development. There are plenty of ruined croft houses on that island which could be put to better use than merely shelter for sheep.

Coll has a series of magnificent beaches. On my last morning I stood above one of the finest, Feall Bay, situated on the Coales peninsula at the island's tail. Behind me spikes of marram grass covered a wilderness of undulating dunes; before me Atlantic rollers beat on to a half-moon of yellow sand.

I listened to their roar and hiss and watched the sun slanting on the distant moor. Its rays drew nearer, illuminating the wet beach, then running with a glitter of fire across seaweed and spume. The sea turned a radiant blue and the waves rose and fell, rose and fell.

I needed nothing but their ancient music, satisfying as the wind's ripple through grass, the thunder of surf on rock, the rotation of the year's flowers on the machair. It is for these rhythms of nature that people come here, I thought. To experience them is like lowering a bucket into a deep well and drawing it up full of the clear waters of life. An indispensable source of human health and strength.

On Coll, I reflected, it is not only buildings that are restored. People too.

Although Coll and Tiree are only a few miles apart, with a regular steamer service running between them, they have little other communication. On each of them I was asked what possessed me to visit the other. Geographically they are similar; both swept by fierce winds, both treeless, both oceanic in flavour. But there the resemblance ends. Their ways of life are different. The large Coll farms are in private hands, and a number of the croft houses are being turned into holiday homes. Tiree, on the other hand, blessed with miles of fertile machair and the highest long-term average of sun in Britain, is a crofter's paradise.

St Columba called Tiree his granary and it has always been known as Tir Iodh, the Land of Corn. Through the centuries wind has blown shell-sand from its magnificent beaches to overlay its gneiss rock, and this has resulted in a fertile plain on which crops, cattle and sheep flourish. Tiree's population is one thousand, almost nine times the number of Coll, and crofting is their chief occupation. No farm is larger than sixty acres; the land is divided up into nearly three hundred small crofts, and these are worked by individual families, and by clubs of crofters who hold grazing rights.

Brilliant sunshine greeted me as I landed in Tiree. White houses clustered round the pier and strung themselves out to the village of Scarinish and beyond along the two-mile stretch of dazzling sand which fringes Hynish Bay. I turned inland, where a thousand-acre plain, the Reef, stretches to the west coast. The RAF established an airport there during the War and it still functions, providing regular flights to the mainland.

Driving across the Reef, much of which is below sea-level, is like sailing on a shimmering emerald ocean. A church or a house on the horizon rises into view like a ship at sea. The sun, unimpeded in the vast skyscape, casts a purity of light radiant as a jewel. I drove through these immensities and reached Cornaigmore and Cornaigbeg, townships on the north-west coast. Fields of yellow oats and barley bound by dry-stone walls alternated with haystacks and vivid green pasture. Cattle grazed right down to the shore, then wandered along it in search of salt.

Cornaig School has one hundred and thirty pupils and thirteen staff.

'Flora Mary, Mairi, Iain, Hamish,' called the nimble physical training instructress as the bright-eyed, red-cheeked boys and girls ran to their places in the class I watched. The children looked healthy, happy and uninhibited. Ninety per cent of them come from Gaelic-speaking homes. They grow up entirely on the island, but once their schooling is finished they have to leave, for a croft cannot support more than one son. The girls go into banking, nursing and teaching. A few stay in Coll's one knitwear factory (a second may soon open). Many of the boys enter the Merchant Navy; some become teachers. An ex-Cornaig pupil is now head of the Celtic Department of Glasgow University.

I remarked on the immaculate appearance of the houses on Tiree.

'Yes, they're well-kept indeed,' the teacher replied. 'Of course, they have to be redecorated often because of the elements. But there's also a certain amount of keeping up with the Joneses. No one wants a shabby house in comparison to their neighbours.'

The Duke of Argyll owns Tiree. The Campbells took it over in 1674 when the MacLeans of Tiree who had espoused the

Stuart cause, lost their estates through forfeiture. But for all practical purposes the future of the island is in the hands of the crofters. Through wise re-allocation of land (achieved after the First World War, when the big farms were divided and the very small crofts enlarged), Tiree has become, with Skye, the most heavily crofted island in the west. The crofting townships are close-knit and have a thriving community life. This is reinforced in the summer when expatriate sons and daughters fly in for the holidays bringing their children with them to experience the island's charms. Thus the live Gaelic tradition is handed on.

Tiree's crofters are helped by fertile soil, low rainfall and good transport. But even more by housing grants from the Department of Agriculture, and an intelligent interest which encourages crofting as a way of life. These are the aids, I thought, which Raasay needs: improvement of transport, grants for new houses, development of roads. If the miasma of neglect which broods over that island could be lifted, there is no reason why the indigenous people of Raasay should not achieve as successful an existence as those of Tiree.

I left Tiree with regret. I felt saturated with sun and sea; moved also by its remote beauty and heartened by the unexpected prosperity I had found.

The *Columba* steamed slowly across a vivid sea and other islands rose like beacons on the horizon – Eigg, Rhum, Skye, Islay, Jura, Colonsay. All now familiar to me. The space and clarity of light gave the voyage an epic quality, a journey over fabled waters to fabled shores. Soon it would end. Only two more islands remained for me to visit – Mull and Iona. Mull, famed in song and legend. Iona, the holy isle at its tip.

Mull resembles Skye in size and in its dramatic scenery. But unlike Skye it is a sporting island with deer forests, three very large farms, and a number of smaller ones of about 4,000 acres. Crofting is minimal, compared to Skye, and most of the farms are owned by incomers. Mull's mountains are volcanic (Ben More, the highest, was originally one of the chain of volcanoes which stretched up the west coast) and this gives the landscape a romantic brooding quality which is enhanced by rain-filled clouds and sombre light. In contrast Tobermory, the island's capital, seems gay. Its eighteenth-century houses with their colour-washed walls of pink, yellow, dark-red and dark-blue, have a Continental air, and the fine harbour they face is crammed with yachts, fishing boats, pleasure-cruisers and the ubiquitous MacBrayne steamers, bound for Coll, Tiree and the Outer Isles.

I landed at Tobermory and took the inland road over the hills to the village of Dervaig. I wondered why its main street looked familiar, and then remembered that it had been built at the same time and on the same plan as Arinagour in Coll. The then laird of Coll had also owned Quinish estate in Mull (where I was bound) and had established both villages at the turn of the eighteenth century.

Nothing much seems to have changed since then, I thought, as the car ricocheted up the serrated access road to the house of my friends.

My host greeted me in a kilt tattered enough to have been worn at Culloden. After a hearty kiss, 'Come round the farm,' he said. We piled into an old Land-Rover and bumped round his policies. Fields bound by dry-stone walls lay gold and green under the autumn sun. Beyond, grass slopes rose to heather moors and in the distance shone the sea.

I learned that all my host's 2000 acres were looked after by himself with the help of only one other man, a shepherd from the Ross of Mull.

'We have about one hundred cattle, fifty or so of them breeding cows, and five hundred sheep. It's damned hard work but you have to face that, if you elect to farm on an island. And a lot of other problems, too.'

'Such as . . . ?'

'High transport costs for instance. Everything costs more and takes longer to get here.'

'And sales of stock are all on the mainland?'

'Yes. We used to send our stock loose on the steamer, and all the owners had to turn out to load it. Loading cattle and sheep at six am on a winter morning was no joke, but in a way it was good for local morale. Everyone was in it together. Now the sheep travel in floats, direct to the Oban market, one hundred in each float, two storeys high.'

'And the prices?'

'They vary. Island farmers are at a disadvantage. We *have* to sell. Can't bring the stock home again. We don't want special treatment, only fair prices, but we don't always get them.'

I had heard the same story from the MacLeod shepherds in Raasay.

'Yes,' he continued, 'it's a struggle to keep going. I have to sell off land and possessions from time to time to carry on. But we all love the island, it's where we want to be, and you have to make sacrifices to live where you want to. Mull hasn't been spoilt yet by tourists, like Skye. Personally, I'm thankful for MacBrayne's high steamer costs. Keeps out the casual visitors who scatter their litter on the roads and empty their san-cans in the burns.'

He stubbed out his cigarette savagely, visualizing an offending camper, then said, 'As a matter of fact, I deal in tourists myself. I let seven houses to visitors in the summer, and some all the year round. That has its problems, too. But most of the people who come here love the place and return to it year after year. That's the kind of tourist we want – people who *give* something to the island. Not morons in immense coaches who do nothing but tear up our narrow roads!'

I drove along those roads the next day, skirting the west coast with its spectacular islands: the Treshnish, where grey Atlantic seals breed, Ulva, and green Inch Kenneth, visited by Johnson and Boswell on their way to Iona and described by Boswell as 'furnished with unexpected neatness and convenience . . . the kindness of hospitality and refinement of courtesy', in contrast to 'the gloom of desolation' which was his impression of Mull.

The road unfolded below green slopes, an occasional hayfield glowing near an old stone cottage. Hump-back bridges spanned small burns, and in the sea-loch bracken slopes were reflected in a glassy calm, moved only by long tide ripples and the shapes of purple and silver clouds. Over all brooded the high Mull mountains, sombre and mist-clad like a Landseer print.

The atmosphere of romance deepened and reached its apex at Duart Castle on the south coast. This picturesque residence, ancestral home of the MacLeans, is built on a crag – Dhu Ard, black rock – which towers high above the junction of three waterways; the Sound of Mull, the Firth of Lorn and Loch Linnhe. It was part of the defence system of the Lords of the Isles, and MacLeans lived there from 1390 until their support for the Stuart cause led to the forfeiture of their lands in 1715. Their home fell into ruin but was restored in 1912 by Sir Fitzroy Donald MacLean. Now his son, the twenty-seventh chief of his line, lives there. A more romantic setting would be hard to conceive. The castle is open to tourists ('home-baking' a speciality) and they flock there. Its benign owner welcomes them with grace and aplomb, rather like the late Dame Flora MacLeod in Skye. I encountered him on the battlements, standing where the guns used to give a warning shot to any ship passing below who failed to salute the Duart flag. He informed me with a wry smile that his family had always fought on the wrong side.

Mull has another resource, in addition to farming and tourists – forestry. In recent years the Forestry Commission has planted over 14,000 acres in central Mull and given employment to fifty-five full-time workers.

'The Forestry Commission practically owns Mull,' my Dervaig host had said, bitterly. Farmers do resent the acquisition of land which they would like to see used for grazing, but anything which brings employment to Mull should be welcomed. Driving past the neat colonies of pines and larches I deplored their intrusion into the wild scenery, but wished at the same time that the same resource could be developed in Raasay, where the only remaining forest is left untended, and no new trees are planted.

So at last I came to the long Ross of Mull and the road to Iona. The day was overcast and Ben More was hidden under storm clouds. The waters of Loch Scridain moved restlessly, throwing up flecks of foam. Mull, the rain-fall island – poetic, sombre, splendid – drew away. And as her hills receded, a shaft of brilliant light burst through the clouds and illumined the way ahead like a searchlight, bathing sea and land in an ethereal blue.

I felt excited and apprehensive. Could Iona be all that I expected? I was ready to worship at Columba's shrine yet fearful of what I might find. Was it possible that his spirit, breathed into the place fourteen hundred years ago, might still remain?

I parked my car at Fionnphort on the tip of the Ross peninsula and joined the queue of tourists laden with wind-jackets, cameras, binoculars and plastic bags. We waited for the ferry, gazing hopefully at the long green smudge on the horizon. What, I wondered, had brought us all here, to pick our way carefully over slippery rocks and sit uncomfortably in a small boat on a choppy sea? The faces around me were tired, pale with indoor living, lined with anxiety. Were we the modern counterparts of the pilgrims who had made this same crossing, year after year, century after century? Or were we merely the victims of present-day tourist exploitation and of the restlessness which forces people to leave their homes and travel away, anywhere, to relieve the tedium of daily life?

The boat landed us at a jetty adjacent to a row of stone houses called The Street, and we straggled along the half-mile to the Abbey in light rain. The macadam road, the carefully placed signs, even Dr Johnson's famous appreciation of Iona reproduced on a bronze plaque nailed to a wall, all seemed a far cry from St Columba's original foundation with its simple piety and remote peace.

The Abbey stands like a massive castle in the midst of a green plain. I entered through the west door and immediately the coolness, the space and the silence laid my fears to rest. People disappeared through stone arches, the size of the building swallowed up its visitors, and quite soon each felt alone.

The greater part of the Abbey dates from 1420 when it was rebuilt after fifty years of neglect. None of St Columba's original foundation remains, but somehow his spirit has been captured within these walls. The medieval remnants like the Romanesque carvings on the capitals of the south aisle arches, and the sacristy doorway with its trefoil arch, are interesting and beautiful. But what matters most is the building's abiding peace. Outside, facing the west door, is a green hillock, Tor Abb, and on top of it are the stones which were the foundations of Columba's cell. Here he slept on bare rock, his monks below him, the lands they cultivated stretching away beyond the boundary wall.

One of the monks was St Oran, who accompanied Columba from Ireland and who, legend says, was the first to die. He was buried in the Reilig Oran, the graveyard to the south-west of the Abbey, and is commemorated there by a small eleventh-century chapel.

With him lie Kenneth MacAlpine, first King of united Scotland and Pictland, Macbeth and Duncan, Somerled's son Reginald of Islay, Kings and Lords of the Isles, and many Highland Chiefs. All were carried up the processional Street of the Dead and laid in St Oran's windswept cemetery by the sea.

Iona was a holy place and a centre for worship even before Columba's time. The Druids were there – Iona's Gaelic name was Innis nan Druinish (the Isle of the Druidic Hermits) – and in all its fortunes, waxing and waning throughout the years, the island's unique atmosphere has survived. Many times the Abbey has risen phoenix-like from its ruins; its last restoration was early this century. Today the Iona Community keeps alight the ancient flame. It has restored all the monastic buildings, and forged links between workers in industrial towns on the mainland and ministers of the Church of Scotland who together laid the stones.

St Columba lived in folk memory for centuries. He was invoked in the people's daily tasks.

By the housewife:

> In the name of Columba kindly
> I will set the eggs on Thursday.

By the weaver:

In the name of Columba, just and potent
Consecrate the four posts of my loom.

By the milkmaid:

The first flow for Columba of my love,
'Tis he clothed for thee each pit and smoothed for the
each hill,
'Tis he who guided thee home tonight unharmed.

The sailor on the sea prayed for his blessing:

I myself will sit down at the helm
It is God's own Son who will give me guidance.
As he gave to St Columba the mild
What time he set stay to sails.

In the folk imagination he watched over humble people, and cared also for animals and birds; the weary crane whose arrival on the shores of Iona he foresaw, giving direction that it should be succoured, and thanking the monk who saved it with the words, 'God bless you, my son, because you have tended well the pilgrim guest.' The swan, which tradition says he found wounded and dying.

'Whence thy journey
Swan of mourning?'
Said Columba of my love.
'From Erin by swimming
From the Fiann of my wounding
The sharp wound of my death.'

'White swan of Erin
A friend am I to the needy;
The eye of Christ be on thy wound,
The eye of affection and mercy,

The eye of kindness and love,
Making thee whole.

Swan of Erin
No harm shall touch thee,
Whole be thy wounds.'

Adamnan, his biographer, tells us that when Columba was eighty years old and near death, 'a white horse came to him, the obedient servant who was accustomed to carry the milk vessels between the pasture and the monastery . . . It began to mourn, and like a human being to let tears fall freely on the lap of the saint, and, foaming much, to weep aloud.'

The horse's attendant would have driven it away, but the saint forbade him saying, 'Let him that loves me pour out the tears of most bitter grief here in my bosom. To this brute and unreasoning animal the Creator has, in what way he would, revealed clearly that its master is going to depart from it.'

So Columba blessed his servant and his horse. And soon after, on 9 June 597, he died before the altar of his church.

His mission had been accomplished without martyrdom. But two hundred years later violence erupted on Iona. Vikings sacked the Abbey in 794, and Norse pirates destroyed it again three times, on the last occasion in 985 murdering the Abbot and fifteen of his monks. But Columba's message survived. It had already spread far, carried by pilgrims who flocked to his shrine in the two centuries after his death, by members of his far-flung foundations, and by St Aidan and his monks who, at Lindisfarne on Holy Island in Northumbria, created a second Iona. The teaching of Columba, the dove, was stronger than physical destruction. It remained inviolate.

I thought of these things as I sat in the Nunnery of St Mary, one of the most beautiful ruins in the Isles. It lies on the way from the pier to the Abbey. Reginald, King of the Isles, built it for the Benedictine Order around 1203 and made his sister Beatrice the first Abbess. Much of it still stands.

The sun sent long shadows across the grass, and the perfume of wild flowers hanging from the rose-red stones and bordering the top of the cloister walls, carried faintly in the soft air. The evening sounds – woodpigeons' coo, rooks' chatter – accentuated the stillness. It seemed that the peace of the ancient nuns had spilled over into this place, causing the grass to shine greener, the flowers to bloom brighter, the high walls to glow more roseate with their beautiful irregular pink stones. Anxious striving for identity, so important in the outer world, was here submerged and sank to rest.

I remembered the prayer with which Columba had sent forth his monks:

May the wisdom of God guide you
May the strength of God uphold you
May the peace of God possess you
May the love of God enfold you
Now and to the end of days.

I envied the simplicity and faith with which those disciples had journeyed, facing difficulties and dangers more extreme but also more tangible than today's.

Perhaps, I thought, the real problem in the islands I had visited and in Raasay was a lack of direction. The old order was passing but nothing satisfactory had yet emerged to take its place. There was no fire comparable to the one St Columba had lit, no evangelist's fervour which would preserve what was unique in the Isles and extend it to the outer world.

The expatriate sons and daughters from overseas who return to find their roots, the thousands of city dwellers who seek rest and refreshment – all these could testify to the Isles' healing and regenerative powers. But they are birds of passage. Those who actually live there too often experience disillusion, even despair. The Highland character, capable of heroism and sacrifice, of selfless devotion to a cause and of extreme loyalty, finds its worst enemy in the slow erosion of neglect.

On my tour I had seen encouraging developments: forestry in Mull, distilleries in Islay, holiday homes in Coll, viable crofting in Tiree. Both the last two could be applicable to

Raasay. But only here in Iona had I felt that inspiration of faith which is the inescapable basis of any great enterprise, the yeast which assures its growth.

Fourteen hundred years ago Columba had visited Skye. It is possible that he visited Raasay then also. That is a matter for conjecture. But what is certain, I thought, is that a modern version of his dynamic belief, his invincible faith and his overwhelming humanity is what the island most needs today.

PART IV

A Home in the Hebrides

14

Landfall

Glasgow airport was crowded at 9.30 am on a May morning in 1976. The flight from London had left late and I was anxious not to miss my connection to Skye, so I waited impatiently for my suitcase to appear through the luggage hole. Frustration at inactivity gnawed my mind, possessed by an unreasoning urgency.

Why did airports always produce interminable delays?

At last my luggage bumped into view, and seizing it I struggled to the Loganair desk and wrote out a cheque for my ticket.

'Hurry,' said the girl. 'The flight has been called.' The plane was berthed at the farthest departure door; an eight-seater Islander, which looked minute in comparison to the Trident which had brought me north. The day was overcast with low clouds. We would have to fly blind over the high ranges of hills which I knew separated me from Skye.

I and the other passengers climbed on board. The engine revved up to full throttle and the little plane lifted and thrust her nose into thick cloud. Nothing could be seen but the tips of her vibrating wings. The swirling vapour folded us into a private universe, strange yet protective. And suddenly I recognized the sensation. I had felt the same when climbing in mist, poised on a rock face or a ridge, shut away from the exposure all around.

The mountains marched beneath. I knew they were there – the highest range in Scotland – but they held no terror for me. I was safe in my little pulsating box, safe and flying north.

How wonderful to be on my way to Raasay, far from the stresses and demands of the south!

I turned to my neighbour, a pretty young woman with dark hair and clear hazel eyes.

'Have you done this flight before?' I asked.

'Yes, frequently,' she replied. 'I live in Portree. I teach at the school there.'

'Then you'll know the children who go there from Raasay, the Gillies boys. John Alan and Alastair Iain, and the others?'

'Yes, indeed. A nice lot they are. Ten of them this year. I know Raasay, too. I lived there as a child.'

'Really? Do you ever come back?'

'Of course. I've got relations living in Inverarish still and I often visit them.'

I learned later that this girl's name was Janet MacLeod, and that in her early thirties she is the deputy head of the Portree School.

'Five minutes to Skye,' said our pilot. The cloud was still impenetrable and I wondered how and where we would break it. We started to descend, and my eyes strained outwards. Then suddenly I could see Loch Alsh far below, reassuringly clear, curving through the hills to the narrows at the Kyle lighthouse. The summit of Beinn na Caillich was hidden, but all else was visible. We turned west to fly over a flank of the hill and then emerged into the bowl of the wide Broadford valley ringed by the Cuillins and the sea. On the horizon lay Raasay's familiar shape. Not long till I would be there. A final turn brought us into line with the air-strip, and then slowly, gently in a long long glide, we drifted down towards it and landed as smoothly as a homing bird.

By 1976 Raasay had its long-awaited ferry. The Caledonian MacBrayne 68-ton s.s. *Eigg*, carrying six cars, had gone into service in March of the previous year. But Dr Green's objections to a ferry terminal on his land near Raasay House had succeeded. The Court of Sessions (to which he had appealed) had upheld the Inverness County Council's compulsory purchase of his land. But by the time the verdict was known, the two-year delay had escalated the cost of the ferry site to around £200,000, a figure far in excess of the money already voted by the Council. So the project had been abandoned and instead an exposed site at Raasay's new pier had been brought into use. First designated as temporary, it had now been made permanent. Alastair Nicholson, I recalled, had been right in his fears that the procrastinating tactics of Raasay House's absentee owner would deprive the island of the good ferry site with proper harbour facilities which is so desperately needed.

I thought of these events as I awaited the ferry at Sconcer, half an hour's drive from the Broadford air-strip. Though I felt some pangs for the old *Loch Arkaig* steamer, so much bound up with our early days on the island, I was happy to see the s.s. *Eigg* appear. A smart, serviceable boat, she drew up at the concrete slipway beside the new jetty, erected as the terminal on the Skye side, opened her ramp and prepared to take the waiting vehicles aboard.

Alastair Nicholson, skipper of the ferry, greeted me.

'Where have you sprung from?' he asked. 'Did you walk all the way from London?'

'Sure,' I answered. 'Anything to get to Raasay.'

'Well, you'll have a nice short trip across. Only fifteen minutes now.'

'How's business on the ferry, Alastair?'

'Good. We've taken twice as much as this time last year. Transport costs are high of course. But that applies to all the islands.'

'It does indeed. It makes the cost of living soar in the Isles even more than elsewhere.'

'But we've got a good service to Raasay at last. Three times a day, and connections in Skye with buses to Kyle and Portree. Mind you, some of the inhabitants are still complaining, wanting the times different, or the service to run to Portree direct.'

'Always problems.'

'Indeed. And always will be on a small island.'

Alastair left to take his place in his Perspex eyrie on the top deck, and Calum Gillies, who had been appointed his mate, came to stand beside me, ready to conduct the rite of off-loading. As we approached Raasay I could see the concrete slipway for the landing cars which had been built beside the long wooden pier.

'It looks a pretty exposed place to berth a ferry,' I said to Calum.

'It is,' he replied. 'It's not satisfactory at all. It's a pity the Highland Regional Council didn't spend some of the money they used for the jetty at Sconcer to give us proper facilities in Raasay.'

'What was it like in the winter?'

'Terrible! I'd often be lying awake listening to the wind and wondering was the ferry damaging herself, bumping against the pier. And sometimes Alastair and I would be up at two am taking her across to Sconcer or Braes, or heaving to till the wind abated. We had a bad storm in January and a mooring rope snapped. The ferry was swinging against the head of the pier, and a tractor with a hawser attached to her couldn't move her against the wind. There was only one thing we could do – chance the storm conditions in the Sound and sail her to Portree for a safe anchorage. She'd have foundered otherwise and smashed in the pier as well. As it was, her starboard bow was buckled, and we were storm-bound in Portree for a week.'

'At any rate you've *got* a ferry now,' I said. 'People can come and go from the island and the children at Portree School can come home at weekends.'

'Och, yes. Thank goodness for that. I'll not forget what it was like two winters ago when the *Samara* was the only boat serviceable in Raasay. Many a trip she made over to Sconcer to fetch the scholars, and sometimes to fetch the doctor as well. Och, yes, it's much better now.'

Calum straightened up his large oilskinned form and stared ashore.

'But all the same we never got the harbour and the safe anchorage for a fishing boat that we were promised. And we could have had them if Green would have released the land at the old Raasay House pier, or if the Council had put a compulsory order on it sooner. *That's* where the Raasay ferry site should have been.'

Shortly after this, the s.s. *Eigg* was replaced by the s.s. *Raasay*, the boat specially built for the island ferry. By 1978 plans to strengthen the ferry site by filling in the pier, which could then give adequate protection, were accepted by the Highland Council (which had replaced the Inverness County Council in 1975), and the importance of basing the ferry at Raasay and thus securing the three jobs which go with it for Raasay men, was fully recognized and endorsed as future policy. So the long fight for a Raasay ferry had ended in success.

Our house, when I reached it on that May day, was in the first flush of summer. The rowan trees were in full bloom, their heady scent wafting on a breeze which blew the last seeds of pussy-willow across the still air. Four sheep sat munching on the grass, each with her accompanying snow-white lamb. They lifted enquiring faces as I approached, then settled down again deciding that I belonged. A cuckoo sounded across the slopes and, as evening fell, I walked by the sea where a field of yellow iris bloomed close to the shore. Two seals were playing in the glassy water, turning over and over, jostling and bumping one another, surfacing and diving, with a sound as innocent as first life. I sat on a boulder to watch them, and my hand, playing idly with stones, picked one up. I looked at it and saw that it contained an ammonite fossil, something made a hundred million years ago.

I do not exaggerate these marvels. They happened one after the other on that still May evening, adding a magical dimension to my life. I remembered that ten years had passed since we first lived on Raasay, and a series of island vignettes flickered across my mind like scenes from a kaleidoscope when each shake produces a different pattern.

Mackerel fishing at night, the shining fish leaping phosphorescent on the darrows as they emerged from the dark sea; children playing at the water's edge; an owl's shape on the bough of the rowan tree, outlined against the moon; the sound of Diarmaid's pipes skirling from Nefarnin across the hillside; a New Year's reel danced by candlelight; the log fire, stoked up in winter, a pile of books before it; whooper swans flying in echelon with a flurry of spray on to the loch at Fladday.

Golden memories. And then the dark ones: old people, crippled by arthritis, making their slow purchases in the shop; rubbish strewn in the burn; abandoned cars rotting where they stood; untended gardens; sheep and cattle ill through neglect; feuds between neighbours, injurious to the spirit; men unemployed, wondering how to make ends meet.

The light and the dark wove together in my mind. They could not be separated for each was true. In the realm of daily living, each was valid; and while I understood the causes, it was hard to see what answers could be found for neglect and decay, and what could best bring prosperity to Raasay.

In my recent tour I had seen different attempts at a solution on different islands. In Coll, the increasing number of holiday homes; in Tiree a viable crofting economy; in Colonsay an enlightened landlord (but for how long?); in Iona, a shrine drawing pilgrims; in Islay, employment on farms and distilleries; in Mull, forestry plantations; in Jura, jobs on the big sporting estates. Rhum had been taken over as a nature reserve; Canna was self-sufficient with an exceptional laird; Eigg had suffered, like Raasay, from careless neglect amounting to criminal proportions, but was now being rescued by a new owner. Skye had sold its soul to tourism, but had found a measure of prosperity as a result.

What would happen to Raasay? Its unique quality, I thought, comparing it to the other islands, was that it was still completely unspoilt. Its scenery was intact, unblemished by camping or caravan sites, and its people possessed a traditional way of life unaltered throughout the passage of many years. They treasured their privacy and wished to preserve it. Whatever development took place in Raasay, these facts should be taken into account.

So far, I reflected, tourism had been controlled. The Youth Hostel on the hill above the Free Kirk had given many young people – a number of them from overseas – an unforgettable holiday. It was self-sufficient, with its own warden, well-run, tidy, and an asset to the island. Other visitors stayed at the Nicholsons' guest house where a clientele of appreciative Raasay-lovers was building up. Many others came during the summer and stayed with relations in Inverarish, Clachan or Oskaig. All these people appreciated Raasay and what it had to offer. They could be integrated into the life of the island, and the village shop was stocked up to serve them, as well as the islanders who made their purchases in confidential whispers and kept a buzz of Gaelic conversation going in spite of the stares of strangers. The casual camper who defaces his environment had not yet reached Raasay. But with the advent of the car ferry and regular daily services this hazard might lie ahead.

There was also, I reflected, the vexed question of holiday houses. When we renovated our houses at Fearns there was only one other 'incomer' on the island – the Reckitt family who had bought the Manse house by Holoman's Island (which we had seen on our first visit to Raasay) and who had come regularly to Raasay for holidays ever since.

Now there were over a dozen houses which had been restored in various parts of the island. Their owners had brought increased employment at a time when jobs were few and prospects low. Calum Gillies had told me, 'Work on holiday homes tided me over until the ferry came and I could get regular employment. If it hadn't been for the rebuilding of those houses I'd have had to leave the island.'

But this development could bring in its train an alteration to the islanders' closely-knit community. Formerly, although internal feuds existed (and still exist), every Raasay inhabitant knew every other, each was bound to each by ties of kinship and experience. Now a new element was emerging and the old pattern was being broken. Homes, which were unoccupied for the greater part of the year, might provide employment while they were being built but did little thereafter to enrich the life of the community.

I remembered that in neighbouring Skye, Iain Noble, who owns a large part of the former MacDonald land in the Sleat peninsula, refuses to rent or sell any house unless it is occupied all the year round. He is trying to encourage a Gaelic-speaking community (with its own Gaelic college at Sabhan Mor Oskaig) and he considers absentee owners a threat to this conception.

The sun was sinking behind the Cuillins and it was time to leave the beach. I had ventilated Raasay's problems in my mind but reached no immediate solution. Yet of one thing I was sure. Whatever happened to Raasay should evolve in accordance with the inhabitants' general will, and not be an imposed policy enforced by an outside body or a particular island clique.

Later that summer, events began to move. Peter Zinovieff, our neighbour at Fearns, and Lt.-Col. Basil Reckitt of Holoman's Manse (both holiday-home-owners in Raasay since 1963) drew up a scheme for a Raasay Society. This was something Peter had been thinking about for some time. The Society's aims would be to protect the island from harmful tourist exploitation and at the same time to encourage active participation by the community on any worthy projects for development.

Peter came to talk over the scheme with me, and told me that two island men – Calum Bàn from the south, and John Gillies of Balachuirn from the north – had agreed to be on the steering committee, and that a public meeting would take place in November when the whole concept could be discussed.

'Who will take the chair at the meeting?' I asked. Peter replied that this had not yet been decided.

'Why not ask Willie Nicholson, Raasay's District Councillor who lives at Braes?' I suggested. 'He's also a member of the Highland Council in Inverness, and responsible for Raasay's interests.'

'Good idea,' said Peter. 'Someone from outside the island would be objective and non-controversial. Will you come if we sail across in the *Alathea* one evening and see him?'

I agreed with pleasure.

About 4 pm a few days later Peter's little yacht pulled out

from Raasay and headed across the Sound. Peter's daughter Sofka and his son Leo, now teenagers, were on board, and so was Calum Bàn who had agreed to visit Willie Nicholson on behalf of the proposed Raasay Society. Calum was dressed for the occasion in a smart tweed jacket and cap, a Fair Isle jersey, a collar and tie, and well-polished shoes. His appearance put to shame Peter's and my shabby polo-necked sweaters and crumpled jeans.

A stiff breeze sped us over the water and soon we were cruising up the Braes coast with the long tongue of sea which runs into the little harbour of Camus Tianavaig stretching before us. Ben Tianavaig's mass rose sheer from the water, and I recalled the many climbs I had made to its crest from which Raasay had beckoned me, mysterious and unexplored.

Slowly the dots of the white houses on Braes grew larger. Peter turned to Calum.

'Do you know which house is Willie Nicholson's?' he asked.

Calum reflected. 'Well now,' he replied, 'I *used* to know. I used to know his house well. But he's after having moved from that house and I'm not just sure which is his now. But it's somewhere very near.'

We all scanned the coastline, Calum looking for the elusive Nicholson house, Peter for a possible anchorage. A small cove came in view and Peter swung the *Alathea* into its shallows. 'We'll anchor here, anyway,' he said. 'Sofka and Leo can stay with the boat, and we'll go ashore.'

The beach was wet and slippery. I was glad of my wellingtons as I watched Calum in his smart brown shoes, hopping nimbly from rock to rock. We panted up a steep brae and came out on the top of a slope crowned by several similar white houses.

'Which one is Willie's, do you think?' said Peter.

Calum gazed, recovering his breath. 'Well, it might be the one nearest,' he replied. 'And again, it might be the one farthest away. Why don't we try the middle one?' We clumped up the gravel to the geranium-filled porch, and unbelievably Willie Nicholson answered the door.

Ensconced inside in comfortable armchairs, a guarded conversation began. The main topic of our visit could not be broached until the two island men had enquired about each other's health, the health of each other's families, the state of the weather in Skye and Raasay, the prospects of the sheep sales at Inverness and the shocking size of the Raasay ferry prices. This last topic gave signs of being inexhaustible till Willie remarked, 'The only thing that could unite Raasay people would be dissatisfaction with the ferry prices.'

Peter seized his cue and said that he hoped the proposed Raasay Society would also unite them in a more positive way. Willie – friendly, flexible and forthcoming – listened with interest while Peter outlined its aims: to encourage tourism which does not destroy what it seeks out; to protect the island's natural assets; to preserve its agricultural status; to establish a historical and scientific archive; to encourage people to remain on Raasay; to create one 'voice' for the island to tackle problems, such as selfish private ownership of land; and to distribute information so that proper consultation could take place prior to development. Willie, having heard Peter out, pronounced himself in favour of the project. He would try to come to the meeting he said, but could not promise to take the chair. Instead, he suggested Sorley MacLean, the Gaelic poet who was brought up on Raasay, and who was very interested in the island's welfare and preservation.

'I'll try to get some of the Raasay people living in Braes and Portree to come to the meeting, also,' he said. And then, by way of a parting shot, as we took our leave, 'I can promise you,' he concluded, 'that the plan of the Highland Council for Raasay is certainly *not* to turn the island into a kind of Blackpool.'

In November the public meeting to launch the Raasay Society took place. It was held in the school house and turned out to be one of the best attended meetings on Raasay for a long time. Sorley MacLean had unfortunately not been able to take the chair, and the two island men on the steering committee failed to turn up, but nevertheless more than half of the island's population came. They lost no time in voicing their resentment at what they considered to be interference by a group of 'incomers', who appeared to wish to preserve the status quo for their own ends. 'We want Raasay developed,' speaker after speaker declared (although at the same time one castigated Peter Zinovieff for going for a walk on the hill on a Sunday). The general fear seemed to be that the existing local Social Services Committee would be overridden by the proposed Raasay society. All in all, no islander wished to be told what to do by people who were not resident in Raasay the whole year round.

The outcome was a typical Raasay compromise: the formation of two committees; one a Community Council, instigated by the Highland Council in Inverness, on to which most of the former members of the Social Services Committee were voted by Raasay's inhabitants; and the other a new Social Services Committee, the rump of the old one, containing a critical younger element, whose chairman is a crofter's young son and one of whose members is Peter Zinovieff. This Committee organized a Jubilee Party for Raasay's children in 1977, and is currently raising money for a village hall. So a competitive element has entered the realm of Raasay's social services and this could prove to have a stimulating effect.

In spite of the suspicion with which they are sometimes regarded, holiday-home-owners have deep roots in Raasay. Several of them have been coming to the island year after year, in winter and spring as well as in summer. And so have their children. Families of this kind belong to Raasay in spirit if not by birth. And as their children grow up (and some are already teenagers) their attachment to the island will become a factor in its future.

In my own case, not only my children but also my grandchildren have a love of Raasay firmly implanted in their hearts. When in 1965 my son Iain bequeathed me the Island file and left Raasay for East Africa he could hardly have foreseen that in 1970 he would return with a wife, Oria (a Kenyan-born girl of Italian and French parentage), and a small daughter, Saba. Saba spent her first Christmas on Raasay, aged six months, and two years later she came again, this time accompanied by her sister Mara, aged nine months. So both children have known and loved Raasay from an early age.

I have many memories of them there; exploring the beach for fossils, picking wild flowers in the woods, digging for spout-fish (razor fish) in the sand at low tide, tucking them into bed at night with an owl hooting and a candle for company . . . Perhaps the most perfect memory of all is that of a sparkling summer day when, on their last visit with their parents, we decided to sail to Brochel, and all set off in the *Samara,* with Calum Macrae at the wheel. He had provided each child with a fishing line and they trailed them over the side of the boat, their fair heads bent above the water, each tense with anticipation at what the sea might yield. 'Be careful your lines don't tangle,' called Calum. But the warning went unheeded. Only one thing was in their minds.

'What will we catch?'

'Och, you'd never be knowing in these waters. It might be a dolphin, or a mermaid or a whale.'

Saba lifted her head and stared at Calum with widening eyes as he guided the *Samara* round the half-submerged rocks of Rubha na Leac and steered a course across Hallaig's wide and beautiful bay.

'I wouldn't like to catch a mermaid,' she said, anxiously. 'It might hurt her. Couldn't I catch a seal instead?'

'You might. But you'd have to sing to it first.'

'What sort of song?'

'Any sort of song. They love music.'

The little girls exchanged looks, then leant over the water again and their clear thin voices, wooing the seals, floated across the sea. I went aft to stand beside Calum.

'What chance of a fish for our lunch?' I asked.

Calum smiled. 'Well now, I might find you one,' he replied. 'Is it a salmon you'd be wanting?'

Of all the fish that run in those waters the salmon and seatrout are the most delicious. Very occasionally one swims up the burn at Inverarish; an event for the village. But for the most part they remain in the sea. At Brochel Calum was fishing salmon in the big bag-nets which he and some others had recently set up there, tethering their ropes to hooks in the rocks used by former fishermen when Brochel had been a salmon-fishing station. A good number of fish ran into the bag-nets between mid-May and late July, and a salmon caught in this way and eaten direct from the sea was a feast to be remembered.

Calum swung the tiller to port and we steamed into Brochel's spacious bay and were hailed from the shore by Fred Hohler, an Oxford friend of Iain's who had renovated an old croft house opposite the castle and was living there with his wife Sarah and their family. Accompanied by two excited small daughters he rowed out to the *Samara* in Calum's dinghy and soon ferried us all on to the beach.

The first time I had seen the bay below Brochel Castle it had appeared to me an enchanted place, invested with a kind of archaic peace, so calm and so old that it seemed part of an earlier forgotten world. Here the surf had rolled on to the boulders year after year, millennia after millennia, had shaped the great rocks which bound the bay, and moved the pebbles back and forth, back and forth. Seasons had grown and faded, winds had risen and died, and nothing had changed. Only the shapes of the ships sailing across the water had altered and the transitory inhabitants on the shore had come and gone. Everything in nature had remained the same, moulded and protected by the patina of time.

This first impression came back to me, as I saw my own grandchildren and the two little Hohler girls, four bare-footed, fair-haired children, running down to the sea, each as excited as I had been at first exploration. The sun streamed from an unclouded sky and the shimmering water stretched away towards the far mainland hills. Lazily I watched Calum set off across it in his little dinghy in search of our lunch.

And what pleasure could be more simple than this? I thought. Lying on the pebbles in the sun waiting for fish from the sea.

The children returned with the treasures they had collected – shells, a few mussels, pieces of emerald seaweed, small bright stones – and we set off along the beach to collect driftwood for a fire.

By the time we had kindled it Calum was back, a silver burden in his hands.

'I was lucky,' he said. 'I found you a big one.' The beautiful fish still gleamed with its underwater colours, its silver scales fresh from the sea's fragrance. We broiled it on the embers of the fire and ate every morsel down to the last bone, our fingers growing sticky with butter, and the warm pink flesh filling us with a primitive delight. And then, when the last mouthful had been devoured, there was still the castle to climb over, the rock pools to explore, the sea to swim in. The day, like the place, seemed enchanted. On everyone it cast its spell.

At last it was time to board the *Samara* for the homeward journey. My grandchildren were sleepy and, after waving goodbye to the Hohler family until they were out of sight, they snuggled down, one on each side of me, eyelids heavy and yellow heads drooping. A bank of huge cumulus clouds had piled up from behind the hills and was beginning to move slowly across the sky, casting shadows over the slopes and the sea. The *Samara* beat steadily onwards, her wake bubbling across the calm water. Everything else was still. But suddenly the peace was shattered. All around the boat a series of vivid black forms leapt out of the water. One by one they turned, flashed, arched and dived back again, to reappear instantly, jumping even higher and splashing back with greater abandon.

'A school of dolphins.'

Saba and Mara were on their feet at once, sleepiness forgotten, holding their hands out to these magical creatures who had appeared from the sea's depths to show them a rare dance.

The dolphins accompanied us all the way home, adding the final touch of wonder to our day, and leaving us only as we rounded the last headland. The Cuillins loomed out of the sea, their great shapes charged with drama, stark against the flaming setting sun. On our own quiet hillside the four houses of Fearns gleamed white. I gazed at them with love.

'Home,' I said to myself. And home it was. My Hebridean home, so valued, so treasured, my home on this island which had become a deep part of my life. Here my quest had ended.

Here I had found a place where peace and awareness could grow, where the spirit could draw sustenance for its journey, and a way of life exists which possessed a unique quality.

I hoped that it could all be preserved. But not at the cost of stagnation. I longed for Raasay to move away from the years of neglect and to find a more prosperous future. And it seemed that at last this might happen. (In fact, in 1978 there was full employment on the island, with a good prospect of more jobs to come when the new hotel sponsored by the Highlands and Islands Development Board opened.) Yet with these new opportunities the old virtues must not be lost. Fortitude and simplicity, existing here for so long, must remain.

The *Samara* came to rest at her buoy below our house and we climbed into the dinghy to row ashore. Two sleepy children waved goodbye to Calum, and Iain dipped his oars into a transparent sea. We landed, and I walked up the steep path through the wood with a small, cold hand in each of mine. Then we came out into the field below our house. A wisp of smoke rose from its chimney. Its white walls glimmered in the dusk and its upturned eaves seemed to welcome us with a smile.

Saba lifted her tired head.

'Look, Mara,' she said. 'We're home.'

Bibliography

ADAMNAN: *Life of St Columba* (Seventh century), Thomas Nelson & Sons Ltd, 1961

BOSWELL, James: *A Journal of the Tour to the Hebrides with Samuel Johnson – 1785*, Oxford University Press, 1970

BUDGE, Donald: *Jura*, John Smith, 1960

CHADWICK, Norah: *The Celts*, Penguin Books Ltd, 1970

CHILDE, V. Gordon: *Prehistory of Scotland*, Kegan Paul & Co, 1935

COOPER, Derek: *Skye*, George Routledge Ltd, 1970

CROSSLEY-HOLLAND, Kevin: *Pieces of Land*, Victor Gollancz Ltd, 1972

DAICHES, David: *Charles Edward Stuart*, Thames & Hudson Ltd, 1973

DARLING, F. Fraser: *Island Years*, G. Bell & Sons Ltd, 1940

DARLING, F. Fraser and J. Morton Boyd: *The Highlands and Islands*, William Collins Sons & Co Ltd, 1969

DE BEER, E.S.: *Raasay To-Day*, A paper read to the Johnson Club, 16 March 1951. Published privately.

DILLON, Myles and Norah Chadwick: *The Celtic Realms*, George Weidenfeld & Nicholson Ltd, 1967

DONALD, Graham: *The Foundations of Islay*, The House of Islay, 1965

FRASER, Marjory Kennedy and Kenneth Macleod: *Songs of the Hebrides*, Boosey & Co, 1909

GIBSON, John S.: *Ships of the '45*, Hutchinson & Co Ltd, 1967

JOHNSON, Samuel: *Journey to the Western Isles of Scotland*, W. Strahan & T. Cadell, 1775

LEHANE, Brendan: *Quest of Three Abbots*, John Murray Ltd, 1968

LINKLATER, Eric: *The Prince in the Heather*, Hodder & Stoughton Ltd, 1965

MACCORMICK, John: *The Isle of Mull*, A. Maclaren & Sons, Glasgow, 1923

MACGREGOR, Alastair Alpine: *The Western Isles*, Robert Hale & Co, 1949

MACGREGOR, Alastair Alpine: *Skye and the Inner Hebrides*, Robert Hale & Co, 1953

MACKAY, Angus: *A Collection of Ancient Piobaireachd*, Aberdeen, 1838; reprinted by E. P. Publishing Co, Wakefield, Yorks., 1972

MACLAREN, Moray: *The Highland Jaunt*, Jarrolds Publishers Ltd, 1954

MACPHEE, John: *The Crofter and the Laird*, Angus & Robertson Ltd, 1972

MALLOY, Robert B.: *The Isle of Raasay*, Framingham Center, Massachusetts, 1975

MALONEY, Eileen: *Portraits of Islands*, Dennis Dobson (Dobson Books Ltd), 1941

MARTIN, Martin: *Description of the Western Islands*, London, 1705

MAXWELL, Gavin: *Harpoon at a Venture*, Rupert Hart-Davis Ltd, 1952

MAXWELL, Gavin: *Ring of Bright Water*, Longmans Ltd, 1960

MONCRIEFF, G. Scott: *The Scottish Islands*, Oliver & Boyd, 1961

MORRISON, Alick: *The Macleods of Raasay*, Associated Clan Macleod, Edinburgh, 1974

MURRAY, W. H.: *Mountaineering in Scotland*, J. M. Dent & Sons Ltd, 1947

MURRAY, W. H.: *The Hebrides*, William Heinemann Ltd, 1966

MURRAY, W. H.: *The Islands of Western Scotland*, Methuen & Co Ltd, 1973

NICOLSON, Alexander: *A History of Skye*, A. Maclaren & Sons, Glasgow, 1930

PREBBLE, John: *Culloden*, Martin Secker & Warburg Ltd, 1961

PREBBLE, John: *The Highland Clearances*, Martin Secker & Warburg Ltd, 1963

SETON, Gordon: *The Land of the Hills and the Glens*, Cassell & Co Ltd, 1920

SHARPE, Richard: *Raasay, A Study in Island History*, Grant & Cutler Ltd, 1977

SIMPSON, W. Douglas: *Portrait of Skye and the Outer Hebrides*, Robert Hale & Co, 1973

Index